NAVAL INNOVATION
FOR THE 21ST CENTURY

NAVAL INNOVATION
FOR THE 21ST CENTURY

THE OFFICE OF NAVAL RESEARCH
SINCE THE END OF THE COLD WAR

ROBERT BUDERI

Naval Institute Press
Annapolis, Maryland

Naval Institute Press
291 Wood Road
Annapolis, MD 21402

Library of Congress Cataloging-in-Publication Data
Buderi, Robert.
   Naval innovation for the 21st century : the Office of Naval Research in the post-Cold War era / Robert Buderi.
   1 online resource.
   Summary: "The Office of Naval Research, known widely as ONR, was formed in 1946 largely to support the pursuit of basic science to help ensure future U.S. naval dominance—and as such, it set the model for the subsequently created National Science Foundation. But everything changed after the Cold War. The U.S. entered a period of greater fiscal constraints and the concept of warfare shifted from conventional land and sea battles and super-power conflicts to an era of asymmetric warfare, where the country might be engaged in many smaller fights in unconventional arenas. Naval Innovation is a narrative account of ONR's efforts to respond to this transformation amidst increasing pressure to focus on programs directly relevant to the Navy, but without sacrificing the "seed corn" of fundamental science the organization helped pioneer. Told through the eyes of the admirals leading ONR and the department heads who oversee key programs, the book follows the organization as it responds to the fall of the Soviet Union, the terrorist attack on the USS Cole in 2000, and subsequent wars in Iraq and Afghanistan. These events are inspiring an array of innovations, for land and sea. Consider unmanned undersea vehicles that can patrol strategic coastlines for months on end, novel types of landing craft that can travel up to 2,500 nautical miles without refueling, and precision shipborne "rail guns" whose GPS-guided shells can hit targets from hundreds of miles off. Other efforts include advanced electronics designed to swap out scores of antennas on ships for two solid-state apertures, greatly increasing speed and stealth and speed; virtual training methods that spare the environment by avoid the need to fire tons of live shells, and new ways to protect Marines from improvised explosive devices. All these programs, some pursued in conventional manner and some set up as "skunk works" designed to spur out-of-the-box thinking, are part of an ongoing evolution that seeks to connect scientific investment more directly to the warfighter without forsaking the Navy's longer-term future. Naval Innovation is a narrative history, and a story of organizational change, centered around the struggles of management and key personnel to adapt to shifting priorities while holding on to their historic core mission of supporting longer-term research. As such, it holds great lessons and insights for how the U.S. government should fund and maintain military R&D in a new era of "small ball" conflicts—and how the country must prepare for the future of warfare. "— Provided by publisher.
   Includes bibliographical references and index.
   Description based on print version record and CIP data provided by publisher; resource not viewed.
   ISBN 978-1-61251-514-4 (epub) — ISBN 978-1-61251-514-4 (mobi) — ISBN 978-1-61251-306-5 (hbk. : alk. paper) 1. United States. Office of Naval Research—History. 2. Naval research—United States—History. 3. Naval art and science—Technological innovations—United States. I. Title. II. Title: Office of Naval Research in the post-Cold War era.
   V394.O34
   359'.070973—dc23
                                                                                    2013032222

○∞ Print editions meet the requirements of ANSI/NISO z39.48-1992 (Permanence of Paper).
Printed in the United States of America.

21 20 19 18 17 16 15 14 13   9 8 7 6 5 4 3 2 1
First printing

CONTENTS

ILLUSTRATIONS AND GRAPHICS

FOREWORD

The technology that enabled U.S. Navy SEALs and their other service colleagues to safely and effectively deliver justice to terrorists—especially Osama bin Laden—one day will be known to the public. When it is revealed, the contribution of sustained research in science and technology and the critical investment in American innovation that are the hallmarks of the ONR will be recognized as a vital factor in America's military and economic successes.

This book captures the challenge that the nation and the U.S. Navy face in balancing basic university and laboratory discoveries, which provide fuel for the engines that power our economy and security in the future, with the need to deliver real-world, cutting-edge technology and capabilities to our sailors and Marines who are in harm's way today. Robert Buderi has skillfully captured that tension in what is arguably one of the most successful sponsors of research and results—ONR—as it transitioned from a relatively stable, forty-five-year Cold War footing to the more agile, full-spectrum science and technology organization that discovers and delivers "game-changing" and life-saving capability to warfighters when and where they need it to be victorious in combat.

This is this story of ONR moving from its "Naval Science Foundation" roots dating back to 1946 to the "Office of Naval Relevance" today. Although it focuses on ONR's organizational history during the post-Cold War era from 1990 through early 2007, it concludes with profiles of some of the potentially game-changing programs that will likely endure well into the twenty-first century and shape the future of naval warfare. The transformation Buderi describes is filled with drama, intrigue, missteps, and successes like few other government agencies have experienced. With this book's commissioning, it is the hope of all, but especially the post–Cold War Chiefs of Naval Research and dedicated civilian and military scientific leadership, that officers, Sailors, Marines, policymakers, researchers, entrepreneurs, and industrialists will better understand that "technology transition" is a creative contact sport not for the timid.

The continuum of basic research through successful prototype demonstration—"discovery to deployment"—is why Congress continues its strong support of ONR and its dedicated government and civilian researchers, program managers, and partners.

Human nature changes slowly, institutional intrigue is a fact of life, and budget priorities are forever in flux. Fifty and even one hundred years from now, when the Secretary of the Navy, Chief of Naval Operations, Commandant of the Marine Corps or Chief of Naval Research contemplate what the role of ONR should be for the twenty-second-century Navy, this book may well offer valuable insights into how mission success can be achieved.

Rear Adm. Jay M. Cohen, USN (Ret.)
Chief of Naval Research, 2000–2006

ACKNOWLEDGMENTS

This book could not have happened without the vision and support of Rear Adm. Jay Cohen, USN (Ret.). I first met Jay sometime in 2000, when he was Chief of Naval Research. He invited me to the Office of Naval Research (ONR) to give a lunchtime talk about my recently released book *Engines of Tomorrow*, which chronicles the history of industrial research and the way modern companies are struggling to adapt their research operations to modern, globally competitive times. The admiral, still new to his job, was keenly interested in how corporations managed research and development (R&D): after all, he had the same job for the Navy and faced many of the same pressures.

Fast-forward to August of 2001, when he first brought up the idea of a post–Cold War history of ONR to pick up where Harvey Sapolsky's original ONR history, *Science and the Navy*, had left off. It wasn't until 2004 that the stars aligned and I had the time to tackle the project. The admiral then found the resources to support the project and opened ONR for me, with no strings attached. I would write it not as an academic (which I'm not) but in a narrative, journalistic style. And while the Navy had a right to review the manuscript for factual errors, I had the final say in all matters. It would have been impossible for me to write under any other circumstances. That he readily agreed to this is a testament to Jay's interest in the importance of history—and in my ability to tell it. My heartfelt thanks!

The other great pillar of support in this project was Owen Cote Jr., himself a great military historian and historian of technology and the longtime associate director of the MIT Security Studies Program (SSP). Owen encouraged the project and helped me find a home as a Fellow in the department. He was also a great sounding board throughout the project—though I am not sure he helped me with my fantasy football team. And, indeed, the entire staff at SSP was great and supportive for the two years I was in its offices, especially Magdalena Rieb, who was my daily point of contact and helped on numerous issues, big and small. Thank you to one and all.

A number of researchers and reporter/researchers helped with this project. They include Corinna Wu, who did the bulk of reporting and initial draft of chapter 10, "Persistent Littoral Undersea Surveillance"; Jennifer Boyce, who did a great reporting job on chapter 9, "New Eye for the New Navy; and highly talented MIT graduate students (at the time) Jessica Karnis and Kelly Grieco, who worked as my research assistants. May you be so lucky to find your own Jessicas and Kellys someday. I also got some much needed research help from Erika Jonietz, and fact checking from the lightning-fast, impeccably accurate Anne Alonzo.

I would also like to thank the people of ONR, past and present, who made themselves available to sit with me (or talk on the phone or e-mail) and answer my questions, and then more questions, and then more questions. This runs from former CNRs Paul Gaffney, William C. "Bill" Miller, Marc Pelaez, and former technical director Fred Saalfeld, all the way down the line to department heads, project managers, administrators, and everyone in between.

There are far too many of these great folks to name here, but they are all identified in my list of interviews. Two former ONR personnel who are not in the list of interviews are Dan Dayton and Chris Christopher, who worked in communications during the time I researched the book. I'd also like to thank John F. Williams of ONR, who helped dig up photos and organization charts and the like, and the overall support of the ONR corporate strategic communications office. This great team worked hard to get other answers and material I needed and were always friendly, true professionals. Thanks to you as well.

Finally, thanks as always to my family, who once again supported me on a long book project.

ABBREVIATIONS

AIEWS   advanced integrated electronic warfare
AMRF-C   Advanced Multi-Function Radio Frequency
     Concept (aka "Amerf")
ASN   Assistant Secretary of the Navy
ASN RDA   Assistant Secretary of the Navy for research,
     development, and acquisition
AUV   autonomous underwater vehicle
BAA   broad agency announcement
BFTT   Battle Force Tactical Trainer (aka "Beef-it")
BMH   BMH Associates
C4ISR   command, control, communications, computers,
     intelligence, surveillance, and reconnaissance
CAMS   central atmosphere monitor system
CNO   Chief of Naval Operations
CNR   Chief of Naval Research
DARPA   Defense Advanced Research Projects Agency
ELB   Extending the Littoral Battlespace
EM gun   electromagnetic railgun
ERC   explosive resistant
FNC   Future Naval Capabilities
"Glo"   gunnery liaison officer
GWOT   global war on terror
HME   hull, maintenance, and electrical
IED   improvised explosive devices
INP   Innovative Naval Prototypes
IPT   interdisciplinary planning teams
ISR   intelligence, surveillance, and reconnaissance
JTF WARNET   Joint Task Force Wide-Area Relay Network
LCAC   landing craft air-cushion
LST   littoral combat ship
MFEW   multifunction electronic warfare
MPF(F)   Maritime Preposition Force (Future)
MRT3   Mission Rehearsal Tactical Team Trainer
MSR   Maritime Synthetic Range
NASA   National Aeronautics and Space Administration

NavAir	Naval Air Systems Command
NavMat	Naval Material Command
NavSea	Naval Sea Systems Command
NRAC	Naval Research Advisory Committee
NRL	Naval Research Laboratory
NSF	National Science Foundation
OAT	Office of Advanced Technology
OCRD	Office of the Coordinator of Research and Development
ONR	Office of Naval Research
ONT	Office of Naval Technology
OODA	observe, orient, decide, act
OPM	other people's money
OpNav	Office of the Chief of Naval Operations
ORI	Office of Research and Inventions
OSD	Office of the Secretary of Defense
OSRD	Office of Scientific Research and Development
PEO	program executive office
PLUSNet	persistent littoral undersea surveillance network (aka PLUS)
POM	program objectives memorandum
PPBE	planning, programming, budgeting, and execution
PSY OPS	psychological operations
R&D	research and development
RDT&E	research, development, technology, and engineering
S&T	science and technology
SAP	Science Advisors Program
SOSUS	sound surveillance system
SSP	Security Studies Program
TAP	Technology Area Plans
TRACES	Technology in Retrospect and Critical Events in Science
TTL	tagging, tracking, and locating
UAV	unmanned aerial vehicle
VAST	virtual at-sea training
VCNR	Vice Chief of Naval Research
VFST	virtual fire support trainer

Office of Naval Research

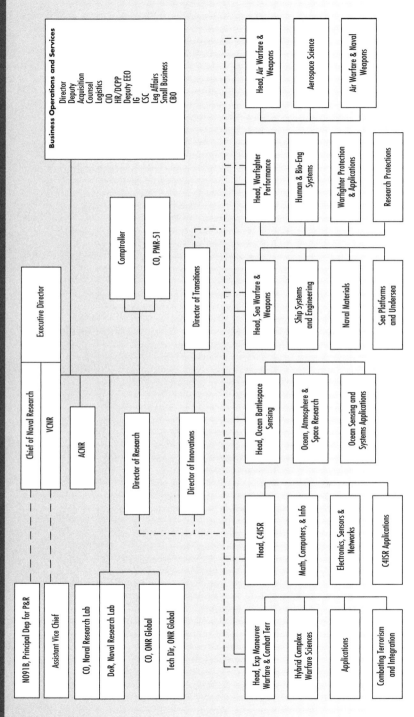

Business Operations and Services

Director
Deputy
Acquisition
Counsel
Logistics
CIO
HR/DCPP
Deputy EEO
IG
CSC
Leg Affairs
Small Business
CBO

Chief of Naval Research

Executive Director

VCNR

ACNR

Comptroller

CO, PMR-51

Director of Research

Director of Innovations

Director of Transitions

N091B, Principal Dep for P&R

Assistant Vice Chief

CO, Naval Research Lab

DoR, Naval Research Lab

CO, ONR Global

Tech Dir, ONR Global

Head, Exp Maneuver Warfare & Combat Terr

Hybrid Complex Warfare Sciences

Applications

Combating Terrorism and Integration

Head, C4ISR

Math, Computers, & Info

Electronics, Sensors & Networks

C4ISR Applications

Head, Ocean Battlespace Sensing

Ocean, Atmosphere & Space Research

Ocean Sensing and Systems Applications

Head, Sea Warfare & Weapons

Ship Systems and Engineering

Naval Materials

Sea Platforms and Undersea

Head, Warfighter Performance

Human & Bio-Eng Systems

Warfighter Protection & Applications

Research Protections

Head, Air Warfare & Weapons

Aerospace Science

Air Warfare & Naval Weapons

PART I

ORGANIZATIONAL HISTORY

The Office of Naval Relevance

The morning of October 12, 2000, began typically enough for the 293 crewmembers of the USS *Cole*. The high-tech Aegis guided-missile destroyer, based at Norfolk Naval Station, was two months into a four-month deployment to the Mediterranean and Red Sea as part of the George Washington Battle Group. She had steamed south from the Mediterranean through the Suez Canal and the Red Sea, arriving in the sprawling Port of Aden on Yemen's southern coast early that day. As planned, the 500-foot, 8,300-ton *Arleigh Burke*–class warship maneuvered to a commercially operated dolphin, or water-borne platform, some six hundred meters offshore for refueling. It was a "gas-and-go" stop: the *Cole* was bound for patrol duty in the Gulf of Aden, where she would ply the waters between Yemen to the north and Somalia on the southern horizon.[1]

The *Cole*'s crew consisted of 249 men and 44 women. Their average age was twenty-two. The warship was operating under Threat Condition Bravo, the second highest of four levels of alert observed in the Fifth Fleet, to which the *Cole* belonged at the time. Condition Bravo indicated an "increased and more predictable threat of terrorist activity." Crewmembers, carrying binoculars and unloaded shotguns (following protocol, the shells remained in their ammo belts), were assigned fore and aft to watch the small craft motoring around the harbor.

The refueling, slated to last five or six hours, began around 10:30 a.m. Despite the threat condition, no one felt a strong sense of danger: U.S. warships had been refueling regularly in the port for two years. Several minutes after 11:00, though, a small white craft began motoring toward the *Cole*. The sailors on watch could see two men in the tiny boat. One waved amiably, and several crewmembers reported later that they figured the men were trash haulers.

But they weren't garbage collectors—or friendly. Hidden on the craft were several hundred pounds of C-4 explosive, a restricted military plastic explosive not approved for commercial use. The small craft turned away from the bow and puttered amidships, where, at 11:18 a.m., the two men reportedly stood to attention and saluted the *Cole* just before detonating their deadly cargo.

It was not the sort of attack the *Cole* was built to combat. She was designed for an era when modern warfare meant fighting off attacks from Soviet jets and missiles, not a bomb delivered amidships by a small craft. The blast force moved upward and sideways along her curved hull, ripping a forty-foot by forty-foot hole and almost severing the ship in half, by some accounts. A few sailors were lining up outside the galley for the fajita lunch. In the messroom, others were sitting back to watch *Mission: Impossible* on the ship's video system. Some reported feeling like the *Cole* had caught a wave and gone surfing. Then the grim truth became apparent. Fuel oil rained over the deck and mixed with water flooding into the ship. Severed electrical cables sparked and arced as most of the ship plunged into blackness. When sailors spilled out into the passageways they found men and women with shattered jaws and broken legs calling for help. Other shipmates lay silent, unconscious or dead.

Some crewmembers panicked. But most remembered their training. The executive officer, Lt. Cdr. Chris Peterschmidt, was holding a morale meeting to determine whether to buy new thirty-two-inch TVs for the crew when the explosion knocked an existing TV out of its wall brackets. According to *Newsweek*, "Peterschmidt went into the passageway to find chaos. Panicked sailors were pushing their way on deck while equally frightened seamen were running below to take cover. Steadier hands were going to battle stations."[2]

As the *Cole*'s second-in-command hurried into the passageway, he wanted to stop and help his injured shipmates. But his training dictated that he ignore their pleas and assume his post in the central control station in the ship's belly. "Inside the CCS," *Newsweek* continued, "bells were ringing, sirens whooping, klaxons blaring. Computer screens signaled massive breakdowns in the ship's systems."[3] Lt. Cdr. Deborah Courtney, the chief engineering officer, joined Peterschmidt. Courtney had been blown out of her stateroom chair by the explosion. She had snatched up an oxygen mask and fought through the smoke to the CCS.

Peterschmidt issued orders to rig emergency electrical wiring and contain the flooding. Crewmembers set up a bucket brigade and installed emergency submersible pumps to dewater the vessel. It was near bedlam. The ship was without power. They were in Yemen, with no friendly forces around. No one knew whether another attack was imminent.

As it turned out, no other attack took place. The *Cole*, though, would not be repaired and recommissioned until eighteen months after the attack. Along with the two attackers, seventeen sailors were killed and thirty-nine injured in the blast.

U.S. and Yemeni intelligence forces learned over the next few years that the al-Qaeda operatives of Osama bin Laden had been planning a suicide attack of a ship off the Yemen coast since at least 1998. The original plan focused on a commercial oil tanker, but bin Laden pressed his operational commanders to target a U.S. warship in its place. In January 2000 a team had been assembled to blow up an American naval vessel in the port of Aden. However, the assault craft was apparently so heavily laden with explosives that it sank before the attack could be carried out. When the *Cole* arrived some nine months later, the plan was revived and refined. This time it worked.

The *Cole* event sent shockwaves through military and intelligence circles and highlighted the need for significant revisions not just in military procedures but also in more general antiterrorism plans and programs. The full report of the quickly convened Cole Commission, issued in January 2001, was never made public. However, the commission did release an executive summary that included seven national policy and procedural improvements that could bolster antiterrorism and force protection capabilities. One of its suggestions dealt specifically with the need for improved research and development to meet the terrorist threat.

Within about a month of the attack on the *Cole*, even before the rec-ommendation was released, the Chief of Naval Research, Rear Adm. Jay M. Cohen, was summoned to a meeting with Chief of Naval Operations (CNO) Adm. Vern Clark. Uppermost on Clark's mind was the *Cole* and how in the future the Navy could protect its ships from similar attacks.[4]

"Jay, find a way to prevent the penetration, the puncture of the hull," he directed.[5]

The sense of urgency was palpable, Cohen relates. Even though the *Cole* was formed of high-tensile steel, the plating was relatively thin to save weight, and the blast had easily ripped her apart. It was a huge vulnerability that had to be addressed.

Cohen returned to his office, then in Ballston Towers at 800 North Quincy Street in Arlington, Virginia. He operated out of a corner suite on the ninth floor of the twelve-story building. The office was big enough to fit his expansive desk and a large dining table for work-ing lunches. Against one wall stood the American flag, and next to it flew Cohen's two-star flag. A connecting room led to the office of Fred Saalfeld, ONR's longtime technical director and top-ranking civilian. Cohen, a former submarine commander, had taken command of ONR just nine months earlier, in January 2000. He was only starting to learn his way around the organization and had yet to make his presence felt. It was time for that to change.

ONR's main role is to provide funding to university, government, and private sector labs to address a wide range of Navy needs, from train-ing to ship design to new weapons systems. The Chief of Naval Research asked the various department heads and program officers in his roughly three-hundred-person organization for their ideas, concentrating first on things that could be quickly brought to bear on ship protection. One of those heeding Cohen's call was Roshdy Barsoum, a program officer in what was then called the Ship Hull, Mechanical, and Electrical Systems S&T (science and technology) division. The division funded research into ship and submarine hulls as well as shipboard electrical and mechan-ical systems. Barsoum himself concentrated on supporting both basic and applied studies into ship structures and protection techniques, so this was right up his alley. But there was nothing on his books that dealt specifically with protecting ships against terrorist attacks. "We were not really focusing on those type of events," he remembers.[6]

Still, Barsoum had some ideas about how to proceed. He worked closely with top universities as well as the Naval Surface Warfare Center, whose sprawling Carderock division in West Bethesda, Maryland, had lead responsibility in the Navy for research, development, and testing for surface and undersea vessels. He quickly funded a Carderock study to survey the state of the art in science and technology to make sure there was nothing already out there that might make a big difference in a short amount of time—anything from different types of steel to novel plating arrangements that might better absorb energy from a blast. "We looked at many technologies, from way back since the Second World War, that the Navy has really used and tested and investigated over the past thirty or forty years," he recalls. The team also looked outside Navy work, around the rest of the military and in universities. "Let us look for everything: nothing ignored," is how Barsoum describes their approach.

While Barsoum launched the survey of existing technology, Cohen simultaneously began looking for something completely new. Another possible solution to the CNO's challenge lay in unique composite materials that might safeguard hulls against explosions more effectively than the corrosion-resistant, high-strength, high-toughness steel (similar to that used in bridges) then used in destroyers. ONR had made numerous investments in composite research and basic materials studies over the years. Besides the investigations that the organization funded in universities, its own Naval Research Laboratory (NRL) was a pioneering force in materials research.

As Cohen surveyed the materials work under way, he grew satisfied that his organization had covered the major bases in composites research, and that the projects it funded seemed on track. But while extremely important, these studies were conventional, conducted mainly in world-class university laboratories by top people in their field. What about the unconventional, the Navy research boss asked himself? Who was a leading expert in composites who also specialized in out-of-the-box thinking that might advance the Navy toward its goal more quickly?

His hunt soon led to famed aerodynamic inventor Burt Rutan, creator of the *Voyager* aircraft that in December 1986 had become the first plane to fly around the world without refueling or landing. Rutan worked out of Scaled Composites, his own privately held company in Mojave, California, about sixty miles north of Los Angeles. Scaled Composites specialized in air vehicle design, tooling, and manufacturing as well as specialty composite structure design, analysis, and fabrication.

Rutan was not unknown to the Navy. He was already working on an unmanned combat air vehicle being developed for the service by Northrop Grumman. But he was picky about his projects. Cohen flew to California to make a personal pitch for the hull protection scheme. He arrived in civilian clothes and, after some basic pleasantries, got right to the point.

"Listen Burt, I have a problem. It's called the *Cole.*"[7]

The admiral proceeded to lay out the challenge—find a way to address the penetration problem without changing the hull design of an existing destroyer of the *Arleigh Burke* class so that the Navy didn't have to start from scratch. Cohen told the maverick inventor that he didn't care if a ship was irreparable after an attack as long as the crew was protected from hull penetration. "Show me how to use advanced composites to survive a several hundred pound explosion amidships, or a twelve-knot collision on the bow, or to survive being run aground at twelve knots," Cohen outlined. He offered a large contract to Scaled Composites if it would take the job.

Rutan looked at the admiral who had come across the country to personally offer him funding and said: "I will not take your money."

Cohen was almost flabbergasted. "Mr. Rutan, I really want to understand this. We've just had the *Cole.* I'm offering you money to do this conceptual design. Why won't you take my money?"

The inventor responded bluntly. "You, sir, are a bureaucrat. I've seen your type. You come in here offering the world, but as soon as I take your money, you'll come in looking over my shoulder and tell me, 'No, that's not right.'"

Cohen couldn't help but smile. "I've been called a lot of things in my forty years of service, but I've never been called a bureaucrat," the admiral replied. He promised that if Rutan accepted funding, he would receive no communication from the Navy for six months. Rutan accepted the deal.

Almost a year before the September 11 terrorist attacks that rocked America to its core, the attack on the USS *Cole* set in motion a string of ONR-backed efforts to cope with the age of terror and a type of threat hardly envisioned when today's ships and planes were being designed and modern warfighting plans drawn up. The *Cole*-inspired work would continue for years, spilling onto fronts Cohen and his charges never imagined—a legacy that includes technologies in areas far removed from ships as well as new approaches to how military research should be funded and conducted in the twenty-first century.

Rutan's project, for instance, turned out to have no direct payoff.[8] When Cohen checked in six months later, as promised, the inventor's team reported only modest success. On balance, Rutan confirmed, stick with steel hulls. Still, the work inspired a novel program called SwampWorks, whose mission was to fund out-of-the-box ideas that might not otherwise be pursued: the program would play an important role in the ONR story in the coming years.

When it came to the first order of business—helping ships avoid or mitigate damage from a *Cole*-like attack—it was the parallel, far-more-conventional survey of the current state of the art funded by Barsoum that seemed poised to pay dividends. The Carderock team had quickly narrowed its search down to ten or fifteen areas that it deemed promising. Perhaps the most intriguing was an energy-absorbing polymer coating that could be sprayed or painted on ship hulls to improve their blast resistance. That was especially appealing because such a coating could serve as an add-on to existing shipbuilding techniques—one that did not require new raw materials or radical changes in the way ships were designed and constructed. Says Barsoum, "The whole thing about a coating is it is easy to apply, you can spray it, you can caste it. . . . It is so easy it is going to be appealing to the shipyards and the Navy."

This area of explosive-resistant coatings had a somewhat unexpected source of inspiration: the Air Force and its own experience with terrorism. In June of 1996 members of Hezbollah, possibly supported by

Osama bin Laden, detonated a fuel truck that had been laden with explosives near the Khobar Towers housing complex in Saudi Arabia, killing 19 Air Force personnel and 1 Saudi national and wounding 372 others.[9]

The attackers had been unable to drive into the Khobar compound. However, by packing the truck with as much as five thousand pounds of explosives and parking it in a lot near one building, they were able to inflict heavy damage: many more might have died had an alert sentry not noticed suspicious activity around the truck and begun an evacuation. In the wake of the attack, investigators at the Air Force Research Laboratory at Tyndall Air Force Base in Florida had begun looking into polymer coatings to make buildings less vulnerable to terrorist attack. Funded by the Defense Threat Reduction Agency, the Air Force had developed a polymer coating much like the spray often put in the bed liners of pickup trucks. In this case, however, it was designed to be sprayed onto the back of a masonry wall to provide an affordable, easy-to-implement means of preventing the creation of tiny fragments of flying concrete that were a major cause of injury in an explosion. Tests showed that even in powerful blasts a treated wall might lurch and expand but would settle back to its resting position almost like rubber, with little fragmentation. It was estimated that casualties might be reduced by as much as 50 percent when compared to untreated buildings.

The steel in a ship's hull was vastly different from bricks, of course, with unique properties and failure mechanisms. Still, the work was intriguing. As Barsoum says, "We figured, why don't we try it?" Early in 2001, fewer than six months after the *Cole* attack, the Carderock group began testing the Air Force polymer developed for masonry on the steel used in shipmaking. By late that summer, things were looking good. The coating, consisting of a blend of commercially available polyurethanes, polyureas, and other materials, was very thin and weighed about the same as water, meaning it would not add appreciably to the weight of a ship. Even more exciting, tests showed that while a blast like the one that had ripped apart the *Cole* would cause gross deformation, the hull would not be penetrated. Says Barsoum, "It could really stop the steel from fracturing—and this is steel as thin as in a ship."

Back in August of 2000, a few months before the *Cole* arrived in the Gulf of Aden, Cohen had instituted an annual Naval-Industry R&D Partnership Conference in Washington, D.C., that was designed to improve communication between the service and its industry partners. A year later at the same conference, Barsoum tracked down the admiral at an evening reception at the Ronald Reagan Building and International Trade Center, where the event was being held. Barsoum whipped out photographs showing the effects of a blast on two circular steel plates, one coated with the polymer, one left untreated. The untreated steel had been completely ripped apart. The polymer-coated plate, on the other hand, had buckled but remained intact. "I took him to the corner, I showed it to him," Barsoum recalls. "He was so excited. He said, 'You've got to continue this work.' The next day he introduced me to a couple admirals and told them here is something that can help us."

Barsoum quickly expanded the Navy's research into explosive-resistant coatings. Little was known about the science behind the polymer's blast resistance, so he convened a panel of National Academy of Sciences experts and contracted for university studies into the scientific mechanisms behind the material's properties. Meanwhile, the Carderock team began tweaking the Air Force formula to optimize it for steel hulls, simultaneously beginning the rigorous testing that was essential before a new technology could be deployed to the fleet. As Barsoum explains, "We are on a fast moving track, and we cannot really wait for the science to cross the 't's and dot the 'i's."

Over the next few years, the urgency of the polymer coating work grew dramatically, spilling into other areas beyond ships. On September 11, 2001, barely a month after Admiral Cohen had given the green light to further explosive-resistant-coating efforts, terrorists struck on American soil, destroying the World Trade Center towers in New York and damaging the Pentagon. In early October of 2001 the United States attacked Afghanistan, quickly ousting the Taliban regime that had harbored bin Laden. Then, in March of 2003, the United States began the invasion of Iraq that deposed longtime dictator Saddam Hussein.

In both countries, but especially Iraq, American forces rapidly became encumbered in insurgencies that proved both versatile and deadly. One of the chief weapons in the resistance: improvised explosive devices, or IEDs. Hidden in piles of rubbish or inside dolls and other innocuous looking objects, these makeshift bombs would be detonated as troops passed by. The blasts ripped apart armored vehicles and troop-carrying Humvees, many of them unarmored. By early 2007 more than one thousand U.S. service personnel had lost their lives to IEDs.[10] The inability to protect troops from such attacks even became a focal point of the 2004 presidential debates as challenger Sen. John Kerry assailed President George W. Bush for sending warfighters into harm's way in unprotected vehicles.

Nearly 20 percent of the victims of IEDs were Marines. At ONR, the threat seemed to be felt more keenly with each Marine death. As Barsoum recounts, "Saddam Hussein had stockpiled thousands and thousands of depots with explosives all over the country, so we had road-side bombs and so on from day one. . . . Admiral Cohen came back again and said, 'What can you do for Humvees?'"

On December 12, 2003, Cohen convened a science and technology briefing at NRL for Secretary of the Navy Gordon England. ONR program managers provided overviews of some twenty technologies in the R&D pipeline that they felt could be ramped up and developed relatively quickly to help warfighters in Iraq and Afghanistan. Each pre-senter briefed the secretary on a given technology for ten to fifteen minutes. At the end Cohen, England, and a few other dignitaries and experts convened a closed-door caucus—moving to secure areas when an item was classified—and selected a handful of projects to be fast-tracked for further development.

For Barsoum, the IED threat—and the related problem of land mines—represented another aspect of the challenge involved with thwarting attacks on ships, only this time the target was a land vehicle. His proposal to coat Humvees with the explosive-resistant polymers his team had been developing for hulls was one of the proposals that made the cut.

Barsoum was initially ordered to concentrate on protecting Hum-vees only from land mines. However, the first tests, conducted two months later at the Army Aberdeen Test Center in Aberdeen, Maryland, proved so effective against the mines that he believed the program's scope should be expanded. Anthropomorphic dummies outfitted with accelerometers and other sensors designed to measure what would have happened to a human inside the vehicle when it rolled over a land mine showed that a soldier or Marine would only have incurred slight injuries and nothing life-threatening. "Yes, we blew out tires, we tore out the engine," explains Barsoum. "But the cabin was 100 percent intact."

The ONR project manager was so excited that he telephoned Admiral Cohen that day to report the news. "Admiral, we passed with flying colors," he related. Barsoum then asked if he could proceed to test the coatings against the rest of the threat, meaning things like bombs, bullets, shells, and, especially, improvised explosive devices.

"Proceed," came the response.

Barsoum immediately began drumming up support for what is called an advanced concept technology demonstration program. This is a formal, triservice effort where work in a core area such as explosive-resistant coatings is divvied up among different military branches. Under the plan put forth, the Air Force and Army Corps of Engineers would concentrate on developing explosive-resistant coatings for different types of buildings and structural barriers, and the Navy would focus on protection of ships and Humvees for the Marine Corps. A three-year, $15 million funding plan was completed in late 2005 that sought to fast-track the coatings for service deployment.

In some senses, the cart was being put ahead of the horse. A series of studies to try to unravel the materials' mysteries was still ongoing at the Naval Research Lab and several major universities—MIT, Harvard, the University of Texas, Caltech, Brown, the University of California at San Diego, and Rensselaer Polytechnic Institute. However, heading into 2006, the complex scientific mechanisms behind the polymers were still not completely understood.

Still, it was clear that the polymers—both the original Air Force material and the Navy's tweak of that design—possessed a tremendous capacity to absorb energy that held the potential to change how armor responds to both explosions and projectiles like bullets and tank shells.

Even if the scientific understanding of their properties remained incomplete, that was not going to hold up deployment.

The work was so promising that in early 2006 an agreement was being forged for coalition partners in the United Kingdom and Australia to participate in explosive-resistant-coating development. Barsoum's charges at Carderock were working almost daily with fleet personnel to teach them how to apply the coatings and do the rigorous durability, weather, and battle-condition testing required before it could be widely deployed. Specifications were also being prepared for shipbuilders. Although no one was willing to bet on when the technology would be brought into service, deployment seemed likely well before 2010. "It's going to be a revolution in terms of armor technology," Barsoum proclaims.

Explosive-resistant coatings are just one branch of an increasingly extensive family tree of research stemming from the *Cole* disaster. The materials studies also helped spawn an ONR program to create a new type of armored vehicle far more impervious to attack than even a retrofitted Humvee. Meanwhile, in 2005 ONR was selected as program lead in a multi-government-agency attempt to research ways to defeat the IED threat. Cohen branded the effort a "mini–Manhattan Project" because his office was organizing some of the best scientists into a sequestered team with a single focus: to turn theory quickly into application in much the same way nuclear scientists had been brought into the fold during World War II to develop the atomic bomb.

———————●———————

The Office of Naval Research (ONR), formed in 1946 and based on the inspiration of a group of imaginative World War II officers known as the Bird Dogs, is the U.S. government's pioneering supporter of fundamental university research. It formed the model for the National Science Foundation (NSF), which opened in 1950, and has served ever since as an organizational poster child for the imperative of America's unceasing investment in its scientific and technological future.[11]

ONR's prime mission is to fund research around the country (and sometimes the world) that will ensure the U.S. Navy's technological superiority in the decades to come. The lion's share of the funds is invested with universities. However, a substantial amount goes to industry and government labs as well as the Navy's own facilities, which include the historic Naval Research Laboratory, a sprawling enterprise on the Potomac River that dates back to 1923, nearly a quarter century before ONR sprang to life. Taken as a whole, the recipients of ONR funding are known as the Naval Research Enterprise.

From its loftiest heights as Uncle Sam's sole supporter of basic research, ONR has necessarily receded in stature as NSF and other government organizations—most notably the National Institutes of Health, Department of Energy, National Aeronautics and Space Administration (NASA), and the Defense Advanced Research Projects Agency—have expanded their own basic research sponsorship efforts. However, with a $1.7 billion budget in 2006, including roughly $150 million to run the Naval Research Lab and hundreds of millions in congressional plus-ups or earmarks added to support specific projects legislators consider important, ONR remains a major player in national research funding.[12]

A large fraction of the funds, over $400 million, supports basic research, making ONR by far the most significant military sponsor of fundamental science—studies geared toward advancing knowledge and understanding without necessarily having a specific end-use in mind. The rest is targeted at shorter-term, more applied initiatives spread across a spectrum of areas more directly relevant to the Navy. The entire portfolio—from basic to applied—runs from deep-ocean studies to space research. It encompasses broad areas such as acoustics, aerodynamics, biology, human factors engineering, virtual reality, computer science, physics, chemistry, materials science, nanotechnology, and robotics—and specific fields such as unmanned aerial vehicles, counterterrorism, hypersonic jet engines, advanced hull designs, and low-powered optical communications.

Throughout its sixty-year history, during which it has supported the work of fifty-seven (as of 2007) Nobel Prize winners, ONR has transformed itself or refocused its mission several times. Overall, it has become far more applied in the projects it supports—zeroing in on efforts that can be brought into military service within a few years as opposed to the five years or longer typically required for basic research advances to bear fruit. These changes have come about partly in light of the competition from other government agencies. But they also arise from more systemic changes since the end of the Cold War, including general economic and political pressures that have squeezed federal budgets and heightened the call to support projects with relatively short-term, identifiable results. Finally, they reflect fundamental changes in the nature of war that have increased the pressure for new tools to address realigned military tactics and strategy as well as the fact that U.S. forces have spent roughly half the post–Cold War era engaged in an ever-more-deadly series of conflicts in the Middle East. With each military death, the calls mount for new weapons and technologies to help the warfighter.

In many ways, this shortening of R&D time horizons is exactly what many corporate research organizations have experienced over the past few decades in the face of rising competition from startups and foreign competitors alike. Led by General Electric, IBM, and Bell Labs, vaunted hallmarks of basic research that between them produced eighteen Nobel Prizes, dozens of corporate labs have been forced to abandon most (if not all) of their further-reaching studies in order to concentrate more on areas of far-more-immediate relevance to the bottom line.

In short, ONR, like modern corporations, has been forced to change with the times. It is hard to say one turn of the evolutionary crank was more important than another. However, the latest transformation of the Office of Naval Research—beginning with the end of the Cold War and picking up steam with the attack on the USS *Cole*, September 11, and the rise of the age of terrorism—looms as potentially its most significant realignment in nearly a half century.

Front and center for much of this latest transformation stands Admiral Cohen, who served in the post for almost six years, nearly twice as long as any previous Chief of Naval Research. For him, the *Cole* proved a personal awakening. It brought home the need to better balance long-term investments in science with shorter-term, applied efforts in technology—and to pair tried-and-true practices with some wild efforts that might fall flat but could bring about revolutionary advances if they panned out. Previously, he and other ONR officials explain, the long time frame of many of the organization's investments made it hard for service commanders to see the fruits of its research, bringing ONR a disparaging nickname: the Office of No Results. Cohen's goal, as he often liked to say, was to make it the Office of Naval Relevance.

The new day hardly began with Cohen, however. His predecessors also strove to realign and refashion the organization to improve its relevance to the Navy (as will his successors). But the whole post–Cold War era seems to have led almost inexorably to a higher level of "transformation readiness." Tim Coffey retired in 2001 after two decades as NRL's head of research, its top civilian position. For a brief part of his tenure, during the early 1990s, he doubled as ONR acting technical director. He refers to the "old ONR" and the "new ONR." The former dates from its inception up to about 1992, just after the end of the Cold War. The "new ONR" began in 1992, he says, when applied research and advanced development funding, previously the domain of other Navy organizations, was brought under the ONR umbrella, alongside its basic research responsibilities. "The merger of the two was successful, but it began to change the character of ONR," Coffey relates. "I think that has had an effect on people's view of what they should be doing in science and technology, looking for stuff that will pay off in the shorter term. . . . And that, I think, is a very distinct difference between the old ONR and the new ONR. In some sense you could say neither of them are necessarily bad or good, but they certainly are different."[13]

Walking the halls of ONR, talking to its military staffers and civilian program managers and department heads as well as various former officials, it becomes even more clear that the merger was just one step in ONR's attempts to keep up with the times. In the early 1990s, in addition to the merger issues, ONR found itself embroiled in the indirect costs scandal over how universities charged for their research overhead, forcing changes in how it went about its business. A few years later, under Adm. Paul Gaffney, ONR moved forcefully to align itself better with the Fleet and the Marine Corps, instituting its Future Naval Capabilities program to help move research advances into service more effectively. More recently, it has added a sister program called Innovative Naval

Prototypes, which provides funding for "game-changing" ideas that hold the power to transform warfare—programs that include building electromagnetic weapons with pinpoint accuracy across two hundred miles and creating ocean sensor networks to locate and track terrorists and enemy submarines, anywhere, anytime.

Throughout its entire existence, tension has occasionally run high between ONR's civilian and military personnel—those who doled out grants and preferred the "old ONR" and its traditional support of unfettered basic research and those who backed the "new ONR" and its increased focus on applied results.[14] Such tensions will never disappear, but it is fair to say they probably came to a head in the post–Cold War period, since some of the civilian employees had served for decades and had a hard time embracing this latest, most wrenching transformation. Some accepted the change, some resisted. The dissent caused turmoil, but it also seems to have ensured that the changes were more thoughtfully implemented and carried out than they otherwise would have been.

Depending on how you look at it, this tension is either the organization's Achilles' heel, or its great strength—a checks and balances system that keeps the organization more vibrant and alive.

CHAPTER 2

The Bird Dogs and Admiral Bowen

On the morning of September 2, 1945, nearly three weeks after agreeing to U.S. demands for an unconditional surrender to end World War II, Japanese delegates gathered on the veranda deck of the USS *Missouri*, anchored in Tokyo Bay amid an armada of American, British, Australian, and New Zealand ships. The Japanese were there to formally surrender to Allied forces. With the solemn Japanese officials positioned alongside one of the *Missouri*'s imposing sixteen-inch gun turrets, the scene depicted a total transformation in world sea power. The United States had been brought into the war by the Imperial Japanese Navy's devastating attack on Pearl Harbor on December 7, 1941, an attack that damaged or destroyed twenty-one ships of the U.S. Pacific Fleet and killed 2,403 people, casting into doubt the United States' ability to even wage war in the Pacific. Now, less than four years later, Japan had been brought to its knees (as had Germany a few months earlier), and the U.S. Navy reigned supreme.

On that historic day, as Fleet Admiral Chester W. Nimitz later noted in a postwar "forecast" of his organization's future, "the United States Navy represented the greatest sea power the world had ever known." Its personnel numbered 3 million, including 484,000 Marines and 170,000 members of the U.S. Coast Guard. "In ships and equipment," related Nimitz, "the United States Navy exceeded the total of the world's remaining navies combined."[1] He counted 28 aircraft carriers, 70 escort carriers, 22 heavy cruisers, 48 light cruisers, 2 large cruisers, 373 destroyers, 365 destroyer escorts, 240 submarines, and untold numbers of patrol craft, landing craft, tenders, and other small and auxiliary ships (but he apparently omitted the roughly two dozen U.S. battleships then in service).

The gargantuan sea force, though, could not be maintained during peacetime. The challenge was to continue as the world's unrivaled naval power while cutting fleet size dramatically: the United States would keep barely half its carriers, cruisers, and destroyers, and only a third of its submarines. A small reserve force would comprise hermetically sealed ships that could be returned to service quickly. But, Nimitz stressed, numbers were almost beside the point. "Too many people think of the Navy in terms of equipment—of battleships and aircraft carriers and submarines," he advised. "If another war comes, we may not use even the latest and best of the ships and weapons we are so carefully preserving today. The ships and weapons of our Navy ten, or even five, years from now may be very different from our ships and weapons of today."

Nimitz took a step back to recall "Old Ironsides," the frigate USS *Constitution*. The ship won her legendary victories not just because she had such a splendid crew, he noted, but also because "in her the U.S. Navy had produced a frigate far ahead of her times—a frigate superior by perhaps fifty percent to any frigate possessed by any other nation in the world at that time!"

And therein, he stressed, lay the real challenge for the future— not building more and more ships and planes, but continuing to find the scientific and technological advances that would ensure the Navy's supremacy even in the face of greater numbers. This could only be done through the "combination of the Navy's men, ideas, and knowledge working with the top scientists and laboratories of the nation."

Nimitz expanded on this theme to close out his address:

> What the future Navy will be like, we cannot say as yet. It may include battleships powered by an atomic plant, protected by unbelievedly [*sic*] stout new materials, and firing jet-powered atomic missiles instead of sixteen-inch shells. It may include carriers launching radar and target-directed jet missiles instead of man-piloted airplanes. It may even include submarines of very high speed both

surface and submerged, making long voyages far beneath the sea to surface suddenly again off some distant enemy shore to launch their missiles, and then hiding themselves again in the ocean depths against retaliation. . . .

Yes, there will always be a Navy. Not necessarily a Navy of battleships, or submarines, or carriers, but a Navy in the sense of what the word Navy truly means—a mobile organization using the ocean highways, carrying its own defenses against any weapon directed against it by the enemy, and launching from its mobile platform whatever missiles—rockets, planes, atomic bombs, or anything else—that the Navy as an organization of men and minds has been able to conceive out of the limitless possibilities of science, research, and endeavor.

Embodying the spirit behind Nimitz's words, the Office of Naval Research sprang to life in the afterglow of World War II. Its chief stewards were a small group of Navy Reserve officers, most of them with PhDs in technical fields who worked during the war within the Office of the Secretary of the Navy. Cocky, imaginative, adept at maneuvering in the bowels of the bureaucratic machine, their chief wartime job was to serve as "troubleshooting ambassadors to the naval operating arms," in large part to make sure that the advances of civilian scientists doing war work made their way into the Navy.[2] They liked to view themselves, in the slang of the times, as "lowly skippers of LSD's (Large Steel Desks)."[3] However, because of their skill rooting out and solving interorganizational problems, they became far better known as the Bird Dogs.[4]

The Bird Dogs drew their inspiration for ONR largely from the Office of Scientific Research and Development (OSRD), with which they worked closely during the war. Carnegie Institution president Vannevar Bush founded the OSRD in June 1941 to coordinate all civilian scientific and medical research for the war effort, a sweeping task that grew to include radar, the atomic bomb, and the hunt for a malaria vaccine, among other enterprises.[5]

The OSRD maintained a small advisory council composed of civilian scientists and other officials as well as one representative each from

The Bird Dogs, so named because of their skill in rooting out and solving interorganizational problems, were young Navy Reserve officers, most with PhDs in science and technology fields. In the midst of World War II, working in the Office of the Secretary of the Navy, they advanced a plan for a peacetime office to coordinate naval research and sponsor basic science in universities and other civilian laboratories that might lead to radical new weapons.

Office of Naval Research

the Army and Navy. But this one-person advisory role was not enough for Secretary of the Navy Frank Knox. Spurred by the OSRD's creation, he formed a parallel organization within his service. Called the Office of the Coordinator of Research and Development (OCRD), its specific job was to serve as a bridge between the OSRD and other civilian-run institutions and the Navy's six matériel bureaus while also advising him on broad matters of naval research.

Signing on as its interim head was MIT professor Jerome C. Hunsaker, a Naval Academy graduate who already served as the Navy's representative on the OSRD advisory council. Hunsaker, who had suggested that Knox create the Navy R&D office in the first place, quickly put together a small staff consisting of two regular officers and four reserve officers. He then began to train them, as one of the young recruits recalled, "in the basic elements of sound research program planning, administration, evaluation, and coordination." It was Hunsaker who gave his new reserve officers the moniker "Bird Dogs."

Not long before the December 7, 1941, attack on Pearl Harbor, Hunsaker was named chairman of the National Advisory Committee for Aeronautics, the precursor to NASA. He quickly turned over the OCRD reins to his handpicked successor, Rear Adm. Julius A. Furer, a technologically keen career naval officer who had graduated top of his class at Annapolis and received the Navy Cross during World War I.[6]

During the first three years of the war, the office focused chiefly on creating an effective liaison between the OSRD and the Navy, assisting in planning and establishing research programs, charting their progress, and shepherding advances into the Navy. On several occasions the Bird Dogs met with resistance from career Navy officers adverse to change. But they quickly became adept at wielding their power. Recalled one, then Lieutenant Bruce S. Old, later an influential vice president of the research consulting house A. D. Little, "Whenever we ran into a particularly salty, operational type who was bellowing in a manner destined to hold up the progress of research, we took out notebook and pencil and asked dutifully, 'Would you mind repeating that statement so I could be certain to quote you correctly to the Coordinator of Research? He will be interested in your view, sir.'"

The approach, reported Old, "worked wonders."

Despite having their hands full with the demands of war, from a very early stage the Bird Dogs and their bosses—first Hunsaker, then Furer—also thought about the *end* of the conflict. Chiefly, they worried that the Navy's close ties cultivated with civilian personnel via the OSRD might evaporate in peacetime. Therefore, they began considering the need for a peacetime organization solely dedicated to naval research that would continue to tap into the nation's leading universities and support the basic research considered essential to maintaining America's technological supremacy on the seas. As Old put it, "a gnawing thought occupied the minds of all: how could the Navy better organize and administer its *own* research?"

Early on, Old and fellow Bird Dog Lt. Ralph A. Krause (destined to become president of the Stanford Research Institute) developed a close relationship with George Karelitz of Columbia University. A former Imperial Russian Navy officer, Karelitz was also keenly interested in the Navy's postwar research agenda. Beginning in 1942, still three years before the war ended, he and the two Bird Dogs began holding bimonthly postwar planning meetings. Karelitz died suddenly of a heart attack in 1943. However, writes Old, "Out of these sessions the initial pattern of ONR was almost completely conceived—the essential elements consisting of establishing a central research office in the Office of Secretary of the Navy headed by an admiral, receiving funds from Congress for research projects, and having a powerful research advisory committee made up of top scientists."

When Vannevar Bush announced in the spring of 1944 that the OSRD would disband with the end of war, the Bird Dogs and their boss began honing their plans. By the following September, Old and Krause, then lieutenant commanders, joined with a third Bird Dog, Lt. John T. Burwell, and submitted a draft organizational chart for what they called the Office of Naval Research to the new Secretary of the Navy, James V. Forrestal, who had taken over that spring following the death of Knox after a series of heart attacks. Their more specific proposal entailed naming a rear admiral as director (later chief) of naval research and giving the new organization equal status with the matériel bureaus to protect it from diehards in the fleet. Under their plan, the Naval Research Laboratory, a bastion of the Navy's R&D since its founding in 1923, would also fall under the purview of the new office.

Both Bush and Hunsaker threw their support behind the plan. The encouraged Bird Dogs wanted their leader, Furer, to head the envisioned

NRL: The Navy's Corporate Research Lab

In 1915, at the urging of Thomas A. Edison, the Naval Consulting Board was created to help screen the roughly 40,000 inventions submitted to the service during World War I.[1] In the words of the military analyst and historian Harvey Sapolsky, "The only memorable contribution of the board was the suggestion that the Navy establish a central laboratory equivalent to those already found in industry for the exploratory development of new concepts."[2] It took awhile, but in 1923 this advice led to the creation of the Naval Experimental and Research Laboratory. This facility, on the banks of the Potomac River in Washington, D.C., later changed its name to the Naval Research Laboratory.

NRL, as it is now widely known, grew into one of the world's greatest research laboratories, pioneering in basic and applied research. Today it reports to the Chief of Naval Research and as of 2007 draws about $150 million of its roughly $1 billion budget from ONR. The bulk of the ONR funds, $100 million in total, goes to basic research. The other $50 million is directed to applied research. NRL typically wins about $200 million more in ONR contracts by competing with industry and government labs for specific projects. The rest of its funds, about $650 million annually, comes through other contracts with a variety of organizations, including all the Navy labs, the Army, the Air Force, the Defense Advanced Research Projects Agency, NASA, the Department of Energy, and various industrial organizations.

Management of NRL is split between a civilian director of research and the commanding officer, usually a Navy captain. NRL consists of roughly three thousand scientists, engineers, and technical support personnel focused on seven main areas of research: battlespace environments, materials and chemistry, electromagnetic warfare, undersea warfare, electronics, information technology, and space.

The lab is by far the U.S. military's most famous and successful research entity. Over the years its achievements include creating the world's first pulsed radar system; developing and launching the first intelligence satellite; playing a pivotal role in inventing the global positioning system; and joining the ranks of the world's top facilities in materials science, nanotechnology, laser technology, electronics, and more. In 1985 two of its researchers, Jerome Karle and Herbert Hauptman, shared the Nobel Prize for their work in turning X-ray diffraction into a powerful and versatile tool for studying molecules and materials.

Since the Cold War NRL has competed more vigorously for outside funds. It has also experienced many of the other changes gripping industrial labs. Among other things, NRL has dramatically stepped up efforts to license its many inventions. In fiscal year 2007 it received some $866,000 in royalty and license income, by far the most of any U.S. military lab and just over 6 percent of all Defense Department licensing income. In 1992 the Naval Oceanographic and Atmospheric Research Laboratory, with operations in Mississippi and California, merged with NRL to form what was formally called "the Navy's corporate laboratory."

---

1. The main sources for this sidebar are Amato, *Pushing the Horizon*; Sapolsky, *Science and the Navy*; and Coffey interviews.
2. Sapolsky, *Science and the Navy*, 102.

organization, so they used their extensive contacts to secure an audience with President Franklin Roosevelt in April 1945, hoping to seal the deal. However, events conspired against them. The president was stricken that month with a massive cerebral hemorrhage while on vacation at Warm Springs, Georgia, and died before the meeting could take place. Forrestal, who had other ideas about how to proceed, received their idea frostily. Within a month of Roosevelt's death, Forrestal created what he called the Office of Research and Inventions (ORI). On May 19, 1945, the OCRD, home to Furer and the Bird Dogs, was subsumed by this body. Also placed under the new organization's rubric was the Naval Research Laboratory and the Office of Patents and Inventions, which had been formed six months earlier to try to mitigate the expensive patent infringement claims that the Navy expected to be hit with after the war.[7]

If the Bird Dogs were dismayed to see their plans thwarted by the new Secretary of the Navy, they were even more chagrined at the man he put in charge: Rear Adm. Harold G. Bowen, the hardheaded erstwhile director of the Naval Research Laboratory.[8] Bowen had come a circuitous route to regain authority over NRL, as well as all Navy research. A former chief engineer of the Navy, he had been exiled to the Navy's lab on the Potomac River in the fall of 1939. At the same time he was appointed technical aide to then Secretary of the Navy Charles Edison, son of Thomas Edison. The jobs were plums offered up by Edison to help Bowen save face after he had made too many enemies inside the Navy through his attempts to push superheated steam power for ships over the objections of the Bureau of Construction and Repair.

Along the way Bowen had made it clear that he was no friend to the civilian scientists the Bird Dogs hoped to cultivate after the war. Wearing his technical aide hat, he had been responsible for the Navy's liaison with civilian scientists. But he smarted over eggheads who assumed they knew better than he what technologies and weapons the Navy required. To counter their influence, he had pressed for a naval research center with bureau status to have sole charge of introducing new technology into the Navy. Edison may have been receptive. However, when the new Secretary of the Navy, Frank Knox, took over, Bowen's influence waned dramatically. Knox brought in Hunsaker to advise him and killed Bowen's idea for a naval research center in favor of the far more civilian-friendly Office of the Coordinator for Research and Development. To make matters worse for Bowen, authority over the Naval Research Laboratory was transferred from the Secretary's office to the Bureau of Ships, home to Bowen's fiercest enemies. Bowen had suffered through an agonizing time until his tour at NRL was over, and then barely survived a forced retirement, hanging onto his Navy career by a thread.

Knox's untimely death and the promotion of Forrestal may have saved him. The new Secretary of the Navy offered Bowen shelter in his office, heading up the Office of Patents and Inventions. But the job was merely a holding pen, designed to give Bowen a foot in the door in planning postwar research. He was really being primed to take over the newly formed Office of Research when it got going in the fall of 1945, subsuming NRL and virtually all matters of Navy research. Now, with Bowen back on top and Furer out, the Bird Dogs were completely dismayed. As one history of those early days put it: "Four years after his defeat, Admiral Bowen was once again dominant. He was in charge of an office that absorbed the office established to placate the scientists he had offended."[9]

Hard as it was for the Bird Dogs to imagine, in many ways Bowen emerged as the true founder of ONR. The admiral's real agenda seems to have been to use his position to drive research and development of nuclear propulsion, to create the "nuclear Navy." He was destined to lose this battle to his old nemesis, the Bureau of Ships, and a group led by Capt. (eventually admiral) Hyman G. Rickover. However, as he pursued his goal, Bowen apparently seized on the Bird Dogs' vision as the best way to realize his aims. "To the amazement of the Bird Dogs," recounts the historian Harvey M. Sapolsky, "Admiral Bowen had immediately set about implementing their plan to make the Navy a patron of academic science."[10]

A first order of business was to line up academic support for the new Navy research office. Bowen and the Bird Dogs knew it would be a tough sell. War-weary scientists were skeptical of government contracts, which typically came with a lot of controls and red tape, not to mention tedious meetings with Navy officers who often lacked a true scientific understanding and instead sought to impose ceaseless military demands. But Bowen dispatched Capt. Robert Dexter Conrad, head of ORI's planning division, on a cross-country trip to drum up support from university presidents and key scientists. In the last months of 1945 Conrad teamed with Bruce Old and some fellow Bird Dogs and visited a slew of top universities, including MIT, Harvard, University of Chicago, Caltech, and Cal-Berkeley.

It was a traveling road show, an R&D sales pitch. The group promised that Navy red tape would end. They promised to sponsor unclassified, truly fundamental research and not "Navy" projects—and guaranteed scientists freedom to publish their findings. Their ideas, coupled with Conrad's persuasive abilities, quickly wore away the resistance. "There was a definite feeling on the part of the scientists after four years of war to wish to forget the Navy and return to former pursuits," remembered Old. "But Conrad was able to crumble all opposition by making superb speeches around the country, and by working with legal and contract people to pioneer an acceptable contract system. This would permit one over-all contract with a university with new task orders to be attached as agreed upon, permit basic research to be contracted for, and permit the work to be unclassified and publishable."[11] In the midst of his seemingly heroic efforts, Conrad was stricken with leukemia and forced to retire: the Navy later created an oceanographic research vessel and a research award in his name.

As Conrad worked his magic with universities, Bowen worked the legislative front, detailing Old and Krause to draft a bill aimed at ensuring the new naval research arm would become a permanent agency. The Vinson Bill, named for longtime congressman Carl Vinson, who served a record twenty-nine years as chairman of the House Naval Affairs and Armed Services committees, passed with flying colors and became Public Law 588. On August 3, 1946, President Harry S. Truman signed the legislation that created the Office of Naval Research. The language of the bill was almost verbatim to the 1945 Bird Dogs' draft. Its charter read in part: "to plan, foster, and encourage scientific research in recognition of its paramount importance as related to the maintenance of future naval power, and the preservation of national security."

————————●————————

ONR was born in building T-8, a gray warren of officialdom on Constitution Avenue in Washington that had served as a "temporary" wartime office space but lingered on after the conflict. The organization was Uncle Sam's first peacetime foray into large-scale sponsorship of basic science, and it hit the ground running. Joining Bowen as chief scientist shortly after the Japanese surrender was former Yale university physicist Alan T. Waterman, who had served as an OSRD official during the war. Already by the time of its formal creation in August 1946, ONR oversaw 177 contracts totaling $24 million (about $261 million in 2009 dollars) with 81 institutions, including university and industrial or private laboratories. All told, it was backing some six hundred academic projects involving two thousand scientists and another two thousand graduate students. Some of the nation's top universities already found it provided the mainstay of much of their research.

None of the key players dreamed things would play out as they did. ONR was formed amid tense debate in Congress and the government over the creation of a national science foundation. It turned out the battle would rage for nearly another four years, until March 1950. Even then, the National Science Foundation (NSF) would not receive significant funding until the launch of Sputnik in 1957 spurred a huge push in U.S. science research. Neither, for at least a decade after World War II, did the nascent National Institutes of Health.[12]

In the meantime, when it came to providing research funds to universities, there was essentially only ONR. Recalls Old, "The Navy found itself the sole government agency with the power to move into the void created by the phasing out of the OSRD at the end of the War."[13]

ONR moved aggressively to fill the void. Bowen went on terminal leave soon after the office was created, retiring officially in 1947 with the rank of vice admiral. But the organization did not miss a beat, taking great pains to fulfill its promises, made by Conrad, Old, and the Bird Dogs, to minimize red tape and make it as painless as possible for university scientists to take its money. The Chief of Naval Research and chief scientist divided the agency's research support among scientific areas or disciplines. However, the choice of funding specific projects was handed to civilian program officers, who were themselves top scientists in the disciplines they served. University professors were encouraged to submit proposals for the work they would like to undertake, regardless of how directly it related to the Navy, "as the belief then within ONR was that all basic research had potential naval applications," summed up historian Sapolsky.[14] The contracts were then awarded on the merits of the proposals, and the scientists behind them. Professors were encouraged to include support for graduate assistants in their proposals. Unlike other government agencies, ONR did not require monthly or quarterly activity statements, usually just an annual report. And in almost every case, professors were free to publish: just fifteen of some seven hundred contracts awarded in 1948 were apparently deemed to involve classified research. Writes Sapolsky, "It is doubtful scientists had ever encountered a more accommodating patron."[15]

By early 1949, under the third Chief of Naval Research, Rear Adm. Thorvald A. Solberg, ONR counted 1,131 projects at some 200 institutions. Three-quarters of its efforts were focused on the physical sciences, encompassing low-temperature physics, cosmic rays, and white dwarf stars as well as cyclotron projects and other research into particle accelerators. But it also found room to support studies in cancer diagnosis and the structure of proteins. All told, ONR boasted credit for supporting 40 percent of the nation's total endeavors into basic science.[16]

In this way, one of ONR's greatest legacies—perhaps its *greatest* legacy—was to set the tone for how science would be funded in the United States. Notes historian Sapolsky,

> Acting then as the Office of National Research, ONR helped formulate America's postwar science policies, many of which are still with us. It aided the development of academic science, selecting the fields, individuals, and institutions to be supported. It helped devise the contractual forms, the financial arrangements, and the support

services for university-based research. It championed the budget for basic science both within and outside government. There was hardly an aspect of the scientific enterprise in America in which ONR was not centrally and constructively involved during the period between the Second World War and the Korean War. Without its sensitive management of what has to be considered limited resources by current standards, the sturdy foundations upon which America's success in science has been built would not have existed.[17]

ONR quickly became the model for other military research offices and, especially, the National Science Foundation. Indeed, NSF adopted much of the same form and practice of evaluating and handing out research funds to university professors. Tapped as NSF's first director when it finally formed in 1950 was Waterman, until then ONR's chief scientist. Seven of NSF's top ten officers had an ONR or Navy connection.[18]

At NSF, Waterman, known for his prudence and given only limited funding, moved slowly. NSF's initial budget was modest and, besides, he didn't want to take on the vastly more powerful Defense Department. NSF's first real appropriation didn't come until 1952, when it received $14 million, but Congress was unenthusiastic about the agency and cut funding to $3.5 million: ONR funding for that year was $73 million.

ONR plowed ahead as the nation's leading supporter of basic scientific research until around the time of the Sputnik crisis in 1957. For over thirty years from its creation, the office's influence on university campuses and in setting the national research agenda waned as agencies such as NSF, National Institutes of Health, Department of Energy, and NASA grew in stature and reach.

Nevertheless, many of the projects that ONR backed throughout the Cold War proved of fundamental importance. All told, it has backed the work of fifty-seven Nobel laureates—and in some cases provided support for the investigations that won science's top honor. More to the point, it funded thousands of projects, small and large, that shaped not just military life but science and life in general—amassing a record no military agency could hope to match.

The work ran the scientific gamut, spanning the physical sciences, biology, and sociology. Under these vast umbrellas, ONR's funding produced major contributions too numerous to mention in domains as wide ranging as satellite sensing of the environment, GPS positioning, operations research, risk theory, oceanography, weather prediction, protein structure, genetics, sound propagation, turbulence, submersibles, robotic vehicles, human performance, jet fighters, high-strength steel alloys, fire-control, missiles, solid-state electronics, ion implantation for semiconductor fabrication, and digital computing, not to mention more mainstream, consumer-interest areas like fighting tooth decay and the invention of Glad trash bags.

A very short list of some of the highlights, arranged by decade, from the work ONR supported over its first forty-odd years:[19]

Tenth Anniversary Milestones

- **Maser,** microwave amplification by stimulated emission of radiation. Leads to Charles Townes of Columbia University winning 1964 Nobel Prize.
- **Whirlwind,** a pioneering digital computer that employs magnetic core memory; the backbone of computer memories until rise of the integrated circuit.
- **Thin films.** Basic research on friction properties spurs advances that reduce the weight of submarines by several tons.
- **Vertical Take Off and Landing,** VTOL aircraft designed to take off and land vertically; led to modern Osprey tilt-rotor plane.
- **Molecular beam.** Harvard's Norman Ramsey developed the first molecular beam apparatus for spectroscopy. Separated oscillatory field method proved crucial in atomic clocks; earned Ramsey the 1989 Nobel Prize.
- **Particle accelerators.** In the aftermath of World War II, before the rise of the Atomic Energy Commission, ONR was

leading sponsor of new physics research in the United States, funding most of the accelerators on university campuses.

Twentieth Anniversary Milestones

- **Owens Valley radio dish** at Caltech. ONR is the leading sponsor of U.S. radio astronomy. Related work helps understand atmospherics and communication.
- **Oceanography.** ONR is credited with largely creating the field of oceanography through work funded in this period.
- **Laser.** Townes and his brother-in-law, Arthur Schawlow, among others, extend maser techniques to optical frequency.
- **Submersibles.** ONR-funded bathyscaphe *Trieste* sets a dive record of 35,800 feet in January 1960; *Alvin* submarine from Woods Hole Oceanographic Institution achieves unprecedented speed, endurance, range, and maneuverability, and helps find hydrogen bomb lost off Spain.
- **Monster buoys.** Tested in the mid-1960s, monster buoys opened door for new studies of oceanography and weather prediction.

Thirtieth Anniversary Milestones

- **Remote sensing satellites** to image earth, ocean, and clouds.
- **Mobile robots.** Shakey, equipped with TV camera eyes, optical range finder, tactile sensors, and rudimentary navigation, is built at Stanford Research Institute.
- **Spectroscopy.** Laser spectroscopy work continues under ONR funding. Stanford's Schawlow and Harvard's Nicolaas Bloembergen will share the 1981 Nobel Prize in physics.
- **Lithium batteries.** The lithium-thionyl chloride battery, the highest energy-density commercial battery, is developed in early 1970s at GTE Laboratories with ONR support.
- **SOSUS.** The SOund SUrveillance System, initially sponsored by ONR in the 1950s, evolved into a major Cold War tool. A network of fixed arrays, it provided deep-water, long-range detection of submarines via their acoustic signals.

Fortieth Anniversary Milestones

- **Acoustic microscope,** used to inspect electronic components like transistors on semiconductors, becomes available commercially.
- **Sidewinder missile.** ONR plays key role in the development of the first highly effective air-to-air missile.
- *Titanic.* Argo, an unmanned deep-diving submersible built with ONR funding at Woods Hole Oceanographic Institution, locates the wreck of RMS *Titanic* in September 1985. The following summer, its discoverer, Robert Ballard, returns in Alvin, a manned submersible also funded by ONR.
- **Ion implantation.** The Naval Research Laboratory helps pioneer ion implantation, a materials process that becomes key to semiconductor "doping."
- **Aegis combat system.** ONR-funded studies contributed to many aspects of this revolutionary integrated missile guidance system for ships, including improved target tracking and high-speed logic.

Fiftieth Anniversary Milestones

- **Ultra-high-strength steel,** strong, durable, and corrosion resistant. Used in landing gear of FA-18E/F Hornet aircraft, among other uses, this steel provides significant life-cycle and cost savings.
- **Hull fouling.** ONR launched a molecular biology study of marine organism bioadhesion to prevent or reduce hull fouling by crusts, barnacles, and slimes that cost the Navy and Marine Corps more than $3 billion in annual cleanup and maintenance.
- **Synthetic diamonds.** In 1991, using chemical vapor deposition, ONR-funded researchers dramatically enhanced the mass production of synthetic diamonds used in high-speed missiles, engine bearings, and other machinery.
- **Neural networking chips.** Intel Corp. developed the Ni1000 computer chip in 1992 with ONR funding. Based on neural

networking technology, it heralds a new era of intelligent machines.

Throughout its first forty-plus years, the Navy's pioneering research arm endured much scrutiny and a few challenges to its very existence (as we discuss in the next chapter), but it always found a way to survive. One of the core arguments for its continuation was that even as other agencies took over the lion's share of basic research funding in the United States, they would never be supporting areas targeted specifically at benefiting the Navy. Part and parcel with this argument came a gradual but important shift at ONR, toward supporting more applied research and "directed" basic research into such areas as underwater acoustics or oceanography that are strategic to the Navy but not core to other agencies.

This realignment stood in stark contrast to the largely unfettered studies supported in ONR's formative years. Nevertheless, much of the organization's pathos continued to be derived from its support of fundamental science. The psyche of its program officers, the outward face it showed to the public, and how it identified its accomplishments all remained largely geared toward ONR's contributions in basic research, what the Defense Department calls 6.1 research.

As the Cold War ended, though, bringing a change in budgets and accountability and, soon, a transformation in the nature of warfare, the pressure mounted to concentrate on shorter-term, more applied research with obvious payoffs that could be related to Congress and the Fleet. Adapting to this new imperative proved a rude awakening for all. The "Old ONR's" time had come. Long live the "New ONR."

CHAPTER 3

Urge to Merge

Everyone gathered in the hotel banquet room for the all-hands meeting. An ever-growing Office of the Chief of Naval Research had sprawled into parts of three buildings—including the two large structures known as Ballston Towers—on Quincy and Randolph streets in Arlington, Virginia. But because none of these edifices held an auditorium big enough to hold the approximately 350 collective workers, everyone had piled into buses that had ferried them to the West Park Hotel in nearby Roslyn.[1]

Inside the meeting room, organizational diagrams and charts were posted on walls or bulletin boards, showing potential realignments of ONR. Not surprisingly, people anxiously scanned the posters to see what might become of their group or department. Charles R. Paoletti, who had been in various jobs since 1974, remembers finally finding his spot on the organization chart. To his consternation, Paoletti saw a big question mark there.

The date was December 4, 1992. Before long, the Chief of Naval Research (CNR) took the podium. Adm. William C. Miller was about a year and a half into the job. He explained in straightforward terms that his domain—their domain—was in some senses out of control. Piecemeal moves by Navy planners had expanded his responsibilities beyond the office's original charter of basic research into applied research and advanced technology development and demonstration. However, each stage of the R&D process was managed by its own separate organization, which partially explained the sprawl across three buildings. Instead of one program in a given area—materials, electron-

36

ics, undersea warfare, and so on—there were typically two or even three. As Miller later described it, "It was kind of like a New England house. You have another kid, you build another room."[2]

It wasn't exactly the seamless, cohesively designed organization the Navy was looking for in those days of budget cuts and mandates for efficiencies of scale and scope. What was in order, he stated, was a more logical management framework and strategy under one organization, not three. The exact form remained undetermined, Miller explained. But rather than being organized by military funding category, the new ONR would likely be organized by area or discipline, enabling one person or team to shepherd an idea from inception to handoff to the Fleet. That would not only save money through the efficiencies it created, it should also enable a faster and smoother transition of technologies into actual use.

The staff members in the auditorium had known that some sort of reorganization was coming. Special planning teams had been meeting for months, discussing various possibilities, some of which were reflected in the draft charts on the banquet room walls. But then again, virtually every new CNR had engineered some sort of reorganization, if only to put his personal stamp on the office. Maybe this was nothing different. Duck your head, wait for the storm to pass, and go on with business as usual was a common response, not just at ONR but throughout the Pentagon and Washington.

But this turned out to be very different because Miller had some more news that rocked to the core many of those gathered before him. The admiral was a student of organizational change. As he explains, "One of the key reasons why major change does not succeed in taking root in an organization is there is no perceived need to change. Everyone is comfortable and can just wait it out. That's especially true in government. So I needed to have a crisis. I needed to have people understand that they couldn't stay where they were. So I blew up the whole organization."

As Miller told those assembled, "I am disestablishing everybody's job except mine. All your jobs, they don't exist."

Miller's words heralded the end of an era. ONR had come under fire before. In fact, from almost its earliest days and continuing for some forty-five years, the office had endured a series of investigations, special committee hearings, and other challenges—from inside the Navy and from outside—that had questioned the worth of its investment in basic research and, therefore, its very existence.

ONR: The Relevance Wars

Almost since its inception, ONR has come under fire from those in the Navy who challenge its relevance to the fleet as well as from broader government forces unconvinced of the merits of investing in fundamental university research. Indeed, a series of studies and reviews have attempted to refocus ONR's mission on more applied R&D activities or to close down the organization entirely. ONR and the scientific community have responded with their own studies that showcase the virtues of basic research. And time and time again, ONR has been saved from its detractors by war and other crises that made tight budgets disappear or critics turn their focus elsewhere. Some highlights of the decades-long "relevance wars" include the following:

1950

A few years after World War II, President Harry Truman hit the new Defense Department hard with budget cuts. In January 1950 CNO Forrest Sherman tapped Vice Adm. Oscar C. Badger, a Medal of Honor recipient, to review ONR's portfolio for potential savings. The Badger review intended to dismiss any project that only offered benefits to the civilian economy. As Badger quipped: "Leave Mrs. Badger out of this."

A few months after the Badger review identified only minimal cuts, the general board of the Navy examination took a harsher line. The report stated: "The Board recognizes the necessity for basic research in the overall scientific development of the United States. However, expenditures for this purpose should be assigned a relatively lower priority if further curtailment of the total research and development budget is necessary."

Response: The naval rationale for projects was enhanced. Funded efforts often were renamed or given two descriptions, one for the Navy and one for the scientific community. "High-power broadly tunable laser action in the ultraviolet spectrum" was renamed "Weaponry-lasers for increased damaged effectiveness." An exploration of Pacific Island cultures became the study of favorable amphibious assault sites.

More substantive changes likely would have been forced upon ONR. However, when the Korean War broke out in June 1950, the voices for change subsided and the Navy shifted its attention to the conflict in Asia.

1953

New Secretary of Defense Charles Wilson, former chairman of General Motors, sarcastically slammed unfettered support for basic research. The term "pure research," he opined, meant that "if successful, it could not be of any possible use to the people who put up the money for it—that made it pure." Wilson imposed broad cuts for the fiscal year 1954 budget on Navy R&D as a whole, in the end reducing allocations 16 percent. ONR's contract research program, however, declined 25 percent on top of some previous cuts. After reaching a high of some $50 million in the early 1950s, the budget fell to under $30 million, languishing at around that level throughout Wilson's term, which ended in October 1957.

Response: ONR countered that any cuts in its university research program would adversely affect its ability to provide the engineering and technical base required to maintain future U.S. naval power. It also argued that the program served as a "listening post" on key fields of science that might prove vital to the Navy.

Wilson's tenure ended just days after the Soviet Union launched Sputnik on October 4, 1957. Soon billions of new dollars flowed into defense budgets. The Naval Research Advisory Committee (NRAC) endorsed a proposal for a 40 percent increase in ONR allocations to university science. What had been a $30 million program in fiscal year 1957 quickly rose to $50 million, then soared to $82 million by fiscal year 1960. NRAC also directed ONR to fund a study of the potential importance of basic research to Navy research and development. Leading the effort was former Bird Dog Bruce Old, then a vice president at Arthur D. Little. Unsurprisingly, the study concluded that future development of naval weapons might be undermined if support for university research was hampered again.

1960s

Seeking more accountability in military R&D processes, Secretary of Defense Robert McNamara looked unfavorably to ONR's support of basic science. Under McNamara, the research budget stagnated and new budget classifications and cost effectiveness analyses increased the pressure to quantify the relevance and benefits of science investments. This trend continued throughout the 1960s, accentuated by the Vietnam War, which increased the pressure for practical results from R&D. Campus unrest over the war and protests against university acceptance of military funding further strained the partnership between universities and ONR.

1966
In the mid-1960s, the director of defense research and engineering initiated Project Hindsight. A response to House Defense Appropriation Subcommittee criticism of the value of substantial investments in scientific research, the study concluded that basic research contributed little to operational weapons systems—implying that it should not be supported by the Defense Department.

Response: The Project Hindsight methodology was challenged by scientists as being shortsighted and ignoring the contributions of basic research to many practical inventions. The National Science Foundation sponsored a counter study, Technology in Retrospect and Critical Events in Science (TRACES). Although no weapons systems were included in the study, it documented many practical advances that resulted from basic or undirected scientific work, concluding that funding efforts should not be curtailed.

1970
An amendment to the Military Procurement Authorization Act legislated that "none of the funds authorized to be appropriated by this Act may be used to carry out any research project or study unless such project or study has a direct or apparent relationship to a specific military operation or function." Dubbed the Mansfield Amendment (the bill was actually proposed by Sen. William Fulbright, chairman of the Foreign Relations Committee) after its most vocal supporter, Montana senator Mike Mansfield, its intent was to reduce research community dependence on the Defense Department, sometimes called "the backdoor NSF."

Response: On paper, the Mansfield Amendment had relatively little effect. The Department of Defense cancelled about four hundred projects totaling less than $10 million in research funding. Only a handful of Navy projects were scuttled. (This partly reflected the fact that ONR and other defense agencies had already terminated basic research studies totally bereft of military rationale.) However, the act had a bigger impact at the operating level, as increasingly elaborate reviews were required to win approval for fundamental research projects.

1986

The Goldwater-Nichols Department of Defense Reorganization Act sparked the most significant defense reorganization since the Defense Department was established in 1947. Sponsored by Sen. Barry Goldwater and Rep. William "Bill" Nichols, it centralized operational authority of the U.S. military through the chairman of the Joint Chiefs, as opposed to individual service chiefs. The act's widespread ramifications for Navy R&D, and especially ONR, are the focus of much of this chapter.

The key source for this is Sapolsky, *Science and the Navy*, esp. 57–79. All quotes are from this material. The ongoing struggle to justify ONR's relevance is supported by multiple ONR interviews with civilians and military officials.

Over the years, ONR had made continual accommodations to its critics, significantly increasing its funding of research more directly relevant to the Navy. Yet the office had survived every challenge with its prime mission of supporting basic research in universities largely intact.

Until Miller's pronouncement. But while the disestablishment of ONR took place in one fell swoop, the forces leading up to the decision had been mounting for almost a decade on a variety of fronts. One was a somewhat loose but much smaller counterpart to ONR called the Office of Naval Technology (ONT). Its place in the ONR story is especially significant.

The government identified seven stages of R&D—classified as budget categories 6.1 through 6.7—that spanned everything from basic research to operational systems development (see table 3.1).

TABLE 3.1   Government Categories of RDT&E

Categories of Research, Development, Technology, and Engineering	
ONR Science and Technology Portfolio	Acquisitions, Operations, and Maintenance
6.1 Basic Research	6.4 Advanced Component Development & Prototypes
6.2 Applied Research	
6.3 Advanced Technology Development	6.5 System Development & Demonstration
	6.6 RDT&E Management Support
	6.7 Operational System Development

By charter, ONR's purview had always been the first level—basic research. This meant its leaders strategized on what the 6.1 budget should be, how much should be spent in a given science or technology area, and who should perform it—and then allocated and oversaw the contracts for doing that research once the overall plan was approved in the Chief of Naval Operations office.[3]

ONT, meanwhile, was responsible for the similar planning of applied research, category 6.2. In dollar terms, this represented a slightly bigger piece of the pie than ONR, roughly $500 million a year versus $400 million for basic research in the early 1980s. But perhaps because the work it funded was further up the R&D chain and tended to involve fewer projects with bigger price tags, ONT's staff size, with roughly thirty civilians and a dozen Navy officers, was barely a tenth of ONR's.

ONT had been created in 1980 inside the Naval Material Command. It was headed by a civilian who reported to a two-star admiral, the Deputy Chief of Naval Material. (The Material Command itself was headed by a four-star admiral.) This person was none other than the CNR, who was double-hatted with the Material Command position. It was a natural arrangement in one way, since the 6.2 area that ONT controlled was typically an outgrowth of the 6.1 research backed by ONR. Moreover, sometime in the first few years of ONT's life, it moved to Ballston Towers to facilitate a working relationship with ONR. It still reported to NavMat, as the Naval Material Command was known.

In 1986, though, as the Cold War was winding down, the Naval Material Command was eliminated. That left ONT without an organizational home. However, because the ONT director had long reported to the CNR, the Navy simply transferred the organizational reporting lines from NavMat to the CNR, who shed his material command hat.[4]

An important distinction lurked in this arrangement. On an organizational chart, ONT reported to what was formally called the Office of the Chief of Naval Research, as opposed to ONR. That was because ONT and ONR were to remain completely separate entities, even though both were overseen by the CNR. This odd but somewhat classic military convolution is where things stood throughout the second half of the 1980s and into the early 1990s, even as the Navy began a series of overhauls to its R&D structure.

Enter Gerald A. "Jerry" Cann. At the end of the Cold War, the razor-sharp Cann was counted as one of the nation's most accomplished veterans of military R&D programs. Back in the 1960s, at age twenty-nine, he had been named test manager of the Air Force's Titan I missile launcher, part of the overall Titan I program. After a stint at defense contractor TRW, he became a government employee and then worked in a series of increasingly important defense positions, including seven years as Principal Deputy Assistant Secretary of the Navy for research, engineering, and systems.

Cann left the job in 1985 after a dispute, part personal and part professional, with his boss, then Secretary of Defense John Lehman. Cann next spent four years in private industry, the last two as a vice president at General Dynamics Corp., before being tapped by newly elected president George H. W. Bush in 1989 to take a huge pay cut and return to government service. In March 1990, after a grueling seven-month-long process, he was finally confirmed as Assistant Secretary of the Navy for research, development, and acquisition. It was his first political appointment, and once was enough. "Potomac fever, well that cured me," he recalls.[5]

Cann was the nation's first "ASN RDA," in government acronym-ese. Previously, the Navy had employed two assistant secretaries whose responsibilities were combined into the new position. One, the ASN for research and development, contracted for R&D into new ships, weapons, and so forth. The ASN for shipbuilding and logistics, meanwhile, was responsible for all major Navy acquisitions programs, meaning he or she handled the purchase and integration into the Navy of things that made it successfully through the research and development pipeline.

One problem with this arrangement was that a lot of tension existed between the two positions. On the shipbuilding and logistics end, says Cann, the view was that the R&D people did not do enough to make sure that what came through their pipeline was ready for mass production and acquisition. While there was some truth in the argument, he notes, it was not uncommon for the ASN for shipbuilding and logistics and his staff to award the big production and acquisition contracts without even consulting their R&D counterparts. Cann had struggled with this arrangement since his principal deputy days. "Our view in R&D was this was ridiculous," he recalls. "We have overseen R&D, and all of a sudden they go into production and want to cut R&D management people out."

Cann's confirmation as ASN RDA ended this situation by putting everything in the hands of one office. Making it work, though, proved a daunting proposition. Cann was quickly swamped in the details of creating a brand new organization, one that also involved rewriting the lines of reporting for program managers and executive officers. It took about six months to get on top of this task, he says. To make things even harder, the Berlin Wall had fallen and the Cold War was over, causing a major rethinking in defense programs. Cann's job was to save money and improve efficiencies in a time of defense downsizing, which everyone soon took to calling "right-sizing." All in all, he found it an extremely unhappy period. "I had a miserable time because every time I made a decision, I had one happy person and about one hundred unhappy people."[6]

Behind this stressful situation lurked the Goldwater-Nichols Department of Defense Reorganization Act of 1986. Authored by Sen. Barry Goldwater and Rep. William "Bill" Nichols, the act heralded the most extensive reorganization since the Department of Defense was created by the National Security Act of 1947. It centralized operational authority of the U.S. military through the Chairman of the Joint Chiefs, replacing the old practice of relying on individual service chiefs who planned, executed, and evaluated wartime activities independently. The act also emphasized the new doctrine of "jointness" by realigning various peacetime activities such as procurement and creation of doctrine, which had been tailored for each service in relative isolation. Goldwater-Nichols had widespread ramifications for virtually every operation within the services. As part of this upheaval, the entire R&D system of the military was up for reexamination, including its processes and establishments.

At the top of Cann's agenda was to pursue reforms for the Navy's technical infrastructure. A main area of focus was the Navy's sprawling laboratory system. At the time, the service maintained seven major laboratories and research, development, technology, and engineering (RDT&E) centers as well as at least twenty-nine additional satellite labs and smaller engineering facilities. Most of these operations were focused on development and testing, covering key areas such as undersea warfare, airpower, and shipboard engineering and systems. An extensive review, begun by the early fall of 1990 by Genie McBurnett, the principal deputy ASN RDA, eventually led to the January 2, 1992, consolidation of the system under four new warfare centers: the Space and Naval Warfare Systems Center (then called the Naval Command, Control and Ocean Surveillance Center); the Naval Surface Warfare Center; the Naval Undersea Warfare Center; and the Naval Air Warfare Center. The rejiggering saved money by shutting down many redundant activities. It also aligned R&D efforts more clearly with the platforms they supported so all work on underwater weapons was overseen by the Undersea Warfare Center, and so on down the line. The nearly seventy-year-old Naval Research Laboratory in Washington, D.C., was left largely alone. It represented a fifth major Navy research center.[7]

The lab closure and realignment dealt with how research and development was performed. This affected ONR because ONR worked with virtually every Navy lab, providing financial support for a host of projects and striving to make sure that the university research it funded was successfully transitioned to the Fleet. Another change orchestrated by Cann, meanwhile, related to how the Navy apportioned funds to many of those same activities. Developments on this front would have a much more direct and profound effect on ONR.

Part of this involved the previous incorporation of ONT and its 6.2 funding program into the ONR fold. The last piece of the puzzle critical to forming the modern ONR had to do with budget category 6.3, advanced technology development. Until this time, 6.3 funding had been handled inside the CNO office by representatives of the various systems commands—or OpNav codes.[8] Dispatched from different branches of the Navy such as surface ship, undersea, and aviation, these were one-star admirals who diligently represented their commands, advocating for, planning, and then parceling out funding for projects relating to their areas. Because of their power and influence, they were known as the "one-star barons."

In the new era of centralized efficiency, this system also came under scrutiny by the Navy's civilian leadership. Within months of taking office in May 1989 Secretary of the Navy Henry L. Garrett III stripped the barons of their roles and formed a separate office dedicated to handling the 6.3 technology development and demonstration money.

Christened the Office of Advanced Technology (OAT), the new organization was opened in August 1990, a few months after Cann took office. Tapped as its inaugural director was James DeCorpo, a former NRL researcher who had become an R&D manager at the Naval Sea Systems Command. DeCorpo had a clear mandate. The view in the Navy Secretary's office, he says, was that the money budgeted for 6.3 projects was part of the service's investment in its science and technology future. Yet it had been all too often wielded by the barons as a plug to fill short-term holes in various technical programs. "No one was making the corporate decision over where the investment should go," says DeCorpo.[9]

Creating a central administration for these funds—DeCorpo's job—was meant to correct that situation. And because the intent was to further bolster the Navy's science and technology future, the new organization was housed inside the Office of the Chief of Naval Research, alongside ONR and ONT. Garrett made the move as part of his "Transformation of the Navy" initiative. His instruction letter mandated that OAT/CNR act as "the honest broker" across all warfare areas.

It was quite a domain that was being assembled in Ballston Towers. ONR had always taken responsibility for 6.1, basic research. ONT, which also reported to the Office of the Chief of Naval Research, oversaw the 6.2 programs that strove to apply that basic knowledge to Navy needs. Now OAT was meant to pick up the ball so that the proof of concept could be demonstrated to the systems commands. In terms of personnel, OAT was a much smaller organization than its counterparts. It had about seven staff members, compared to forty-three (thirty civilians and thirteen officers) for ONT, and roughly three hundred for

ONR. On the other hand, because technologies became more expensive (although the number of active programs was much smaller) as they moved up the research chain and into demonstration, the new office had a budget of approximately $700 million (in fiscal year 2005 dollars). ONT, by contrast, oversaw about $500 million, and ONR, around $400 million (see figure 3.1).[10]

These expansions of the CNR's purview all probably had another aim as well: to help shed ONR of the "Office of No Results" epithet that had been stuck on it sometime in this period. The idea was to give the organization a greater role in funding more advanced stages of R&D, where projects and programs were more Fleet-relevant than the far-out fundamental research that was ONR's charter area of responsibility.

But while the general idea of handing responsibility for more applied work to the CNR made sense, the moves presented a formidable set of challenges. When the new CNR, Rear Adm. William Miller, arrived in the summer of 1990, he was handed the reins to two separate organizations inside the same building: the Office of Naval Research and the Office of Naval Technology. After OAT got up and running soon thereafter, he became responsible for a third organization. Suddenly, he

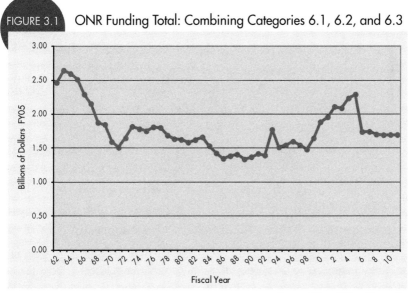

FIGURE 3.1   ONR Funding Total: Combining Categories 6.1, 6.2, and 6.3

Source: Office of Naval Research

found himself overseeing programs spanning three budget categories: 6.1, 6.2, and 6.3.

"That sounds really neat in a linear fashion," Miller says. "But technology isn't developed in a linear fashion." Instead, he points out, it involves messy interactions and back-and-forth efforts all along the chain. Rather than three smooth, clearly delineated science and technology areas, Miller found overlapping programs inside a triad of organizations that each had separate staffs to handle the same areas of technology, leading to his New England house analogy.

It was a messy, thorny problem. Ultimately Miller concluded that organizing around budget categories wasn't the best way to ensure the Fleet got new technologies as speedily as possible. In fact, if things got all muddled up in three different organizations, it could slow down the pace of technology transfer and harm ONR's reputation inside the Navy.

Miller hadn't served in Vietnam. But when considering the future of ONR, he soon found himself uttering a sorrowful phrase adapted from that war: "The way to save it was to blow it up."

This was the main path leading to the all-hands meeting at the West Park Hotel nearly two years later and the most important—and wrenching—organizational change since ONR's founding in 1946. The decision to raze ONR and resurrect its three disparate offices as one, though, wasn't made based on one issue. The momentum for change built over most of 1991 before gathering critical mass early in 1992, as ONR and Miller were caught in a perfect storm of events that virtually forced dramatic action.

In a way Miller's trajectory seemed to point him toward ONR almost from the start of his Navy career. Raised in Los Angeles, the first day he ever spent east of the Mississippi was the day he was sworn in at the Naval Academy in 1962. After graduation, he served a year on a destroyer, then took advantage of an advanced scientific education program for warfighters to devour anything he could get his hands on in math, science, and engineering. Through the service, he earned a master's and a doctorate in electrical engineering at Stanford University:

James DeCorpo of OAT praised him as "an industrial strength technical guy." He then alternated between various jobs at sea and ashore,
rising to captain two surface ships as well as to teach at his alma mater,
the Naval Academy. Over the years, Miller spent more time in science,
technology, and research jobs. He served as founding director of the
Navy's stealth technology office, called the low observables technology
office, and at a similar program in the Defense Department. He had also
served as chief executive of the Naval Research Laboratory.

In 1990 Miller was tapped to replace Adm. J. R. "Smoke" Wilson
Jr. as the new CNR. But, just as had happened with Cann, his civilian
boss, Miller's first year on the job was usurped by crises and controversy
that forced to the back burner thoughts about how the organization was
structured.

Right away he had been selected to serve on Genie McBurnett's
RDT&E facilities consolidation working group that evaluated the Navy
lab organization. In the midst of this, Iraq invaded Kuwait, leading to
the opening of the Gulf War in early 1991. ONR was responsible for
"the Navy after next." But Miller wanted ONR to play a role in the current conflict. His staff canvassed industry and NRL for technologies that
might be culled from ongoing projects, looking especially for ways to
detect and defend against Saddam Hussein's expected chemical or biological weapons. NRL scientists were particularly responsive, says Miller.
Bypassing all the acquisition processes that normally applied, he notes,
"they came up with some really neat stuff that went right to the Gulf War
from the lab bench." He won't say what NRL contributed, except that
"they ended up doing a couple dozen of some very important things."

All this was enough for any job. However, two other raging fires far
more directly related to ONR burned up the lion's share of Miller's time
during the first twelve to eighteen months of his tenure. First up was an
idea from the Defense Department to consolidate all military science
and technology under the Office of the Secretary of Defense (OSD).
It was a bit like the Navy lab consolidation effort, only it ambitiously
sought to combine work across the Navy, Army, and Air Force.

All the services objected to this plan. First and foremost, no branch
wanted control of its work distanced from the warfighters who benefited

from it. Plus, some science and technology programs were so service-specific—such as underwater research for the Navy—that they feared it would be marginalized if it were transferred to OSD control. Another factor was a natural organizational response to defend one's turf. Miller was hardly alone in seeing the plan as a power grab by the Secretary of Defense. "There was a big push by some empire builders in DOD to take S&T money from the services, and they were going to manage it better," he scoffs.

In looking back at this same period of consolidation and upheaval in industrial R&D, former IBM vice president for science and technology John A. Armstrong remarked that there was nothing like a crisis to help seemingly disparate interests find common aims. "Adversity brings people together," he said. So it was for the science and technology hierarchy of the three main military branches.

Until this time the S&T leaders of the three services were part of a loose working group called Joint Directors of the Laboratories, which in essence existed mostly as a kaffeeklatsch that met a few times a year to share basic information. Now, though, the confederation suddenly took on greater importance. Within a few months of arriving at his new billet and faced with rumors of the OSD plan, Miller met with his coffee colleagues from the Air Force and Army to see what they could do to counter the threat. As Miller puts it, "We got together and decided how we can jointly rely on each other to do better than OSD could." They aptly christened their collective effort Project Reliance.

The driving force behind the meeting seems to have been the Air Force representative, Maj. Gen. Robert R. Rankine Jr., recently named deputy chief of staff for technology, Headquarters Air Force Systems Command. On the Army end of things was a civilian, George T. Singley III, Deputy Assistant Secretary for research and technology. As the effort quickly won support higher up the chains of command at all three services, the men told their staffs to form teams according to scientific discipline and jointly evaluate all the programs each service supported in a given area. The charge was then to figure out which research should be pursued separately, which could be relinquished, and which should be combined and managed jointly. They called the reports "Technology Area Plans" (TAP). Miller, Singley, and Rankine would then hear the TAP recommendations and decide together what actions to recommend— as a group—to their superiors.

Project Reliance kicked off in the fall of 1990. Managing the ONR end of the effort was Phil Selwyn, director of ONT. "We tried to do it in a way where there was an operating principle, which was we tried to coordinate in areas where common sense said it made sense to coordinate," he says. He describes the first step as a surgical process of analyzing everybody's program. Things that were service-specific—such as antisubmarine warfare and submarine technology in the Navy's case—were kept off the table because the other military branches had no relevant work in that area. Other fields, including explosives, aircraft, materials, and electronics, were of triservice interest. In those cases, plans were developed to coordinate the work, typically by centralizing many aspects of the R&D and giving one service lead responsibility for managing it. This enabled all services to save costs by avoiding duplicative work and streamlining facilities and equipment costs.

The teams decided, for example, that the Air Force should take responsibility for all fixed-wing aircraft technology, something both the other services delved into but on a much lesser scale. The Army, meanwhile, would be responsible for rotary wing technology, so that it oversaw helicopter R&D for all services. The Navy was left to concentrate on things like takeoff catapults for aircraft carriers and the problems associated with operating planes in a corrosive marine environment— issues unique to naval aviation. Critically, all three services continued to pay for a proportionate share of the joint work.

Reliance's evaluation and recommendation period occupied all of 1991 and ran into 1992. Then Capt. Paul Gaffney, who served as Assistant Chief of Naval Research beginning in 1989 under Smoke Wilson and continued in that role when Miller took command in 1990, contends that he worked on countering the threatened Defense Department takeover nearly seven days a week for two years. He says ONR and its counterparts tried to drive home the point that while some centralization of R&D would save money and improve operating efficiencies, it was critical not to take things too far by ceding control to Secretary of Defense. "We fought off making such an organization for lots of reasons," he sums up. "But the most important was not to separate the people in the science and technology business from the warfighter that they supported."[11]

That argument ultimately carried the day. Buoyed by the strength of a joint proposal from top science and technology officials at all three military branches, Project Reliance set a new standard for interservice R&D cooperation and efficiency. A 1996 report assessing the progress of it and other laboratory reform efforts concluded, "Project Reliance created a more condensed, corporate and cooperative approach to laboratory and T&E management by establishing areas of RDT&E capability and 'Lead' military departments for Lab/T&E focus area." The report noted that Project Reliance had evolved into an important initiative for joint planning and management of R&D programs. "This participative approach to overseeing the DoD RDT&E program greatly improves the focus, quality, timeliness and customer satisfaction of the DoD RDT&E investment," it stated.[12]

The same paper hailed Project Reliance as one of three critical efforts—along with the Base Closure and Realignment Act of 1990 and a laboratory-quality improvement program—to streamline and improve the Defense Department's RDT&E management. The report didn't break out the relative contributions of each. However, these efforts, joined by several smaller programs from the early 1990s, were expected to reduce total military lab personnel by 29 percent between fiscal years 1992 and 2001, reducing the overall workforce from 121,000 to 86,000.

"It was an effort designed out of necessity and self-defense rather than out of just logic," concludes Miller. But it became one of the most important programs ever to streamline military R&D.

Miller's stress load didn't end there. Even as Project Reliance was unfolding largely behind the scenes, a second crisis that had surfaced just before Miller took office in July 1990 erupted into a national firestorm. At the center of events was Paul Biddle, ONR's representative at Stanford University, who alleged that going back to 1981 the school had dramatically overcharged the U.S. government by hundreds of millions of dollars for overhead costs associated with research Uncle Sam funded on campus.

ONR—and especially Miller—was caught in a whirlwind of controversy. Biddle filed a whistle-blower lawsuit under the False Claims Act that would have allowed him to receive a portion of any recouped funds; he then quit ONR to run (unsuccessfully, as it turned out) for Congress. His accusations, meanwhile, led to two congressional hearings on the matter and seemed to have precipitated the 1991 resignation of longtime Stanford president Donald Kennedy, who took special heat when it turned out that some of what the university had billed as research-related overhead went to maintaining a yacht and furnishing the president's home with cedar-lined closets. In the midst of this brouhaha, the new CNR was repeatedly called to testify before Congress, appeared on an investigative segment by ABC's *20/20* show, and toiled night and day to overhaul the rules for how schools could charge for such overhead costs.[13]

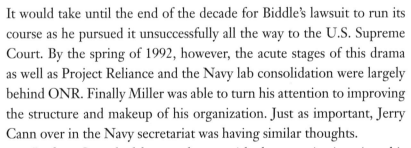

It would take until the end of the decade for Biddle's lawsuit to run its course as he pursued it unsuccessfully all the way to the U.S. Supreme Court. By the spring of 1992, however, the acute stages of this drama as well as Project Reliance and the Navy lab consolidation were largely behind ONR. Finally Miller was able to turn his attention to improving the structure and makeup of his organization. Just as important, Jerry Cann over in the Navy secretariat was having similar thoughts.

In fact, Cann had been unhappy with the organization since his principal deputy days. In particular, he had considered it a disaster when ONT was transferred to the CNR's purview with the disbandment of the Naval Material Command in 1985. The reason: until then ONT had worked very closely with the systems commands in developing and transferring technology because it was part of an organization that directly supported the Fleet. With the shift to the Office of the Chief of Naval Research, ONT was now part of an organization whose entire history was geared toward supporting basic research often far removed from the direct needs of the systems commands. Says Cann, "That was a huge mistake because it broke the connection between people doing development in aircraft and so forth . . . and the people doing R&D to support them, and pushed them away from each other."

The transfer of OAT to the CNR's domain hadn't helped, Cann says, because the mentality at the ONR hadn't changed. Now, both the ONT and ONR were removed from the people doing development work in the systems commands. Remembers Cann, "The big picture from my point of view is there was no connectivity between what ONR was doing and the development programs. In other words, stuff was not flowing from ONR to NavAir, NavSea, and other places in a way that I thought made sense—and they were spending a lot of money. . . . What I wanted to do was get a much better connection between the work that was going on in the 6.3a world and the 6.2 world and the people doing the development."

Cann's executive assistant was a Navy captain named Marc Pelaez. Sometime probably early in 1992, as Pelaez remembers it, "We from the secretariat [had] told him [Miller] that the organization as it was needed to change."[14]

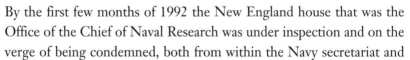

By the first few months of 1992 the New England house that was the Office of the Chief of Naval Research was under inspection and on the verge of being condemned, both from within the Navy secretariat and by the ONR's own management.

As former staffers of both organizations recount the travails of that period, a one-word term is almost universally used to describe the issue at hand: stovepipes. The reality had dawned on everyone that ONR, ONT, and OAT were all standalone organizations not used to sharing information or working together. In fact, they operated like individual fiefdoms, for 6.1 basic research, 6.2 applied research, and 6.3 technology development and demonstration, respectively. As Miller explains, "I had these three stovepipe organizations . . . all reporting to me and I'm the integrator. That's not good. The CEO shouldn't be the integrator."

With some urgency Miller began holding hearings with key personnel about how to reorganize and revitalize his office. Both he and

Cann agreed they should also get outside perspective. To that end Cann sent over Marc Pelaez, his executive assistant. Others came from the various systems commands to provide input on how ONR's "customers" would like to see things reconfigured. Their idea was simple, says Pelaez: "'Look, we're going to abolish the stovepipes.'"

The reviews lasted months. "I think that a lot of people during this period were very confused about what an ONR, OAT, ONT, OCNR was," reflects Phil Selwyn, the director of ONT. His own office, smack in the middle of this chain, received intense scrutiny. "There was a very, very extended review of the management of the 6.2 program, the ONT," says Selwyn. "That was a very arduous time for me."[15]

This intense examination reflected the imperative of adapting to a changing world. When money was flowing throughout much of the Cold War, few in the Navy cared deeply about what was happening at ONR. But now the Soviet Bloc had crumbled, and the overall budget for science and technology was slipping. Especially in the face of the just-concluded Gulf War and the prospect for an increasing number of smaller regional conflicts, the pressure was more intense than ever to make the relevance of the work ONR supported more clear to the Fleet and to Congress—and to deliver technologies for the here and now.

"There was a lot of angst over that, because budgets were being cut across the board in many cases," says Pelaez. "Many, many programs were impacted. And ONR was sort of in this insular world over there, off to the side." All told, some $1.5 billion was flowing into the three programs under the ONR auspices. But on the operational side of the Navy in particular, he notes, "they weren't sure what they were getting out of it, because ONR, frankly, for a long time always pushed back to these one or two things that they had done, and that doesn't justify over a billion dollars a year of investment. They'd talk about inventing radar at NRL. I mean that stuff was still being used. So you had a big disconnect that had occurred."

Tension over this issue seems to have permeated the building. At the top of the agenda was how to better connect the basic science efforts that ONR funded, some of which looked ten or fifteen years down the road, to the applied research and technology development and demonstration sides of its house. "How do we make that a more continuous flow?" explains Pelaez. "It doesn't mean that everything you start in one area ends up flowing to the next. But how do you connect them in a logical way that shows the value of the investment?" However, while people generally agreed on the overall necessity of integrating things better, a consensus on how to proceed proved elusive. "Everybody had a different viewpoint," remembers Fred Saalfeld, who was chief science officer of the 6.1 program at ONR.[16]

The effort apparently dragged on into the fall. Teams studied the different offices, trying to identify the various roles each organization and job inside them played. Once those results were in, says Selwyn, the ONT director, "a drill began where people started working on a possible reorganization." New organizational charts were then created, but no names were put in.

Finally, Miller figured he had enough information and called the all-hands meeting. The idea he ended up embracing was to form one big organization under a single scientific or technical director, not three. He didn't have all the details worked out, not by a long shot. But he made it clear to Selwyn in advance of the all-hands that the top job would likely not be his. "I was not a happy camper," says Selwyn. Consequently, he decided to skip the meeting.

Almost no one else stayed away, however. It was a full ONR-ONT-OAT house that poured into the ballroom at the West Park Hotel in Roslyn. At this point, the general staff was well aware of the intense ongoing examination but still largely unaware of the course it was taking. Says Selwyn, "People knew something was up, and people knew that the trend was to consolidate. But people didn't know who was going to be responsible for what box." It was all still very vague.

Surrounded by the posters showing a few early ideas of how ONR might look in the future, Miller got right to the job of clearing things up. He told the crowd that the three organizations they now represented were going to be blown up and reconstituted as a single entity. The CNR stressed that it was still a work in progress, and that everyone would have a chance to provide input. But the basic idea was that it would be restructured along discipline lines, not the 6.1, 6.2, 6.3 budget categories that currently divided things. As he put it: "We are going to spend the next year reorganizing our efforts so that we are all complementary along logical lines rather than budget lines."

Then, to shake staffers out of the bureaucratic complacency that he feared would set in, Miller dropped the bombshell about disestablishing ONR and abandoning everyone's billet. He stressed, however, that even though individual jobs no longer existed, no one was going to be fired. "We're not going to let you go," he said. "Your pay is protected but not your work assignment."

Job security was no doubt a big consolation to many present. But Saalfeld still describes the general tone of the meeting as: "Shock. Shock."[17]

Selwyn puts it another way, even though he didn't attend the meeting. The demolition announcement took place on December 4, a Friday, and went into effect the next day. Fridays weren't generally considered good days to deliver major bad news, largely because they left everyone the weekend to stew about events in isolation. But, Selwyn notes, the Navy wanted to move quickly; and the news couldn't wait until the following Monday because that was December 7. No one wanted to deliver such bad tidings on Pearl Harbor Day.

Still, to Selwyn and no doubt many others, December 4 was also a day that would live in infamy.

CHAPTER 4

The New ONR

All through the holidays, ONR existed in suspended animation. No one knew what his or her job would be. No one knew the structure of the forthcoming organization. No one knew who the bosses would be. "Everybody was in limbo," sums up Fred Saalfeld.[1]

With the New Year, things chug-a-lugged into action. As if confronting an organizational Humpty Dumpty, Bill Miller set about putting ONR back together again, in a different form. The admiral launched a national hunt for a technical or scientific director to head the civilian side of the house. New teams formed to study existing personnel and programs in finer detail and develop recommendations for a structure that better blended basic research, applied research, and advanced technology development. Suggestion lists even went up beside all the elevator banks to solicit feedback from staffers, so that no one felt excluded.

Everything took place against the specter of looming changes in leadership, both in the Navy Secretary's office and at ONR itself. A presidential election had just been held, and George H. W. Bush would not be returned to office. As of January 20, 1993, the day that President Bill Clinton was sworn in, a new Secretary of the Navy would be needed.[2] Tough-minded ASN RDA Jerry Cann, a main force in the changes the organization was trying to implement, would also be out of work. If that weren't enough, Admiral Miller was two and a half years into a three-year tour as Chief of Naval Research. By the coming summer a successor for his job would be needed as well.

As it turned out, Cann had begun preparing for his own departure long before the election. Not only did he consider it possible that

President Bush would be defeated, he wasn't sure that he would stay on the job even if the president were reelected. A big part of those preparations centered on ONR. In the months leading up to Election Day, the Assistant Navy Secretary brokered a deal with CNO Frank B. Kelso II to move Cann's executive assistant, Marc Pelaez, into the CNR job when Miller's tour ended. Earlier in 1992, Pelaez had been selected for his admiral's star and was waiting for a position to open. So the fit seemed perfect. The pending assignment was one reason Pelaez had been so involved in ONR's study sessions throughout the second half of 1992, mainly sitting on the sidelines and kibitzing, as he termed it, but also gathering ideas for his own tour.[3]

Now, as 1993 opened, Pelaez worked even more closely with Miller and the ONR team to get a new structure up and running. Hiring the technical director—the top civilian position and in essence the overall number two official at ONR—headed the list of action items. The position was absolutely critical to making the new structure work. In many ways, it superseded the importance of the CNR, since CNRs would come and go every few years but the technical director might serve in the role for a decade or longer. It was vital to find someone well regarded in the university community who would continue to nurture ONR's long-standing ties to academe. But he or she also had to be comfortable with applied research and development in order to transition products and technologies to the Fleet with much greater urgency than in the past.

As Miller began scouring the country for a technical director, he also had three potential internal candidates: the heads of his recently disbanded fiefdoms, Saalfeld from ONR, Selwyn at ONT, and DeCorpo at OAT. Although he had already discouraged Selwyn from applying, Miller told all three they were free to compete for the post. "I don't think anybody was happy with me for that," he says. Selwyn didn't bother. The respected former ONT director would soon decline a lesser position offered to him and go off to a successful career in industry. Saalfeld and DeCorpo, though, threw their hats into the ring.

On top of those two, a slew of strong external candidates applied for the position, including officials from several national laboratories.

Miller formed a selection committee that included his successor, Pelaez. But the final decision was Miller's: he was the "deciding official." As one of the last acts of his tenure, he chose Saalfeld.

The choice of the longtime ONR veteran wasn't a universal crowd pleaser. Jerry Cann, for one, would have preferred someone with experience in industrial R&D. Still, it was hard to argue with Saalfeld's bona fides. Armed with a PhD in physical chemistry, he'd been in the Navy research fold for thirty years. He had started out at the Naval Research Laboratory as a young researcher, rising to head NRL's chemistry division. In 1979 he had been tapped to oversee the London office of ONR and had returned as associate director of the organization. For the last six years, since 1986, he had been ONR's scientific director. He was greatly respected in academe and among the staff. But he also had experience beyond the world of basic research. While at NRL he had managed a program that solved one of the top ten problems in the submarine fleet: how to test and maintain onboard air quality. Working with Perkin-Elmer, Saalfeld and his team had pioneered a central atmosphere monitor system (CAMS) that enabled crew members to reliably gauge air quality in real time. He had helped transfer that and many subsequent technologies to the Navy. Years later, when it came time to apply for the new ONR technical director job, he says, "That was my calling card."

Saalfeld understood the necessity of the changes descending on his organization. "ONR had become almost exclusively in its mind a

A chemist by training, Fred Saalfeld joined the Naval Research Laboratory in 1962, where he worked for some twenty years before moving to ONR as director of its research department. In 1993 he was appointed technical director of ONR and Deputy Chief of Naval Research, the highest-ranking civilian post. As such, he oversaw Navy and Marine Corps science and technology programs from basic research to exploratory and advanced technology development. He remained in this post until his retirement from ONR in 2002, although his title was subsequently changed to executive director and technical director of ONR.

Office of Naval Research

basic research organization," he says. "And putting it all together [with applied research and technology demonstration] to me always made a lot of sense."

Despite his credentials, winning the job was quite a coup for Fred Saalfeld for another reason: he was in the hospital at the time, just out of a coma. Saalfeld didn't return to work until June 5, 1993. His official title then became Deputy Chief of Naval Research and technical director of ONR.

How ONR Saved Fred Saalfeld's Life

Fred Saalfeld retired in 2002 after forty years in Navy research, first at the Naval Research Laboratory and then at ONR, where for the last decade of his career he served as Vice Chief of Naval Research and technical director. Saalfeld was named to ONR's top civilian post in the spring of 1993. But if not for a shrewd insight by an ONR program officer, he likely would not even have been alive.

Saalfeld's ordeal started that February. After slogging through the paperwork to apply for ONR's head civilian job, he decided to have an operation to replace his ailing arthritic hip. Just before checking into the hospital, however, he developed a serious infection in the joint. He barely made it into the emergency room when he went into septic shock and then fell into a coma.

As bacteria riddled his body, it seemed likely that Saalfeld would never recover. For Adm. William Miller, then Chief of Naval Research, what happened next really showed what a special place ONR was. "It really talked to the culture of the institution. It wasn't 'The boss is sick,' it was, 'Hey, Fred's sick,'" he relates. "You'd go over to the waiting room, it would be full of ONR scientists."

At one such point a doctor came up to Fred's wife, Liz, in the waiting room, wanting to talk candidly about her husband. As usual, a group of ONR people gathered round.

"Can we talk to you privately?" the doctor asked.

"No," Liz replied. "These are my family."

"Does he have a living will?"

But even at that low point, no one gave up. ONR's scientific staff kept coming up with questions about Saalfeld's condition the doctors couldn't answer. Then an ONR program manager named Jeannie Maejda stepped to the fore.

Maejda's expertise in this area turned out to be strong, and in a big way she had Saalfeld to thank. As director of ONR's basic research program, Saalfeld had earlier instituted a policy to encourage his program officers to publish scientific papers to help keep them academically current. Maejda, a biologist, had decided to write a paper on a sometimes deadly bacteria called *haemophilus parainfluenzae* (this bacteria took the life of Muppet creator Jim Henson).

Saalfeld hadn't been impressed with the topic and wanted to nix it, but Maejda's immediate supervisor stressed its importance to the Navy, so he relented. Maejda realized her boss had this very infection and was able to make treatment recommendations to the doctor. Saalfeld was given a new batch of drugs, and within a few days—after a month in a coma—he awoke. Marvels Saalfeld, "Jeannie was studying the very bacteria that I had been infected by. Boy, that shows what kind of a director I am: I want to cut the program that eventually saves my life."

Soon thereafter, Miller came to see him in the hospital, wondering if he was going to retire or return to work. A grateful Saalfeld said he "absolutely" planned to come back.

That's when the admiral offered him the top civilian job. "So ONR saved Fred's life," says Miller. "Right during the competition, I had decided he was going to be the person, but then he went into shock. We kind of held the job for him until he was on his feet."

The story of Fred Saalfeld's battle with *haemophilus parainfluenzae* is derived chiefly from interviews with Saalfeld (October 17, 2006) and Miller (September 1, 2006).

In Saalfeld's absence, ONR's scientific program was overseen by Tim Coffey, who'd been dispatched to Ballston Towers from the Naval Research Laboratory. Coffey had attended MIT in his hometown of Cambridge, Massachusetts, and ultimately earned his PhD in physics at the University of Michigan. In 1971, after a few years in industry, he had joined NRL as head of a plasma physics division branch. He rose through the ranks and in 1982 was named director of research. As NRL's top civilian, Coffey had line authority over the organization and its 1,400 government scientists and engineers.

Many ONR staff scientists and program officers were unhappy with the merger plan, he relates. The latest round of studies of possible structures for the organization ran three or four months while he was there. "The big driving force was to integrate these stovepipes," Coffey notes. But people held widely different views of what "integrate" meant. As the reality of the changes grew more clear, debates raged over what form they should take. "That was a bit ugly at the time," he says.[4]

Miller tried to hold the debate out in the sunshine, conscientiously avoiding the imagery of plotting decisions in a smoke-filled room. It was his idea to post potential drafts of the organization on bulletin boards near the elevators. Staffers were encouraged to mark up the drafts with their own ideas. "It was as much team-building as it was organization at that time. We didn't want people to feel excluded," says Miller. After a few months nobody scribbled on the sheets anymore. Then he knew they were close.

None of this was completely resolved by the time Saalfeld returned in early June; the challenge of combining three organizations into one and then recasting the roles of some 350 or 400 government staffers made for slow going. Plus, of course, existing work had to go on. As Saalfeld puts it, "We had to keep all the programs running while we underwent a rather major institutional change and cultural change."

Making the job harder was the fact that in the face of the government's budget woes, overall billet strength—the number of jobs allocated to ONR under the latest five-year plan—was being slashed. Over that time, they would lose about a quarter of total personnel, going from nearly four hundred staffers to closer to three hundred. "The work increased and the budget decreased," says Saalfeld. It wasn't a story unique to ONR.

Saalfeld had never had his hip replacement: the joint had been eaten away by the bacteria to the point the operation was no longer feasible. At first confined to a wheelchair, and later building to crutches and finally a cane, he took a month or longer to get up to speed and regain his strength. All that time Coffey stayed in the acting technical director role and proved a godsend, says Saalfeld, helping him refine ideas for "what in the world the new organization should be."

During this same period, Marc Pelaez had also been bivouacked in the ninth-floor executive suite, waiting in the wings to take over. On July 1,

1993, Pelaez put on his admiral's star for the first time and formally assumed command as the new Chief of Naval Research. Only then did he and Saalfeld finally dive fully into the chore before them.

"The first thing I did was I sat down and read in detail every position description of all four hundred and some people," Saalfeld says. Then he formed a new committee, looking at all three organizations as a whole, from their budgets to their technical and administrative staffs. This involved still more meetings, as consultants were brought in to add their voices to the choir. Saalfeld also staked out a spot in a conference room and began interviewing a succession of people about their jobs and what they thought should be done.

From this input Saalfeld constructed a detailed model of the new organization. He reiterated, rehashed, and debated everything with key colleagues, especially Pelaez, who had to approve the final structure. In the end, everyone involved just kept working through the various issues until a solid structure came to light and general agreement was reached on what should be done. Eventually, they were able to account for most of the needed personnel cuts through attrition in nontechnical jobs, such as building maintenance, mailroom, and secretarial staff. "That was stuff I could contract out. I didn't need to use precious billets for it," Saalfeld notes. The last task was to assign staffers to specific areas and positions. "I spread them according to their talents," he says.

This work spanned the first six months of Pelaez's term. The result was the combination of all existing scientific and technical programs into five new science and technology (S&T) departments, or "codes." A sixth, nonscientific department was targeted at increasing ONR's ties to industry, which had been underemphasized in the past.

One of the most hotly contested issues centered on the names for the new departments. "That was always a big argument," recounts Saalfeld. "Do you reach out to the academics . . . or the military? What we did was go for a compromise, which didn't really appease anybody."

When the dust settled, the new arrangement looked like this:

> Code 31: Information, Electronics, and Surveillance
> (S&T department)
> Code 32: Ocean, Atmosphere, and Space (S&T department)

Code 33: Engineering, Materials, and Physical Sciences
(S&T department)
Code 34: Human Systems (S&T department)
Code 35: Special Warfare (S&T department)
Code 36: ONR Industrial and Corporate Programs
department

A civilian scientist would head each of these groups except Code 36. Reflecting the imperative of increasing ties to the Fleet, however, every S&T department was assigned a Navy captain as deputy chief. Nothing like this had previously existed in ONR. "The military guys in ONR had not had very definitive roles prior to that. And we tried to make that really an outreach to them," says Saalfeld. Pelaez, he adds, pushed hard for such changes.

Management of the departments formed another big issue. Where did the leaders come from—ONT, OAT, or the "old ONR?" All three would have their representation. But the choice here was weighted to the traditional science side of the organization. Jim DeCorpo, the former OAT director, was put in charge of Code 32. A veteran of the Office of Naval Technology, Elihu "Eli" Zimet, was given the reins to Code 35. The three remaining scientific department heads came from the "old ONR."

Directly overseeing this structure and reporting straight to Saalfeld were an S&T director and a deputy director. The director, whom Jerry Cann had sponsored into the job, was Art Bisson. He specialized in applied research (6.2) while the deputy director, Bruce Robinson, was from the 6.1 "old ONR" world. In reality, the two were coequals, says Saalfeld. But he and Pelaez reasoned it might send a more positive message to the Fleet if the 6.2 person was in charge.

Many adjustments and refinements would be made to this organization over the coming years as each Chief of Naval Research sought to secure his legacy—and as each step in the organization's evolution made another step possible. But at least for the next fifteen years, this was the essential post–Cold War structure of the Office of Naval Research.

Within a few months of completing the new structure, probably in early 1994 when he was more mobile, Fred Saalfeld found himself in Chicago, surrounded by a group of anxious oceanographers. Everyone had gathered at an airport hotel in the Windy City to attend a scientific meeting. But Saalfeld realized that some of the world's top scientists were as curious about the changes at ONR as they were about the conference agenda. The oceanographers were particularly anxious about the 6.1 contract research program and what the merger would mean for it. The general feeling, he recalls, was one of dread: here was another short-sighted government cutback in basic research that was making it hard to maintain the U.S. lead in science and technology. After all, if the Navy wouldn't fund basic studies of the ocean, who would?

Saalfeld tried to reassure them. "The real big problem was convincing [them] that we weren't just going to be applied research, that we would keep our basic research," he explains. Accompanying him was Jim DeCorpo, now heading Code 32, Ocean, Atmosphere, and Space. "We were trying to make the integration of 6.1, 6.2, and 6.3 seamless," Saalfeld explains. The two then assured their audience that making applied research more integral to ONR did not mean the office was forsaking basic research.

The oceanographers were hardly alone in their concerns. That spring and summer Saalfeld and fellow staffers undertook a road show to MIT, the University of Chicago, the University of California San Diego, and other universities around the country—mindful of the tour Dexter Conrad led to launch ONR—to stress to academics that ONR's contract research program would continue. "I went to a lot of places to try to talk to the communities about where we were going and that we were going to maintain a strong 6.1 interest," Saalfeld recalls. "They were all very frightened that ONR would just leave them high and dry."

That wouldn't be the case. But the coming budget reductions, which had already forced a billet reduction, were about to put ONR funding for 6.1 programs into a deep swoon. In real 2005 dollar terms, ONR's basic research funding reached a post–Cold War high of $522 million in fiscal year 1993. It headed steadily downhill for the next five years, bottoming out at $373 million in 1998 before climbing back up to

$491 million in fiscal year 2005. The next year, though, it turned south once more, falling to $439 million, where it appeared set to level out for at least a few more years.

The funding crunch, coupled with the new organizational framework and mounting pressure to deliver real benefits to the Navy, probably raised the anxiety level at ONR to its highest level of the post–Cold War era. All these changes also altered the character of ONR. The basic science program continued, with hundreds of millions poured into 6.1 research. But the numbers did not tell the whole story. Tim Coffey perceived a change in the mindset of ONR program officers, and dates it to the merger. "I think that has had an effect on people's view of what they should be doing in science and technology—looking for stuff that will pay off in the shorter term, and maybe not looking as much as they should in the longer-term," he says.

To Coffey, and many others, ONR was never again the same kind of place. That was why he spoke of the "old ONR" and the "new ONR." As soon as Saalfeld settled into the job, recalls Coffey, "I came back to NRL as rapidly as my feet would carry me."

This was the climate during Marc Pelaez's first months as Chief of Naval Research. The changes had gone down. Now, he had the task of making it work. Pelaez was the son of two naturalized U.S. citizens, a Spanish-born father and native French mother. He grew up in Miami speaking fluent French and some of his father's language. After high school, he matriculated to the Naval Academy and graduated in the vaunted class of '68, along with future Chiefs of Naval Operations Michael G. Mullen and Jay L. Johnson, future Navy Secretary James Webb Jr. (in 2006 elected to the U.S. Senate from Virginia), Rhodes Scholar and future Director of National Intelligence Dennis Blair, and Oliver North. Ultimately, this class would produce more admirals and Marine Corps generals than any class in history.

After graduation, Pelaez became a nuclear submariner. He eventually rose to command the nuclear-powered attack submarine USS *Sunfish* (SSN 649), which he commanded on special missions from 1984 to 1987, during the waning days of the Cold War. Along the way he served a number of shore tours in Washington, including a stint overseeing submarine R&D at NavSea. In January 1988, after his last sea tour, then Captain Pelaez was dispatched to Defense Advanced Research Projects Agency (DARPA), where he worked on submarine technology. It was in that position that he came to know Jerry Cann, who was then with General Dynamics. When Cann assumed the Assistant Navy Secretary position a few years later, he asked Pelaez to become his executive assistant. The job turned out to be his stepping-stone to Chief of Naval Research.

The new CNR was smart, resourceful, and astute in the ways of Washington. However, Pelaez's task was made harder than it needed to be because he was constrained by a unique situation that no other CNR has faced, before or since: he only had one star.

Traditionally, the Chief of Naval Research was a two-star position, required by law to have the same rank as the heads of the systems commands (in the original law it read bureau chiefs, but the Navy's matériel bureaus had been abandoned in favor of the systems commands). But just prior to Pelaez's term, some legislative maneuvering had removed that provision so that the CNR could even be a civilian. According to Pelaez, it was inserted into a bill by a staff member of the Senate Armed Services Committee, who fancied himself competing for the job. "As a result," notes Pelaez, "the CNR was no longer equivalent to the Syscoms in terms of rank." Largely through the efforts of his former executive assistant, Cdr. Eric Womble, whom Pelaez had arranged to be transferred to the staff of Senate majority leader Trent Lott, they were able to get the old rule reinstated. However, it would apply to all Pelaez's successors, but not the admiral himself.

His lower standing almost certainly handicapped Pelaez because he just didn't have the clout of previous CNRs. He was also hindered by Cann's departure. Relates Saalfeld, "I think had George Herbert Walker Bush been reelected in '92, and Jerry Cann reappointed as ASN, Pelaez would have been enormously more successful, maybe even become a three-star or four-star. But his cover was Jerry Cann. And when he was left hanging as a one-star, he was free game." Shrugs Saalfeld, "In this town, this is the way the game is played."

Still, by all accounts Pelaez played a difficult hand well, diving into the daunting task of creating a single, cohesive ONR from three separate organizations. "It was trying to put together three different cultures," says Jim DeCorpo. The small OAT group DeCorpo had overseen interacted chiefly with the Pentagon, the Fleet, and the various warfare centers. His staff hadn't spent much time in universities. Similarly, the 6.1 program mangers "never set foot in the Pentagon. They were all academic." ONT personnel, DeCorpo says, fell somewhere in between.[5]

Blending these three worlds didn't sit all that well with any of them. "There was a lot of rumbling within the organization," Pelaez acknowledges. Many staff members, he says, felt like they had lost power with the forced breakdown of the barriers between the three groups. But getting people from different organizational cultures to work together was a relatively small part of the challenge because most staffers came from the original ONR in the first place. Potentially far more problematic was the fact that program teams were now expected to manage efforts as they moved across the three budget categories. That meant that people used to working in one world now had to become adept in all three worlds.

The argument for this situation was that it enabled a program manager to take an idea from discovery to deployment, avoiding the headaches that come with handing projects off to an entirely new team. In short, the person with the original vision behind a program could own it all the way from inception to acquisition by the Fleet.

In practice, though, things were rarely that easy. It made the entire portfolio more program manager dependent. Some were good at working across all three areas. Some were not. As DeCorpo puts it, "There are some people who can work at all viscosities. There are some 6.1 and always that way."

Indeed, with the technical director, half the department heads, and almost all the staff from the "old ONR," the new ONR was still dominated by its basic research mentality. Phil Selwyn, the former ONT director, saw that as a big problem. Says Selwyn, "So you had a situation where on the one hand the Navy was supposed to vertically integrate these programs, but the people they had to do it were culturally and [experientially] biased to 6.1."[6] Their lack of experience in other areas could actually slow down the R&D process or, worse, cause good programs to fail.

Pelaez could see the pitfalls. He had helped choose Fred Saalfeld as Vice Chief of Naval Research and technical director of ONR. Yet he knew Saalfeld's roots in basic research loomed as a potential problem. "The 6.1 was so disconnected from anything else. It was stand-alone. It was Fred Saalfeld's baby. He was sort of the guardian of 6.1. He had to broaden beyond that," he says. "And it was all about getting not only Fred but the technical people at ONR to understand what this was all about."

Part of the answer lay in changing the mindset of the ONR scientists. Rather than seeing projects as specific pieces of technology or activities in individual realms of science, Pelaez urged the staff to think in terms of programs that ran all the way from basic research to demonstration. He also extolled the scientific staff to work on the story: how could the Navy one day benefit from what they were funding?

"If you are thinking about things in 6.1, you have to have some vision of what it can yield," explains Pelaez. "You have to articulate that, and that was where I think ONR was failing. They couldn't articulate it in terms that the operational Navy could appreciate. Even the farthest-out scientists would always have to tell me where they saw the applicability to the future Navy. For example, Buckyballs can reduce friction and could ultimately result in longer-running, quieter machinery."

Staff members responded very well to all this, Pelaez says. But even as he coaxed program officers out of their 6.1 mentality, he also worked the other side of the fence—striving to get the Defense Department and the Navy to better appreciate the virtues of what ONR did.

By 1994 defense belt-tightening was threatening to engulf ONR. The Department of Defense put forth a proposed budget that contained huge cuts in the Navy's science funding, far greater than those ultimately enacted. "Over the five-year plan that was submitted, we would have had hundreds of millions of [additional] dollars taken out of science," Pelaez says. To fight off the cuts, he pulled together a list of all the Nobel laureates that ONR had supported over the years—close to fifty. A significant number of those still living, the admiral relates, went directly to Secretary of Defense William J. Perry to plead the case for science. Says Pelaez, "That's how we got the money restored."

The admiral also took part in the ongoing Project Reliance, joining the weekly breakfast club meetings with his counterparts from the Army and Air Force and continuing the practice of divvying up key R&D costs and management responsibilities. Also joining the breakfast club was the new director of defense research and engineering, Anita Jones. She was responsible for managing the Defense Department's S&T program. Her presence, Pelaez says, provided an important vehicle for interacting with the White House on national science policy.[7]

Several other outreach efforts were notable this period. Sometime in late 1994 or early 1995 Pelaez began cultivating ties to Jeremy "Mike" Boorda, who had recently become Chief of Naval Operations. The two quickly developed an unusually good rapport. "We met at least once a month," Pelaez remembers. "We became very close. We could talk about what the Navy needed, where the Navy was going."

Occasionally, Boorda visited ONR for special briefings. These were informal sessions that Pelaez says may not have happened before or since. One day in late 1995 they were walking down the steps of the ONR building after a brief on advanced training techniques to enhance learning when Boorda, an old surface sailor, turned to Pelaez, the former submariner: "I'll tell you what I need your help on," the Navy chief said. "We're all thinking about the next generation of surface ship. My problem is that all the traditional players, the systems commands, are going to give me is an upgraded DDG 51 [guided-missile destroyer]. What we have is pretty good, but I need to know if there is something else we should be thinking about, or a different way to do it."

What CNR could ignore that opening? Pelaez quickly assembled two teams, one from ONR, the other from NRL. He assigned them the task of brainstorming about the next generation of surface ships. Any idea was fair game, he told them. But the process was heavily influenced by experiences in the Gulf War, which had seen the first combat use of Tomahawk cruise missiles launched from ships and submarines. One glaring lesson from that conflict was that the Navy didn't have the capacity to carry enough Tomahawks to regional theaters. Each ship had only so many holds, and some were needed for antiaircraft missiles, antisubmarine rocketry, and other types of weaponry. Pelaez therefore charged his teams with coming up with a ship design concept to address this problem at the lowest possible cost.

Two months later Pelaez met Boorda for breakfast and handed him an idea for a double-hulled ship built to commercial, not military, standards. Maintained by a small crew of under 50, it could carry a stunning 1,042 Tomahawk launchers. "It was all about getting firepower," says Pelaez. "The idea was somebody else would do the targeting, send it to these guys, and they could launch."

That was the genesis of what became known as the arsenal ship program. Boorda jumped on the basic idea and set up a series of meetings involving ONR and ship architects. From those discussions, the initial number of launch tubes was cut by roughly half, to 512. The Naval Sea Systems Command and DARPA were brought to the table. And by March of 1996 a memorandum of agreement to fund the arsenal program was signed by those two groups and ONR. The agreement called for a demonstrator ship to be ready by October 2000. Cost of this first ship was not to exceed $541 million, with the Navy and DARPA agreeing to put up $371 million and $170 million, respectively.

The project kicked off only two months before Boorda committed suicide after learning that *Newsweek* was readying a story questioning the legitimacy of the "V" for valor pin on his Vietnam combat ribbon.[8] Pelaez himself would end his tour that July and leave the Navy. But the arsenal ship project continued through two complete phases before being terminated on December 31, 1997, when then Navy Secretary John Dalton "reluctantly determined that continuation . . . into Phase III and further phases was unachievable," according to an account by the program manager.[9]

Still, Pelaez was particularly proud of the effort. It forced Navy ship planners to think outside their normal box. The next generation of destroyers, the DD(X)—ultimately designated the DDG 1000 *Zumwalt*-class destroyer—incorporated at least some of the arsenal ship concepts, though it could hold only eighty missile launch cells. "The impact on Navy thinking was significant," Pelaez says.

Pelaez's other big outreach efforts were geared to the Fleet. The systems commands had always had trouble seeing the benefits of the fundamental research that ONR supported. But they also groused about the 6.3 program in technology demonstration. Ideally, once a project was successfully demonstrated (and only a percentage from the 6.1 program made it to this stage), the systems commands would be ready, willing, and eager to give it a home. In reality, that was too often not the case. Oftentimes, the demonstrations proved too raw for Fleet representatives to make an informed judgment of an effort's worth. In other cases, it turned out the program officers hadn't worked with the systems commands to make sure that ONR had funded something the Fleet actually wanted.

Recognizing that ONR was part of the problem, early in his tour Pelaez arranged for ONR to take center stage in the Navy's Science Advisors Program (SAP). The SAP, as it was known, was an existing program under which the Navy laboratories sent scientific representatives to work alongside Fleet commanders, usually for a two- or three-year detail. The idea was to help them become more familiar with real-world conditions and concerns, and to provide technical or scientific advice about what could done to make things better. It was a good idea, says Pelaez, "but there was no connection with ONR. I arranged for responsibility for this program to be transferred to the CNR." A dynamic ONR staffer named Susan Bales was put in charge of the program, which Pelaez says immediately made a difference in getting ONR more intimately involved with the Fleet as well. "This led to a series of initiatives and interactions with the Fleet that greatly enhanced the advocacy for ONR and speeded the introduction of new technology to the Fleet—in some cases bypassing the normal acquisition process," he says.

Toward the end of his service, Pelaez tried to cultivate similar ties to the systems commands, inviting them to send representatives to ONR. He designated an office area reserved for these emissaries so that they could follow program progress and interact with staff members— key steps to building the rapport and trust necessary to moving advances into service ever more readily. "It was trying to show that there's not some big conspiracy to hide things from you," Pelaez says. "We're not going to make science and technology decisions by vote, but you can come in and see what's going on." In the end, although the effort was well-intentioned, it met with only marginal success. Only NavAir, the Naval Air Systems Command, really took advantage of it.

———————●———————

Pelaez would lead ONR up to its fiftieth anniversary in the summer of 1996. To celebrate, the organization planned a series of events over several days, including lectures at the National Academy of Sciences by Nobel laureates and other distinguished scientists it had supported over the years.

As he anticipated the celebrations and his imminent retirement from the Navy, Pelaez could look back on the many positive strides the organization had made during his tenure. Some things had worked. Some hadn't. But overall the new ONR was well along toward its pre-merger goal of integrating 6.1, 6.2, and 6.3 research.

The admiral had never shaken his concerns about ONR's standing with the rest of the Navy. In particular, he fretted over how attuned his basic research-oriented staff was to real-world Navy needs. Sometime in the last half of his tour, his angst had prompted him to take another crack at this puzzle.

One day the Chief of Naval Research called an informal meeting of the executive staff in his ninth-floor suite. Joining him were Fred Saalfeld and Art Bisson, the technical director. Pelaez expressed his desire to do better telling the ONR story. "We just needed a better way to articulate what it is we were about," he recalls saying.

The admiral drew a little triangle on a piece of paper. The triangle, he said, represented ONR. At the bottom, he wrote "basic research," the organization's foundation. The base was wide, because it took a lot of exploration to find the nuggets that would turn into real gold. But as you moved up the triangle and began mining the results of basic science into technologies the Navy could use, you naturally narrowed the field. The middle of the triangle, therefore, represented technology development.

"But what's at the top?" someone asked.

"Capabilities," Pelaez responded, writing in that word. "That's the way we should be talking about all our programs." He told Bisson and Saalfeld he didn't want to be briefed on even the most fundamental science project if program officers didn't have some understanding of the capabilities it might produce.

Pelaez calls that meeting a turning point. Soon capabilities became a part of every ONR story. As it turned out, though, no one present had any idea of how really important the discussion would become. That would wait for the next Chief of Naval Research. But if there was one word that summed up what the new ONR had to be all about, it was there on the apex of the triangle: *Capabilities.*

CHAPTER 5

The Valley of Death

ol. Timothy E. Donovan struck an imposing figure—a sturdy Marine tank officer of Irish stock, six-foot-three, 220 pounds, shaved head, full of energy and drive. "I intimidate the shit out of people," he once admitted. "I ask tough questions and don't take prisoners, and I want deliverables."[1]

Donovan arrived at the Office of Naval Research with his gung-ho attitude and almost no track record in science and technology. Yet it did not take long for his enthusiasm, acumen, and passion to make a difference to win over just about everyone, including the scientific staff. He quickly made himself at home.

It was June 1998. Donovan, who had already been selected for brigadier general and would receive his promotion that fall (he would ultimately retire as a major general), had just come on board as the new Vice Chief of Naval Research. In effect, he ranked as the number two on the military side of the organization. Fred Saalfeld, previous Vice Chief and technical director, gladly relinquished his title to accommodate the general. He took the new mantle of "executive director."

With Donovan's arrival, the new ONR accelerated to a higher-octane fuel grade. All the upheaval of the past few years was designed to make the office more streamlined, integrated, and forces-friendly. Donovan represented a much more prominent manifestation of the forces-friendly part of the goal. His appointment marked the first time the Marine Corps had gained anything close to this level of footing at ONR. The move was the result of a shrewd agreement forged by

Marine Corps Commandant General Charles Krulak and the new Chief of Naval Research, Rear Adm. Paul G. Gaffney II. A quid pro quo was involved as well: simultaneously with Donovan's appointment, Gaffney had been named deputy commandant of the Marine Corps for science and technology, or so he thought.[2]

Executed with lightning speed, in bureaucratic terms, these moves were conceived in large part to bring the Marines more front and center at ONR. On a deeper level, though, Gaffney nurtured a more ambitious goal: to address what Saalfeld called the "Valley of Death." This was the executive director's term for the yawning gap between ONR's 6.3 technology development and demonstration efforts and the acquisition world. It referred to the fact that only a handful of the projects that went into demonstration emerged from the "valley" to be accepted by the Fleet.

In Gaffney's view, closer ties to the Marine Corps were one key to bridging the Valley of Death. Because it was much smaller than the Navy, the Marine Corps represented a more manageable test bed for finding better ways to move technologies into service. In that way the Corps could become an incredibly important trailblazer for identifying processes that would benefit the entire Navy. "My philosophy on this was if we were going to try to transition things, it's difficult to transition in a big, huge infrastructure, where you're handing off to big organizations that have their own momentum," explains the admiral. "What I thought was because the Marine Corps is rather small, uncomplicated, and people actually follow orders, one might be able to do a better job learning how to transition and actually transition if we could do more with the Marine Corps."

Even though he had no real track record in science and technology, Donovan had been selected as the Marines' first high-powered liaison to ONR because he had recently been named head of the nearly three-year-old Marine Warfighting Laboratory at Quantico. The lab experimented with "bleeding edge" technologies and strove to accelerate their entry into that service. He was therefore in a prime position to rapidly move ONR projects to the next level, with a minimum of red tape.

The Marines had long been trained to storm the beaches, to be the first forces to gain a critical foothold in war. Now they were being deployed as well to take the beaches in science and technology transition.

———————●———————

As of 2007, Adm. Paul Gaffney was the sole chief from the post–Cold War era to go on to reach vice admiral. The only other CNR to garner a third star was Albert Baciocco, who served in the post from 1978 to 1981.

A big part of Gaffney's success stemmed from the very moves he began almost as soon as he set up his admiral's flag in ONR's ninth-floor executive suite—namely, to cultivate ties to the Marines and take bold steps to bridge the Valley of Death. These took most of his term to make real but proved hallmarks of the office's modern era.

Gaffney had grown up in Ohio, far from the sea. In high school, he'd ranked as the third-best miler in the state. He'd had no intention of becoming a career naval officer. But he had grown interested in oceanography and marine life while spending a good part of each summer visiting his grandmother, who ran a boarding house on Martha's Vineyard. So when the U.S. Naval Academy track coaches came knocking, he decided to apply there. He had vowed to remain with the Navy only as long as it proved challenging. Thirty-five years later, wearing three stars, he finally retired as a vice admiral and president of the National Defense University at Fort McNair, in Washington, D.C.

The new Chief of Naval Research was yet another graduate of the Naval Academy class of 1968. He went immediately on to graduate school, earning a master's degree in ocean engineering at Catholic University under a scholarship program sponsored by the Office of Naval Research. The young ensign then steamed to sea on a minesweeper based in Japan. Gaffney next served as an oceanographic advisor to the Vietnam People's Navy combat hydrographic survey team during the Vietnam War. Over the ensuing years, he held various executive and command positions at sea and ashore, picking up a master's of business administration degree along the way.

As Gaffney took the reins of ONR, it was hardly his first tour at the organization. In fact, it is probably safe to say that no Chief of Naval

Research has spent as much time with the office as the Ohio native. From late 1979 until early 1980, as a lieutenant commander, Gaffney was briefly tapped as acting director of ONR's Arctic and Earth Sciences Division, known as Code 460. Captain Gaffney then served as Assistant Chief of Naval Research from 1989 to 1991 under both "Smoke" Wilson and Bill Miller, putting in long hours to fight off the threatened Defense Department takeover of military labs and deal with the indirect cost of research scandal. He was a big fan of both his former bosses, and knew firsthand how hard they had worked to help the organization adapt to the post–Cold War era. He also had a wealth of respect for the ONR staff. "Because of my strange background, working at ONR several times and even going to sea with civilians, . . . I have no mistrust of, and great faith in, the civil servant," he observes. This view would serve him well in his new position.

After his first tour at Ballston Towers, Gaffney had gone down to the banks of the Potomac River, taking over as commanding officer of the Naval Research Laboratory, which reported to the Office of Naval Research. In 1995, after a three-year term there, he was named commander of ONR's Naval Meteorology and Oceanography Command, located in Bay St. Louis, Mississippi. He held that position when he became Chief of Naval Research in 1996. He would spend four years as CNR, bringing his total ONR/NRL service to more than a decade. "It's unprecedented," he says of his time with the organization.

Gaffney could have used some extra heads as well, for all the hats he wore. The entire first year as Chief of Naval Research he was double-hatted with his old job running the Oceanography and Meteorology center. "So it was a very difficult first year, logistically. Because I essentially worked every working hour of every day for a year until a successor was found for me in Mississippi," he relates.

The agreement he struck with General Krulak earned him a third hat as deputy commandant of the Marine Corps for science and technology. During his tour, too, the OP-098 requirements czar position in the Chief of Naval Operations office was changed. It went from the previous three-star position to a two-star job called OP-091. This post then automatically went to whoever was serving as Chief of Naval

Research—meaning a fourth hat for Gaffney. "If you add up all the stars that those were worth in the early days, it was probably worth about ten stars," he quips.

Given his long experience with ONR, Gaffney nurtured lots of ideas about what to do next. He also knew, though, that the organization had experienced tremendous upheaval in the last few years, and to push on too many fronts risked overwhelming the staff or destroying morale. Now was the time to be methodical and sure-footed and turn structure into action. That was another big reason why he started by concentrating on the Marines: he had long admired the Corps' "professionalism and ability to get things done."

His first meeting with Krulak probably took place in late 1996 or early 1997, after Gaffney had been on the job a little over six months. Gaffney had heard that the general was supportive of science and technology and had even expressed his interest in better employing oceanographic data to support amphibious assaults. "I knew he was sort of enlightened in that regard," says the admiral.

Almost simultaneously, Gaffney met with Gen. Alfred M. Gray Jr., who had served as Marine Commandant until 1991. The general was retired and therefore had no official standing at the Corps, but he had a lot of unofficial influence. He and Gaffney became quite friendly as they discussed ideas for how to better link the Marines with first-class science and technology.

As a result of these feeling-out sessions, a watershed meeting took place at the Marine Corps headquarters on February 17, 1998. Besides Krulak, a four-star general, a trio of three-star generals were in the room, along with other staff. At the meeting, Gaffney briefed the Marine officers on the programs at ONR and how they could help the Marine Corps. He then formally broached the idea of ONR taking formal responsibility for the relatively small existing Marine science and technology program, more than thirty separate efforts in total. In return he proposed a Marine brigadier general becoming Vice Chief of Naval Research, with direct line of succession should the CNR become debilitated.

Col. Thomas "Joe" Singleton, a Marine pilot who had been detailed to ONR since 1993, was blown away by Gaffney's presentation. "He was masterful in the briefing," Singleton says. "He just made an incredibly powerful argument."[3] On the spot, Krulak embraced this plan and stressed that if ONR was going to make its number two a Marine, then the research organization ought to have better standing in the Corps as well. He then pledged to create the vice commandant for science and technology position and either then or soon thereafter made the offer even stronger by putting the terms in writing. As all this was unfolding, the two got down to discussing the right Marine for the ONR job.

It would take more than another year for everything to be formalized, including the transfer of six Marine science and technology billets—three military, three civilian—to the Office of Naval Research. This was the staff of the amphibious warfare technology laboratory at Quantico, Virginia, which became the core of a new group at ONR, the Expeditionary Warfare division.

There was a fly in the ointment, however. It turned out that the legal staff would not allow Gaffney to be appointed deputy commandant of the Marine Corps for science and technology. Joe Singleton handled a lot of the discussions with the lawyers. By his account, the issue was that the Chief of Naval Research had already been named as S&T advisor to both the Chief of Naval Operations and the Marine Corps Commandant. To create a position that gave him the role again and made him a member of the Marines in the process was not possible. Gaffney was apparently never aware of this decision. Since it didn't affect his role or standing, Singleton and others chose not to tell him. "We just left it alone," Singleton says. The "myth" of the Marine Corps appointment was apparently handed down to Gaffney's successors as well. They thought they had that title, but they didn't.[4]

All this took until mid-1999 to unfold. However, the more immediate result of these negotiations was that in March 1998 a card arrived for Colonel Donovan, who at the time was serving as director of the Marine air-ground task force staff training program at Quantico, one of the service's prime training grounds for general officers. The note said something along the lines of: "Congratulations on your selection to Brigadier General. Call me."[5]

Donovan looked at the card in a kind of shock. It was signed by an admiral named Gaffney, of the Office of Naval Research. As the newly selected Marine general relates, "My reaction was, 'ONR? What the hell is ONR? What the hell does this guy want to talk to me for?'"

Gaffney had been on the job for nearly two years when Donovan arrived that June. The admiral had been swamped the whole time, still wearing his oceanographic hat the first year and filling in his knowledge of the staff and programs. Now it was time to reach for the next level. Getting the Marines into the front office marked the first big step. Next on the agenda was finding new ways to push development of technological advances the Marine Corps could really use. That, in turn, would help him identify transition strategies that could benefit the entire Navy.

Donovan's arrival crystallized his plans. Lauds Gaffney, "What really was the spark, the thing that really got it going for me, was Tim Donovan came in as Vice CNR, or VCNR. He's such a dynamic guy. . . . Very good on his feet, enthusiastic, well-accepted by scientists. . . . He was an evangelist for the program."

It was a mutual admiration society, too. Part of Donovan's enthusiasm stemmed from the impressions he had gained of Gaffney after an introductory lunch with the admiral in Ballston Towers even before he had formally come on board. "He was not a typical Navy admiral," says the Marine general. "Tremendous background and enthusiasm. I just said to myself, 'This is a guy I could work with.' I told him I knew nothing about science and technology, but I learned pretty quickly what had to be done." Donovan also took a quick shine to Saalfeld. They had offices in opposite corners of the ninth-floor executive suite and soon began working "hand in glove," in Donovan's words.

The Marine threw himself into his new task with characteristic fervor. The twin assignments running the Marine Warfighting Laboratory and serving as Vice Chief of Naval Research were his first as a general officer. He split his time almost 50/50 between the two, typically spending three weekdays in Arlington and the rest of his on-duty time at Quantico. He loved having two jobs. "If I didn't have two jobs, I wasn't working," he quips.

At the time, ONR carried a few projects on its books to help the Marines. These included one in shallow-water mine warfare and another looking into an advanced amphibious assault vehicle. A Corps officer was typically assigned duties at the office as well. But these largely were second-tier efforts, at least in Donovan's view. "ONR prior to my arrival, you had a colonel up there doing Marine Corps matters type of thing," says Donovan. That was Singleton, who would be there at least another decade, even after he retired from the Corps. The colonel was a great believer in what ONR did and how it could help the Corps. But, says Donovan, there wasn't a lot of passion for the office within the Marine Corps hierarchy. "For a lot of people, they just viewed it as get the Marine Corps share of the Navy research budget. I told Fred Saalfeld, I'm not here to get money. I'm here to leverage the technologies and what ONR is doing. And if it's not doing something of benefit, we will do it."

It didn't take Donovan long to see the essence of the Valley of Death problem. "The hardest piece with S&T is [finding] somebody to pick it up in the R&D process. That was what was broken," he says. Too often, despite good progress with a project, ONR program officers could find no customer to adopt it on the service end. In that case, notes Donovan, "You are at ground zero. You wasted all that S&T time."

Because he also ran the Marine Warfighting Laboratory, Donovan offered a unique way to avoid that trap. "The thing I brought was an execution arm," he relates. "I had the lab, which meant I could take the stuff out of ONR and take it to the field and start getting the visibility with the operating forces." The first big effort they pursued was tied to Urban Warrior, a project ongoing at the Marine lab. In the coming age of asymmetric warfare, it was believed, Marines would increasingly find themselves engaging the enemy in cities. How did you fight in close quarters? How did you land troops, communicate, support? "So I was looking at technical solutions to the urban fight," says Donovan.

ONR could definitely help with that. In fact, Code 31, then called the Information, Electronics, and Surveillance department, was already backing a series of experiments in digitizing the battlefield. They dovetailed with, but were not part of, a program called Extending the Littoral

Battlespace (ELB), which was also incorporated into Urban Warrior. "Littoral" in this case covered everything from shallow coastal seas to an amphibious assault and troop support one hundred miles inland. The ELB effort had started in 1997 as an advanced concept technology demonstration program. This meant it consisted entirely of 6.3 advanced technology development funding.

The ultimate aim was to fulfill the Defense Department's "Joint Vision 2010" concept of supporting joint force operations. Its main focus was to provide accurate firepower, command and control, communications, and sensing throughout the littoral space. Code 31 soon initiated a follow-on effort to ELB that sought to further the goal of seamless command and control between the Army, Air Force, Marine Corps, and Navy: this was through a wireless network called JTF WARNET (Joint Task Force Wide-Area Relay Network) that could provide a shared picture of the battlefield to everyone from an offshore ship commander to a lone rifleman miles inland. One vision of such systems was that Marines would carry laptop displays on which to view battlefield data.[6] It was a hot concept that even had Bill Gates excited. In his 1999 book, *Business @ the Speed of Thought*, the Microsoft founder wrote: "Marines testing the system today are operating what is essentially a battlefield Internet. It ties together all the key players—marines in the field, Command and Control, and friendly aircraft overhead—with up-to-the-second information and real-time messaging."[7]

Overall funding for ELB, which at the time ran around $150 million and covered a four-year period, was being provided by PACOM, the joint Pacific Command. ONR was using part of the funds to push development of core technologies underlying the concept. Until his arrival, though, says Donovan, the effort had been on a relatively slow track. "It had been moving along but it had not been moving along at the light speed that I wanted it to," he notes.

Donovan's Warfighting Lab was gearing up to demonstrate its Urban Warrior efforts during an upcoming urban security and disaster relief exercise scheduled at an old naval hospital facility called Oaknoll and the Naval Air Station at Alameda in March 1999. The exercise was part of a biannual effort called Kernel Blitz that involved some 15 ships and 12,000 sailors and Marines, and was being conducted that spring in three phases in the San Francisco Bay Area and at Camp Pendleton, further down the California coast.

Several ONR demonstrations were slated for these same exercises, including a few that overlapped with the Marine lab's efforts. Donovan pushed everything along at a faster pace. Among the technologies tested by the two organizations: artificial intelligence software "agents" developed by the California Polytechnic Institution (Caltech) that synthesized data from disparate sources, and a Jet Propulsion Laboratory computer program that automatically processed information no matter what application it had originally been written in. Since a variety of programs and systems were being melded together, such synthesis was key to providing a unified picture of the battlefield. Some hardware was being tested as well, including a new type of squad radio. Traditionally, Marines had carried walkie-talkies, where it was necessary to push a button when speaking. Under Urban Warrior, they field-tested a hands-free radio with a boom mike, much like the headsets later developed commercially for cell phones.

Some of the Urban Warrior technology soon found a home among the troops. Military personnel patrolling in Iraq after the U.S. invasion of 2003 would employ future iterations of the radio system. Another technology tested also saw widespread deployment in future years.[8] This was an air-ground communications system that was enabled by the transmission of bursts of digitally stored information.

For Donovan, though, one of the most important results of Urban Warrior was what didn't work. "If you go back and pull some of the failures out, that's probably more interesting than some of the successes," he notes. One example: the portable computer display. It rapidly became clear that troops couldn't fight and look at a computer screen. That pointed the way to the development of heads-up displays.

Another glaring lesson brought to light by the trials was the need for better ways for platoon commanders to see the battlefield. A few months after the exercise Donovan and a few representatives from ONR and the Quantico lab visited an NRL team led by future NRL director of research John Montgomery, who at the time headed the electronic warfare division. They told Montgomery they were interested in a small, cheap, unmanned aerial reconnaissance vehicle that could be equipped with special cameras, fly in forty-knot winds, and be repairable with duct tape. If NRL would tackle the challenge, they promised $1 million a year in funding for three years. Montgomery and his team agreed.

Admiral Gaffney was a driving force behind this offer. "With Tim Donovan's agreement, I gave John Montgomery a chunk of money and said I wanted it fast and cheap and consumable and simple," he recalls. "From my time as commanding officer at NRL, I knew John's work with electronic warfare decoys very well—and knew he could deliver. He did." The result was the well-publicized Dragon Eye drone that won a top innovation award from *Popular Science* and accompanied the First Marine Expeditionary Force to Iraq in 2004, where it took part in the battle of Fallujah.[9]

All these projects would prove important to cultivating ties between the Marines and the Office of Naval Research. Still, it was the ongoing ELB that pointed the way to the next major step in the organization's evolution.

As an advanced technology demonstration project, the program resided squarely in the Valley of Death. For Gaffney, it therefore represented a perfect proving ground for honing some ideas he and Fred Saalfeld had been mulling over. He had been getting a lot of heat from the CNO office and other elements of the Navy to transfer ever-more-relevant technology—and at a faster pace. It was an old story, but with the tough budget climate the brass was turning up the heat.

To ease the pressure, Gaffney decided to make ELB the cornerstone of a much broader program to speed the transfer of an entire suite of "capabilities" to help the Navy and Marine Corps. His focus on capabilities was very much related to the push Marc Pelaez had started at the end of his tour. But Gaffney, says Jim DeCorpo, made it "more structured" and "a clear and distinct part of the portfolio."[10]

The core concept was to offer the Fleet a much bigger hand in determining how ONR funded its more applied or advanced projects. In return, the admiral wanted the top brass to agree to back off their long-standing assaults on the relevancy of the rest of the portfolio, specifically basic research.

It was ambitious, bold, and, to some veteran scientists and program managers, outrageous horse-trading that tampered with ONR's heritage and legacy. To Gaffney it was all about delivering more of what the Navy and Marines needed. He called the program Future Naval Capabilities (FNC).

Gaffney once described the plan as "an elegant form of prostitution." That was because ONR was essentially offering to sell some of itself to the Fleet (Navy) and Force (Marines) in return for a favor of its own. "There are nice forms of prostitution—each give," explains the admiral.

The plan was rooted in an acceptance of basic truths about organizational behavior that he felt had virtually ensured attacks on ONR for decades as a succession of high-ranking officials demanded to know what the organization was doing for them now. It was a tough question to answer because traditionally the ONR budget had been invested in basic research that took years to come to fruition. "The blue suit Navy [was] always under-appreciating what ONR did, even though the ONR track record was phenomenal over decades," says Gaffney. "[That's because] they don't think in terms of decades, they think in terms of their job—years."

To beat back the assault, many bones had been thrown to the Navy to protect the core basic research program. But the pressure kept coming. Right after Gaffney took office, his Naval Academy classmate Adm. Jay L. Johnson became Chief of Naval Operations. Word soon came from the CNO's office that the Office of Naval Research needed to reorganize in a way that provided "some tangible proof of relevance," according to one ONR insider. "So there was born the FNCs."

Gaffney put it another way. "A lot of time and effort had been spent by ONR's scientific staff over the years protecting the basic research and early applied research aspects of the program," he explains. "But I knew if [ONR's work] was not connected to the delivery end, we were not going to get [ongoing] support in the budget." Providing that connection was the intent behind Future Naval Capabilities.

To sell this idea, Gaffney initiated a series of meetings with Vice CNO Don Pilling and his staff, as well as with General Krulak at the Marine Corps. During these sessions, he formally proposed to divide ONR's portfolio into two parts. One half he called "discovery and invention." This was the 6.1 and early 6.2 program. It would not be bound by Navy or Marine Corps requirements. The other half, covering the more applied aspects of 6.2 projects and some two-thirds of 6.3, would essentially become the FNC program. Here the old rules would not apply. He offered the Marines and Navy an unprecedented hand in selecting and managing every project that fell under that part of his agenda.

The plan won quick acceptance outside ONR. It took months, though—essentially the rest of Gaffney's term, to iron out the wrinkles and develop a system that everyone signed onto. He and Saalfeld worked closely together to hone the idea, soliciting feedback from senior civilians at ONR and from Navy and Marine Corps officials. Gaffney estimates that he briefed it "to hundreds and hundreds of people. Systems commands, officers, flag officers. . . . Usually I'm not a big process guy, but this was a big process and realignment initiative."

The gist of the idea lay in what Gaffney, the MBA, called "a balanced portfolio."[11] By describing ONR's investment philosophy in this way, he and Saalfeld were in effect stressing to outsiders the importance of balancing ONR's traditional focus on basic research with the calls to deliver shorter-term results.

On the one hand, they noted, ONR by charter needed to invest in long-term, fundamental research. This they described as taking two forms. One was national naval needs, areas such as ocean acoustics, underwater weapons, and naval engineering that were vital to the Navy but which no other national agency or private corporation could be expected to pursue. The other aspect of basic research took the form of grand challenges. These were a set of very difficult but likely achievable scientific or technical problems that ONR challenged the research community to overcome. A grand challenge, for instance, might be to develop a superconducting electric motor for ships. It was far more specific than a national naval need, but it involved far-reaching investigatory research and could take decades to meet.

Grand challenges and national naval needs made up roughly half of ONR's investment portfolio, Gaffney and Saalfeld told anyone who would listen. Most of the rest of its funding would be dedicated to FNC. These were to be essential advantages that the Navy and Marines would need to ensure technical superiority in the years ahead. FNCs were much further along, well into the applied research and advanced technology development stages, and the goal was to find them a home in the Fleet or Force as quickly and efficiently as possible.

The trick, the officer and the scientist argued, was to balance ONR's investments between these two aspects of its mission. The basic research aspect had been pursued for decades. So it was on the FNC program that they focused their energies.

It turned out that one of the big problems facing the organization was that too many projects were funded too far up the R&D ladder. At the basic science level, it made sense for research to be broad-based, exploring a lot of uncharted ground. But as research matured and continued development grew more expensive, only the more promising projects could be selected for advancement. The pot of money simply wasn't big enough to allow for anything different.

ONR officials had always known this, of course, and they did pare down their portfolio significantly at the higher levels. But in Gaffney's view the organization hadn't done as good a job at winnowing out projects as it should have. That was because in order to be ready for transition to the Fleet, projects had to receive a critical mass of funding and effort. If they didn't have that critical mass, it made no sense to keep them on the books because they weren't going to make it out of the Valley of Death anyway. As Gaffney and Saalfeld reexamined the portfolio, they found the budget pie spread too thin. So many efforts were being carried past basic research and into the 6.2 and 6.3 stages that even the most deserving might not achieve critical mass.

"When you try to fund everything, nothing gets over the bar," Gaffney, Saalfeld, and an ONR consultant named John Petrik wrote, describing the FNC concept. The situation was exacerbated in periods when resources declined, they noted. The tendency was to cut back on programs almost equally across the board, making everyone share the pain. This made it even harder for any to reach critical momentum. Their view, therefore, was that rather than trying to support so many programs "with funding that falls short of the level at which research has a chance of being productive," the Navy would be better served by concentrating its higher-category science and technology budget appropriations into "prioritized, desired future Navy and Marine Corps capabilities."

What was needed, they argued, was a reexamination of the portfolio with an eye toward making sure the most important projects made it over the bar. It might mean carrying fewer into the advanced stages of R&D, but it should mean far more making it across the Valley of Death. A graphic depiction of their idea showed ONR's science and technology efforts shaped like a mountain. That base was made up of basic research or supporting technologies. The mountain's midsection consisted of the 6.2 applied research efforts, also called enabling capabilities. From this rose a group of peaks, the 6.3 programs. The key was to identify the most important mountain peaks and make sure they rose up past the level of critical mass while cutting the others loose. Those that did make the cut appeared as spikes, towering above the critical threshold level.

As Saalfeld put it, "Gaffney and I came in and said you got to take some of them [the programs] and decrease them—and spike some so that you really get transitions. We called that spikeology. And these spikes became FNCs."

All around ONR the scientific staff became consumed by spikes and making sure their pet projects rose to the challenge. Some liked the concept. Others saw it as one of those hollow, buzz-phrase ideas management comes up with and uttered the term with a derisive snicker. "The spikes from hell," one staffer complained. "It didn't make any sense to me."

But spikes were an essential part of the FNC concept. The real issue became how to choose which projects to spike. In the past ONR might have worked with other elements of the Navy and Marine Corps to decide what efforts to pursue, or it might not have. Gaffney's predecessor, Marc Pelaez, had seen the imperative of getting the systems commands more involved in ONR's project selection and oversight, offering them offices in Ballston Towers and creating the Science Advisors Program toward the end of this term. But this was a voluntary program, and only NavAir had really taken advantage of it. With the advent of the FNC process, it was to become standard operating procedure through the creation of mandatory teams that would represent the major stakeholders involved in the process: the Office of Naval Research itself, the Marines or the Fleet, and the CNO office.

These joint groups were called integrated product teams. One of their core functions was to identify potential spikes, or FNCs. They would then pass on their nominations to a newly created oversight body, the Department of the Navy science and technology corporate board, usually just called the Navy corporate board. The board consisted of the CNR and the direct deputies of the highest leadership of the Navy, Marines, and Navy secretariat: the Vice Chief of Naval Operations, the Assistant Commandant of the Marine Corps, and the Assistant Secretary of the Navy for research, development, and acquisition. The board's job was to decide which spikes to try and push over the bar. It could accept the recommendations brought before its members, reject them, or suggest modifications. Oftentimes board members were given "prebriefings" to solicit their input and incorporate it into the formal proposal.

The involvement of top-ranking officials was a critical element of the plan because their presence virtually dictated that the final FNCs were incorporated into the all-important program objectives memorandum, or POM. This was the annually updated, rolling five-year plan that prioritized budget spending. It was essential that the FNC programs were accounted for in each year. Otherwise, when it came time to approve a given year's science and technology budget, there would be no money available for them.

Once capabilities were selected, the integrated product teams were responsible for developing and managing them along the transition path. The teams were given three ironclad goals. First was to come up with the technology strategy and operating concepts needed to provide the chosen capability. The second encompassed planning the budget and setting "definite milestones and objectives, concrete deliverables, and a finite end state." The last was to actually demonstrate the technologies and thereby prove their worthiness to move to the acquisition phase and beyond ONR's area of responsibility.

Each team had four core members. The team chair represented the requirements community, meaning those in the CNO office or the Marine Corps combat development command. Its role, in essence, was to say, "This is what we need." The chair then helped prioritize capability goals and approved the investment and management plan for achieving that goal.

ONR provided the science and technology expert, called either the executive manager or the technical working group leader. This person made sure that the goals set by the chair were feasible and then crafted the investment and project management plan to get the job done.

A transition leader would represent the acquisitions community, usually one of the systems commands. He or she would be responsible for ensuring that a transition path was opened for the technologies being developed so they would find a home on the other side of the Valley of Death. Finally, an executive secretary would be responsible for recording progress on a monthly basis and serving as a point of contact for the entire team.

Gaffney saw the first three members of the team—the requirements person, science and technology expert, and acquisitions representative—as the crux of his plan. "If any one of those three legs of the stool is not connected, then transition, I believe, is nearly impossible," he says.

———————●———————

By early 1999, probably shortly after the Urban Warrior exercise, the concept was complete and accepted by the Navy hierarchy. A trio of spikes made it through the initial review as potential FNCs. One was ELB. The others were organic mine countermeasures that sought new ways to detect and defeat mines using a Marine unit's own resources, and destroyer technology, an effort to fast-forward the next generation of destroyer.

Over the next year or so, a variety of new FNCs were added to the list. Destroyer technology was cut altogether while ELB was parceled out and incorporated into other efforts. All told, the first wave of FNCs reached a dozen efforts.

> **Information distribution**. This effort apparently subsumed the bulk of ELB.
>
> **Organic mine countermeasures**. Detects and defeats mines in shallow water, on the beaches, and inland using a Marine unit's own resources.
>
> **Time-critical strike**. Seeks to substantially reduce the time it takes to hit vital mobile targets, such as command centers or ballistic missile launchers.
>
> **Decision support system** (later evolved into **knowledge superiority and assurance**). Integrates and distributes information in a dynamic, interactive network in order to ensure superior situational knowledge.
>
> **Autonomous operations**. Unmanned vehicles and robots capable of operating on land, at sea, and in the air.
>
> **Littoral antisubmarine warfare**. Ways to detect, classify, track, engage, and defeat a new generation of small, quiet, shallow-water submarines expected to characterize the new era of asymmetric warfare.
>
> **Total ownership cost reduction**. Addresses the imperative of lowering costs in building, purchasing, maintaining, and operating Navy and Marine Corps weapons and systems while increasing system readiness.
>
> **Missile defense**. Detecting, identifying, and defeating ballistic and cruise missiles in an age of proliferation.
>
> **Platform protection** (later evolved into **Fleet/Force protection**). Ways to protect ships from terrorist threats and other asymmetric warfare. Includes weapons, sensors, countermeasures, damage control, and stealth operations.
>
> **Expeditionary logistics** (later named **littoral combat and power projection**). Developing the ability to deploy, reconstitute, and supply forces from the sea without a large, shore-based logistical infrastructure.
>
> **Warfighter protection**. New technologies for protecting and caring for sailors and Marines.
>
> **Capable manpower**. Outfitting sailors and Marines with the ability to fight in information-rich, distributed battlefields, taking into account human factors.

By all accounts, the adoption of FNCs marked a milestone in ONR's modern history. The program laid the foundation for an entirely new way of doing business, one much more focused on cultivating a working partnership with the rest of the Navy and Marine Corps—and one that handed the Fleet and the Force vastly greater input into how applied research programs were selected and managed.

"It changed [ONR] from a cottage industry to focused deliverables in my view," says Donovan.

"Another big, seminal change," says DeCorpo, comparing it to the merger of ONR with OAT and ONT.

"It was huge. It was huge," stresses Maribel Soto, a former ONR program manager.[12]

It was hardly all smiles and roses around Ballston Towers, however. "You had all these basic scientists really mad because they lived in a world where they never took direction," says Soto. "Now they were getting direction." Not even the merger was as upsetting, she notes. "When they all blended, it wasn't as threatening as when we FNC'd."

Besides the gut-shock of a new way of doing business, the great worry was that Gaffney and Saalfeld had given away too much of the store. Tim Coffey, at the Naval Research Laboratory, had a close working relationship with Admiral Gaffney, who had always supported NRL and its basic research efforts. NRL's top civilian had also experienced firsthand some of the pressures ongoing at the ONR when he filled in for Fred Saalfeld as technical director. Still, Coffey had his doubts about the new program. "I was originally a proponent of the FNCs," he says.[13] "My position was that any organization with a $1.5 billion budget ought to at any time have things rolling out the other end." But he figured it should be about 10 percent of the portfolio, involving a portion of the 6.3 money. "The way it finally worked out was the FNCs took all the 6.3 money and half the 6.2 money. Coffey was flabbergasted at this."

Coffey knew the argument. Give the rest of the Navy a big hand in half the program in exchange for leaving the rest alone, especially basic science. He didn't buy it. Continuing in his vein of speaking in the third person, he scoffs: "Coffey's position was you got to be kidding. As soon as we give them control of that half, they will be back for the other half."

In a way, he was right.

CHAPTER 6

Out of the Box

ordon England rose to meet his visitor. It was early June 2001, and the Secretary of the Navy had only been on the job about a week. This was his first meeting with the Chief of Naval Research, Rear Adm. Jay Cohen, who had come to the Pentagon to pay a courtesy call on his new boss.

"Good morning, admiral."[1]

"Good morning, Mr. Secretary."

"Before we sit down, I have one question to ask. What am I going to get in twenty years for my basic research investment today?"

The admiral barely missed a beat. "Mr. Secretary, we have never met before. I like to make a good first impression. And you don't make a good first impression by saying, 'I don't know.' But I do know that if we invest nothing today, in twenty years we'll have nothing."

England, short, wiry, gray-haired, and academic-looking, got a sparkle in his eyes when he smiled, as he did then.

"Jay, that's exactly right—that's why we invest in basic research. Come sit down and let's talk."

From that point on, Cohen and the Navy Secretary enjoyed a warm relationship. It was a good thing for the admiral—he needed some protection. He had barely been on the job a year, but he had already ruffled feathers at ONR and in the broader Navy. He was just getting started.

The disruption that trailed in Cohen's wake, and sometimes crossed his bow, was partly the result of personal style. The admiral was an outgoing, charismatic, irreverent, energetic quip machine whose personality bore aspects of a standup comic. He delighted in waxing eloquent on a topic and provoking or shocking his audience.[2]

95

As a boss, he could be a handful. Many ONR veterans just didn't know what to make of Cohen. It didn't help that he kept key details of what he was plotting closer to the vest than his predecessors. At the same time, he proved a veritable Vesuvius of ideas that erupted with such force it was hard for his staff to follow everything, especially those numbed by years of government bureaucracy. Some of his notions were truly inspirational, others just made people shake their heads. And sometimes, after Cohen had decided on a course of action, he might change his mind. A lot of folks simply couldn't handle that in an admiral.

Most importantly, though, Cohen was a change agent. People either liked him or hated him, but one thing was certain: business would not go on as usual. Here was yet another high-achieving member of the Naval Academy class of '68, the third in a row to become Chief of Naval Research. Despite a lack of science background, or more likely because of it, he had been dispatched to ONR by Vice Adm. Jay L. Johnson, the Chief of Naval Operations, and the previous Navy Secretary Richard Danzig, to fast-forward ongoing efforts to better connect the organization to the Fleet and the Force. Their tasking was immediately reaffirmed by Johnson's successor, Vern Clark, as well as by England. It's what inspired Cohen, master of the buzz phrase, to describe his mission as turning ONR from the "Office of No Results" into the "Office of Naval Relevance." "They were not anti–basic research," he says of the Navy leadership. "But their point was, 'My god, Jay, we have got to see some outcome, and it's got to be naval.'"

If the mission sounded familiar, it was with good reason. Essentially the same brief had been given to every CNR who took office in the post–Cold War period (and maybe long before that). Every chief had worked hard to fulfill the order and, when leaving office, felt he had gone a long way toward doing so. And yet in each instance, his successor had been told, in effect, to go clean up the mess over at ONR.

What was going on? There was some merit in what Tim Coffey had feared: give the brass an inch and they'll try to take a mile. But a deeper truth was at work as well: the very definition of relevance changed with the times. Indeed, what had constituted dramatic moves a few years ago were no longer enough. Cohen's orders to make things better didn't mean his predecessors had failed. Instead, the mandate to Cohen (and his predecessors) almost certainly went beyond the Navy just wanting more short-term results at the expense of long-term programs. It spoke to the hunger for evolution and change that pervades organizations. If the demands are unreasonable or out of touch with the times and resources at hand, or if those in the hot seat aren't up to the task, this evolutionary quest kills morale and can take the organization with it. But if the pressures can be met with reasonable demands filtered from the unreasonable and the path to change communicated effectively, it can also spur innovation.

Cohen had a lot going for him in this regard. He listened well to his bosses and strove to anticipate what they wanted, unafraid to disrupt years of tradition at ONR. As one manager said, "He probably takes the cues from the administration much better than other admirals I've seen." He was also a master on Capitol Hill, adept at working legislators and ONR's growing congressional plus-up budget. But he didn't mind shaking up the Navy house either. If the Fleet wanted relevancy and outcomes, well, some of those outcomes might actually be disruptive of common Navy practices and values, or might move into domains the systems commands viewed as theirs alone. That, too, was Cohen.

A scarier world of terrorism and asymmetric warfare colored everything. The twin specters of the USS *Cole* attack in October 2000, followed by September 11, took place during the first eighteen months of Cohen's tour. Coupled with the ensuing fighting in Afghanistan and Iraq, where Marines died almost daily from IEDs, rocket-propelled grenades, mortars, and other attacks, the effects were profound. The admiral's favorite slide, with which he typically started or ended his presentations, showed a battle-weary Marine with a cigarette dangling out of his mouth. Helping that guy, Cohen constantly reminded people, was the reason ONR existed. And if the enemy took a different form than in the past and proved more creative than ever, so too would the Office of Naval Research.

Some other mighty considerations existed as well. Too few people understood and appreciated the substantial progress that had been made in the last few years connecting the organization to the Force and the

Fleet. From the outside, the Office of Naval Research looked pretty much the same. Old-guard scientists still ran most of the departments. The fledgling FNC program, as carefully as it had been planned, was struggling to get off the ground and still years away from making a true difference. ONR had done a poor job at making sure the important things it had accomplished were recognized. Its structure, despite periodic reorganizations, was confusing—and the Web site that provided a critical face to the outside world and to the Navy was an absolute mess. In short, if you were a scientist, a potential partner in industry, or a systems command with a need to fill, it was not easy to figure out what was going on in your area that might help, or even whom at ONR to consult.

Relevancy. Innovation. Transparency. How to deliver the right innovations to the sailor or Marine faster? How to coax, cajole, and inject more creative ways of thinking? And, not to be overlooked, how to take what was great about ONR and make it easier to see and comprehend? These were the challenges Cohen took on. Meeting them became the main focus of his tour. In one sense, they were the same challenges confronted throughout the post–Cold War period. But viewed in another light, much of the previous decade—with the indirect costs scandal, the Navy lab consolidation attempt, and the wrenching merger with the Office of Advanced Technology and the Office of Naval Technology— had been spent managing crisis and upheaval. Admiral Gaffney had made real strides in connecting ONR to the warfighter by moving the Marine Corps front and center and launching the FNC program. Now Cohen sought to make all these changes more seamless and visible to the outside world, and more integrated into the soul of the organization and how its staff members thought of their jobs.

Cohen would end up serving nearly six years, nearly twice as long as any other CNR. As he liked to quip toward the end of his term, "I'm in the sixth year of a three-year tour." As he also liked to say, his long tenure gave him time to make major missteps, and then correct them. The jury is still out on his ultimate effectiveness as of this writing. However, it is clear that in large part because of his lengthy tenure and passion for innovation, Cohen put in what were likely some of the most well-considered and significant changes of the post–Cold War era.

Adm. Jay Cohen arrived at the Office of Naval Research in May 2000 on a steep learning curve. Unlike his three direct predecessors—Gaffney, Pelaez, Miller—he had no previous experience with the organization. This, though, he saw as mainly a good thing: the lack of connection made it easier to make wholesale changes.

Cohen had left the Naval Academy to become a submariner. Early in his career, he had returned to school to earn a joint ocean engineering and master of science in marine engineering and a naval architecture degree from the Massachusetts Institute of Technology. Afterward, he had received nuclear power training: he was interviewed and selected by Adm. Hyman Rickover, father of the nuclear navy. In the late 1980s Cohen had with great pride risen to command the USS *Hyman G. Rickover* (SSN 709). On his watch, the sub earned a coveted Battle Efficiency "E" Award and was designated the best Atlantic Fleet attack submarine for the Battenburg Cup: this honor is given annually to the ship or submarine with the greatest accumulation of crew achievements. His subsequent command, of the USS *L. Y. Spear* (AS 36) in the early 1990s, earned another Battle Efficiency "E" Award and a Meritorious Unit Commendation, among several other honors. Under Cohen, the *Spear* was deployed to the Persian Gulf to support Operation Desert Storm.

Between these sea commands, Cohen's land duties had included a Pentagon stint as director of operational support for the director of naval intelligence. He returned to Washington after leaving the *Spear*, joining the Navy secretariat as Deputy Chief of Legislative Affairs, where he honed his considerable skills on Capitol Hill. He was promoted to rear admiral in 1997 and became Deputy Director for Operations on the Joint Staff. Two years later, Cohen became director of the Navy Y2K project office to prepare for the system upheaval that was expected when the internal clocks inside computers turned over (or rather, didn't) to the new millennium. The next May, the millennium passed without catastrophe, he was ordered to report as Chief of Naval Research.

Cohen greatly admired Paul Gaffney and felt his classmate knew more about ONR than anyone in the Navy. Working with Gaffney during the leadership transition period, he grew increasingly impressed with the outgoing CNR and the recently launched FNC program and other key details of the command. If there was a chink in ONR's armor, Cohen felt it was that the organization remained too insular, too focused on its own world of research. Much had been done over the past decade to correct that situation, but it still had a long way to go.

Three major categories of change characterized Cohen's tenure, all of them addressing the need (or the pressure, depending on how you looked at it) for ONR to break more forcefully out of its decades-long patterns. One big thrust—greatly heightened in urgency by the age of terrorism and, later, the Iraq War—was to continue the push for relevancy that had underscored everything ONR had done during the post–Cold War period. Part and parcel with this, taking a cue from Cohen's iconoclastic personality, came an extensive focus on more innovative projects and programs designed to produce major breakthroughs in warfighting performance. The third area of change was structural. Cohen labored almost throughout his tour to engineer a dramatic reorganization designed to better align ONR with Navy goals and make it easier for people—whether Navy insiders or outsiders—to find what they needed and see the relevancy and innovativeness he and his predecessors had toiled so hard to foster.

In large measure these changes were only possible because of the admiral's uniquely long tenure, which gave him time and opportunity to nudge the big battleship that was ONR onto a new course. In many ways, too, they marked a culmination of all the forces for change that had been building since the fall of the Berlin Wall.

Although it would turn out to be the last thing he finalized, Cohen focused almost from day one on the structural front. Overhauling management had also been part of his tasking from the CNO office (OpNav). Too many people, the OpNav staff felt, had served in top positions too long. The way Cohen summed up his mandate: Make ONR relevant, and "Oh, by the way, refresh the leadership without breaking the fundamental goodness of the organization."

The obvious place to start, in Cohen's view, was the executive director position held by Saalfeld. Gaffney had relied heavily on Saalfeld, and

CNR Day: In March 2005 Chief of Naval Research Rear Adm. Jay Cohen (seated, center) invited all living Chiefs of Naval Research to ONR's headquarters for a day of briefings, lectures, and celebration. Back row, from left to right: Rear Adm. L. S. Kollmorgen (1981–83); Rear Adm. Brad Mooney (1983–87); Rear Adm. Dick Van Orden (1973–75); Vice Adm. Albert Baciocco (1978–81); Rear Adm. R. K. Geiger (1975–78). Front row, left to right: Vice Adm. Paul Gaffney (1996–2000); Cohen (2000–2006); and Rear Adm. William Miller (1990–93). Only those in the front row served in the post–Cold War era covered in this book. Missing from this period are Rear Adm. J. R. "Smoke" Wilson Jr. (1987–90) and Rear Adm. Marc Pelaez (1993–96).

John F. Williams/ONR

Cohen greatly respected his top civilian as well. "Fred comes out as a hero," he once said when speaking for this history. Indeed, the degree to which Saalfeld was held in high esteem by officers and scientists alike was remarkable. Cohen himself instituted the Fred E. Saalfeld Award for Outstanding Lifetime Achievement in Science to recognize outstanding career achievements by naval research scientists: its namesake was the first recipient. But the admiral was nonetheless shocked by all the power that rested with the position, which included line responsibilities for hiring, firing, budget control, and the assignment of all civilians. He wanted more hands-on control than his predecessors. As Cohen put it, "If he did it all, I would not be doing my job."

Saalfeld understood. He was a veteran of government service and knew that conditions and priorities often shifted with new leadership. Says he, "I had everybody except the CNR reporting into the position I held, and Jay Cohen was really uncomfortable with that."[3] Moreover, there was a general movement at this time under CNO Vern Clark to rein in the powers of the Navy's civilian leadership, not just at ONR but at the various systems command labs as well.

In ONR's case, change did not happen overnight. But when Saalfeld retired in early 2002, the executive director role was abolished. Saalfeld's main duties were then bifurcated.[4] A new technical director/chief scientist continued to oversee the basic and applied research programs and personnel. But a hand-picked civilian chief of staff, a former Cohen colleague named Paul Lowell, took over the more administrative and budgetary duties Saalfeld had held.

The most important other management change centered on a position called Navy chief technology officer. This job had been created in 1998 by Lee Buchanan III, then Assistant Secretary of the Navy for research, development, and acquisition. Buchanan had then plucked Jim DeCorpo from ONR to fill the role. DeCorpo kept his ONR title but worked out of the Navy secretariat. His main focus was on transitioning technology from ONR to the Fleet. In effect, it took a layer of responsibility away from the Chief of Naval Research—at the time, Paul Gaffney—and significantly undercut his authority. "It was a real slap in the face to the CNR," says one insider.

DeCorpo was still in the role when Cohen took over. But when George W. Bush assumed the presidency in 2001 and new ASN RDA John Young took office, he found himself without support. Congress even stepped in to change ONR's charter, handing the Chief of Naval Research the authority for transitioning technology to the Navy as part of the Defense Authorization Act of 2001. The original 1946 law establishing ONR had authorized the organization to "plan, foster, and encourage scientific research . . . as related to the maintenance of future naval power, and the preservation of national security."[5] The 2001 act stated that the Chief of Naval Research would "manage the Navy's basic, applied, and advanced research to foster transition from science and technology to higher levels of research, development, test, and evaluation."[6]

Cohen, not surprisingly, was pleased by the change presumably engineered by his predecessor. He started including excerpts from the new and old laws in his presentations. The 2001 changes also set the tone for much of what he tried to do during his tenure. The word "transition," he related toward the end of his stint, "has driven me for the last five years."

The Navy chief technology officer job was eliminated. DeCorpo returned to ONR briefly before departing for a State Department posting, although he was destined to remain a major player in the ONR story. A number of other leading civilians also moved on early in Cohen's tenure. Coffey, the longtime senior scientist at NRL who had briefly filled in for Fred Saalfeld as ONR's top civilian, retired in the fall of 2001. Several department heads took new jobs or retired as well. Meanwhile, the first two technical directors hired in Saalfeld's wake left after only a year or so in the role. All this created a civilian leadership void at ONR in the early 2000s. Looking back, Saalfeld gave Cohen a lot of credit for keeping things moving, but he believed the management holes hurt. "Jay's job could have been even more successful and a helluva lot easier if he had had a good civilian partner [during this period]," he says.

These changes all unfolded amid the specter of terrorism. First the *Cole* and then September 11 spurred ONR to leap into action on a scale not seen in the post–Cold War era. These events also served as trumpet calls for Cohen's push for innovation.

Cohen had responded to the *Cole* tragedy in the fall of 2000 by launching investigations into every project ONR was supporting that might better safeguard hulls from terrorist assault. He had quickly become convinced that the obvious bases were well covered. Indeed, it was a largely conventional effort, led by ONR's Roshdy Barsoum, that had pointed to the development of explosive-resistant coatings to protect hulls and armored vehicles. A few years later this effort resulted in the three-year, multiagency, $15-million plan to fast-track the coatings for service deployment toward the end of the decade, though it was not clear in early 2007 what the outcome would be.

But no matter how important programs like Barsoum's might prove, leaving ONR only to its traditional approaches was out of the question for Cohen. He became almost obsessed with the need to inject mold-breaking thinking into the organization, and into the wider Navy R&D enterprise. ONR, he once remarked, managed a less than $2 billion budget. The systems commands, by contrast, spent approximately $11 billion a year on R&D. The Naval Research Lab counted some three thousand scientists and engineers. The systems command employed closer to ten thousand each. "And they suffer to this day from Not Invented Here. Now that is the antithesis of what you want in a free-ranging, open-ended science and technology environment."

Immediately after the *Cole* attack, Cohen's passion for fresh thinking had led him to the Mohave Desert to talk with aerodynamics pioneer and materials expert Burt Rutan, who specialized in out-of-the-box uses of composites. On the spot, he had offered the inventor a contract to determine whether advanced composites could be used to revolutionize hull strength and blast resistance. Almost simultaneously he began a program aimed at institutionalizing revolutionary and creative thinking inside ONR.

It was called SwampWorks. Cohen modeled the effort on the famous Skunk Works unit created at Lockheed Aerospace Corporation in the 1940s. Run by Clarence L. "Kelly" Johnson, Lockheed's organization was itself named for the secret "Skonk Works" moonshine brewery featured in Li'l Abner cartoons. Designed to operate creatively and outside the normal corporate bureaucracy, the initial team took only forty-three days to build the first U.S. fighter to eclipse five hundred miles per hour.[7]

Nothing was going to be created by ONR in forty-three days in the current era. Even forty-three months would mean setting an almost unbelievable pace. But Cohen's goal was to use the unit to fund very high-risk, high-reward efforts that were so unconventional they would not likely be pursued in the traditional portfolio. This small group was put in the hands of a dynamic civilian named Maribel Soto. In keeping with the SwampWorks image, a visitor could find Soto's office tucked back off a side corridor in a somewhat dingy corner of Ballston Towers. A sign over her door read: "The Swamp."

Admiral Cohen's ambition for the program was to place such risky bets that 90 percent of what it funded should fail. Too often, Soto explained, managers were judged as failures if their program didn't bear fruit. As a consequence, the organization had become too risk adverse. "That mentality has made us less powerful" and incapable of fully capitalizing on the promise of science and technology, she asserted.

Initially SwampWorks was allocated only a few million dollars a year. However, it would soon grow to roughly $20 million, or 1 percent of ONR's total portfolio. All the funding came from the 6.3 advanced technology development budget and was designed to pay off in one to three years, a fraction of the time of most ONR investments. That didn't mean the technologies pursued would be perfected in that period, Soto explained. Rather, the idea was to quickly create working prototypes and even deliver test units to the warfighter for experimentation and evaluation, fast-tracking their movement in the acquisition realm. In terms of both riskiness and the short-turnaround, SwampWorks was a marked departure from the ONR status quo. One ONR staff member called it an "amnesty zone" from conventional organization thinking. No rules: just find important problems, solve them, and align them to naval needs.

SwampWorks' inaugural project was called Swarm. Based on the idea of "swarm" intelligence, the hope was to create a pack of small robotic vehicles that would work cooperatively to fulfill various mission objectives, such as taking out a bunker, thereby reducing human casualties. Another early effort, for which work was funded at Florida State University and General Electric, sought to mitigate noise on F/A-18s. These jets generate a huge amount of noise that can disrupt communities where they are flying. The ONR program, which employed microjet injection technology and nozzle modification to lower output by several decibels, was scheduled for transition to the Fleet in fiscal year 2007. Other efforts that seemed poised for success included a stainless steel monohull design that showed promise in withstanding *Cole*-like attacks, and "Half-Torp," a lightweight torpedo meant to be half the size of a conventional Mark 48. This would enable submarines to carry fifty-two of the weapons—twice the normal number—and make it more economically feasible to use them to blow up mines in littoral waters.

Shortly before he retired from the Navy in early 2006, Admiral Cohen expressed his dissatisfaction with SwampWorks: "After six years, it has not been the success I hoped it would be. Instead of having 10 percent success, we're having 55 percent success. Which means things we thought weren't solvable—we set the bar too low."

Formally kicked off in 2001, SwampWorks proved merely an early salvo in a much wider campaign to spur "leap-ahead" thinking at the organization. On its heels came TechSolutions, which solicited ideas from ordinary sailors and Marines over the Internet. The program was inspired by Master Chief James Blesse, a sailor who in early 2001 sent Cohen an unsolicited letter suggesting a way to improve submarine safety by making periscope displays viewable by the entire control room instead of just one officer. Cohen liked the idea so much that he arranged for Blesse to be transferred to ONR and launched a program to gather ideas from across the Fleet and Force. TechSolutions contributed several concepts that seemed destined to become reality. One of the most interesting was a "flight-deck Zamboni," a machine to automate the previously manual labor job of clearing post–take off debris from aircraft carrier decks, much like Zamboni machines clear and smooth ice between periods of a hockey game.[8]

Cohen pushed innovation and out-of-the-box thinking on many other fronts. Several bigger initiatives grew out of the SwampWorks program. He called them CNR initiatives, because they were driven largely by the Chief of Naval Research, typically in response to Navy and Marine Corps leadership concerns or ideas that were not being met by traditional means. One of the first stemmed from an idea he picked up from his predecessor, Paul Gaffney, for building a new type of high-speed, multimodal ship. Gaffney had called it the Lily Pad ship. Cohen code-named his version X-Craft. This was a prototypical aluminum catamaran capable of speeds of fifty knots. It was designed to hold interchangeable modules that support up to a dozen different mission types, from mine-sweeping to antisubmarine warfare to search and rescue. The craft was renamed *Sea Fighter* at its early 2005 christening.

Later that year, it was successfully handed off to the Fleet and trans-ferred to San Diego, where it underwent further tests by the Navy and Coast Guard. Despite the successful transition, however, the project made Cohen enemies in Naval Sea Systems Command because ONR left the powerful systems command that normally builds ships largely out of the picture in the craft's $80-million development (see the sidebar in chapter 11).

For the most part, CNR initiatives like X-Craft were paid for by "OPM," other people's money. That is, they didn't come from the Navy budget but from congressional plus-ups added to the budget. Still, says Cohen, the perception around the Navy was that he had some-how dipped into programs of record to pay for his innovative programs. Even though this view was unwarranted, it further rankled many offi-cials. The initiatives persisted nonetheless, says Cohen, partly because he didn't care who he upset if the cause was right, and partly because they won the support of Gordon England and top brass in Naval Operations.

In 2003 or 2004, though, another turn of the evolutionary crank took place. One fan of the maverick Chief of Naval Research's quest for innovation was then Vice Chief of Naval Operations Michael G. Mullen, whose job included serving as head of Navy resources. The VCNO, a fellow Navy Academy class of '68 alum, especially liked what he saw in SwampWorks and programs like X-Craft. However, says Cohen, he wanted the CNR to formalize the bigger initiatives, in large part to miti-gate the bad perception they were getting. And rather than restricting such initiatives to just 1 percent of the ONR budget, he told Cohen to make innovative approaches to problems a much bigger thrust, on the order of 10 percent of what the organization funded. Cohen jumped on the $200 million suggestion and turned it into a game-changing pro-gram called Innovative Naval Prototypes (INP).[9]

The aim of Innovative Naval Prototypes was to identify and promote research and development of disruptive technologies and programs to which the acquisition community would be reluctant to commit—and which would therefore likely be cut or left unfunded if not specifically championed by naval leadership. In its risk-taking nature, then, the program was similar to SwampWorks. But INPs, as they became known, were funded chiefly from ONR's 6.2 budget (with some 6.3 funding) and not plus-ups. They had much longer time frames of between four and eight years. Their costs were also significantly higher than SwampWorks efforts, soaring into the tens of millions or even hundreds of millions of dollars as the program evolved.

A major goal of the INPs was to take the chanciness of developing game-changing technologies and push it from the acquisition world into the science and technology realm. The reason was that by the time programs made it to development and acquisition, billions of dollars had already likely been spent. If something failed then, it was a major disaster. That discouraged risk-taking. However, if concepts could be proved at a much earlier stage, meaning ONR was the one willing to stick its neck out, the costs of failure could be reduced to tens of millions. That made it much more feasible to take chances to begin with, especially if top Navy leadership sanctioned the risk. Explains Bobby Junker, a longtime ONR department head, "What you have to have is somebody high up saying this is critical to the future, we need to see what we can do there. The acquisitions people don't have to put money on the table up front."[10]

Cohen loved the high stakes, go-for-broke nature of the program. "I call it the Nike effect," he says. "Just do it." Because there was no real champion in the acquisition world, the program had a "build it and people will come" aspect as well. However, to enhance the chances of INP projects being moved into the acquisition arena later on—thereby making them programs of record—the idea was to align the programs with the five fundamental concepts, or "pillars," laid out as part of *Naval Power 21*, the Navy's vision statement for the early twenty-first century. Three of these pillars—Sea Shield, Sea Strike, and Sea Basing—aimed at enhancing "America's ability to project offensive power, defensive assurance, and operational independence around the globe."[11] They were supported by two additional pillars, the FORCEnet communications and sensor network concept, and Enterprise and Platform Enablers, core technologies that cut across many areas.

The first two INPs, for a shipboard weapons system called the electromagnetic railgun and an array of tactical satellites, were funded in

Innovative Naval Prototypes:
Out to Create Game-Changing Technologies

In 2004 the Navy's science and technology corporate board reviewed the major elements of the service's science and technology portfolio. Its conclusion, according to a summary document: "current S&T plans are appropriately balanced across long-term and mid-term objectives that are vital to our continued ability to maintain technological superiority in a fast changing Naval environment."

On May 3, 2005, the Navy issued a memorandum for the Chief of Naval Research, giving him further guidance about administering the portfolio. The longest section of the three-page memo was devoted to the fledgling INP program. The guidance stated, "Investments should be planned with the critical mass to achieve a level of maturity suitable for transition within 4–8 years. Programs in this category may be disruptive technologies that, for reasons of high risk or radical departure from established requirements and concepts of operation, are unlikely to survive without top leadership endorsement. The CNR, in consultation with other stakeholders . . . will identify candidate projects where a critical mass investment could create a transformational advance in capability."[1]

By the time of the memo, the first four INPs had been approved. All were aligned with naval pillars set out in *Navy Power 21*. All were overseen by ONR program managers.

Electromagnetic railgun: A ship-launched hypervelocity projectile weapon designed to travel up to two hundred nautical miles with unprecedented accuracy. Funded in partnership with the Army and DARPA. Naval Pillars: Sea Shield and Sea Strike.

TacSat: A tactical satellite that costs under $20 million and can be launched within twenty-four hours of a decision to deploy it. A constellation of three satellites is designed to give twenty-four-hour electronic intelligence and communications coverage to a given area. Naval Pillar: FORCEnet.

Seabase Enablers: A wide-ranging program centered on developing T-Craft, a reconfigurable, multimode amphibious transport and landing craft with unprecedented capacity, speed, fuel-efficiency, and weather durability. Naval Pillar: Sea Basing.

Persistent Littoral Undersea Surveillance: Seeks to revolutionize antisubmarine warfare and the monitoring of shoreline areas to prevent terrorism and support expeditionary landings. The idea is to clandestinely deploy undersea surveillance nets, some towed by underwater gliders, that will cover 100,000 square nautical miles. Sonobuoys will pop to the surface and upload information to satellites. Naval Pillars: Sea Shield, Sea Strike, FORCEnet.

1. Willard, Nyland, and Young, "Memorandum for the CNR."

fiscal year 2005. By the time Cohen left office more than a year later, two additional efforts—involving a transformable boat called T-Craft and an undersea surveillance network—were also off the ground, and into the water, so to speak.

In function, the INP program was much like FNC in that representatives from the CNO office, Navy secretariat, Navy systems commands, the Marine Corps, and ONR would identify and recommend promising candidates for funding. The science and technology corporate board would review and approve project recommendations. The FNC program also stemmed from 6.2 and 6.3 funding and had a slightly more compressed time horizon of five to seven years. Its efforts were also governed and approved by the corporate board. However, the FNC program was created to fill specific gaps in identified naval needs with proven or at least well-known technologies, not to take big risks. Moreover, each project generally had a much lower price tag.

Folding the INP program into the ONR portfolio enabled a more complete strategic investment across the spectrum of science and technology. At one end of this range was the basic research effort, which invested in core scientific areas often decades from fruition and with a still vaguely defined relation to Navy needs. At the other end, the most conservative and near-term part of the portfolio, came the FNC program. Perched somewhere in between were the INPs.

Besides filling a hole in the portfolio, INPs had something else going for them: they were hugely sexy with palpable, mouth-watering payoffs. Almost overnight, they became the most exciting part of ONR's portfolio.

ONR had long struggled to win respect around the Navy. This was largely because the studies it had traditionally backed often paid off decades after they had been sponsored and even then might contribute only a piece of understanding to some larger puzzle. Even when the payoffs were highly visible, the university scientist conducting the work typically got the credit, not ONR. "If we did our job right, there is some person in academia who is getting a Nobel Prize or some other world recognition for the work that they did," says Kelly Cooper, manager of the T-Craft effort, one of the first INPs.[12] Program officers like herself, she noted, might have retired by the time the work came to fruition. No wonder that many in the Navy still hadn't heard of the Office of Naval Research and would be stunned to learned it controlled a nearly $2 billion budget.

Just sponsoring and managing the visionary efforts that characterized the first wave of INPs elevated ONR's status as a trailblazing organization. Indeed, the excitement about the program was almost palpable around the office. Geoff Main, a division director who once worked in the department overseeing the electromagnetic railgun, draws similarities between INP initiatives and efforts supported by the Defense Advanced Research Projects Agency (DARPA). The agency, he notes, became legendary for its support of originally far-out projects in computing and the Internet that ended up changing the way people lived. "DARPA takes a lot of longshots," he says. "But if one succeeds, they get a lot of credit for it."[13]

Only time would tell if similar accolades lay in store for the Office of Naval Research. Meanwhile, even as the INP projects were being planned, more pressing events were enveloping ONR. None was more urgent than the war in Iraq.

CHAPTER 7

War Footing

Organizing for a New Era

I t was ONR's version of a county fair. The Naval Research Laboratory bustled with activity early on the morning of December 12, 2003. Visitors streamed through the entrance gate and down the long driveway toward the main buildings near the banks of the Potomac. The impressive guest list included some thirty VIPs, among them at least four admirals, another quartet of generals, two assistant secretaries of the Navy, and the Navy Secretary, Gordon England.[1]

The visitors' first stop was a classified conference room in the large building that housed NRL's tactical electronic warfare work. Awaiting their arrival were NRL's top military and civilian officials, commanding officer Capt. Dave Schubert and director of research John Montgomery. Along with them stood the man who had convened the impressive assembly, Adm. Jay Cohen, his usual effusive self.

Cohen and a host of ONR staffers had been readying this event in conjunction with NRL officials for weeks. It was in many ways their most visible chance to help the Iraq war effort, which had begun with the U.S. invasion that March and was almost daily claiming the lives of American troops through insurgent fire, sniper attacks, and improvised explosive devices. Fittingly, Cohen had named the event "Science and Technology Support for Deploying Warfighters." Privately, they really did call it the county fair.

At around 7:40 a.m., after everyone had grabbed a buffet breakfast, Cohen began his introductory remarks. His short brief was followed by a couple of other quick overviews from high-ranking ONR staffers. Shortly after 8:00 a.m. the group was shown a few classified demos. On a large display they also watched a piped-in real-time unclassified demonstration of the Silver Fox reconnaissance drone as the remote-controlled craft was put through its paces on a distant test range. The Silver Fox was fitted with video and still cameras capable of operating in different regions of the electromagnetic spectrum. It had been fielded initially in Afghanistan with the First Marine Expeditionary Force. Eighteen drones had been deployed to date, and the Navy Secretary was informed that a variety of improvements were on the way, including advanced chemical agent sensors and a high-bandwidth datalink with digital video compression.

Over the next roughly three hours, some fifteen additional technologies were shown to England and his entourage. Most took place in a large open tent set up on the big lawn that lined the main driveway. "We turned the quadrangle at NRL into Tikrit," was how Cohen described the scene. A few, though, were scattered around the NRL campus, including a SwampWorks-funded gunfire detection system developed at the lab. To demonstrate the technology, a "rifleman" fired blanks from the window of an NRL building. The antenna-like contraption, mounted on a Humvee, pinpointed the source of sniper fire through acoustic sensors. Then it slewed around to light up the target with powerful illuminators.

Roshdy Barsoum was one of those in the tent. To bring the Navy Secretary up to speed on the explosive resistant coatings he was helping develop, Barsoum displayed two steel plates of the same type and thickness used in ship hulls. One had been laced with explosive resistant (ERC) "paint" and the other left untreated. Both had been subjected to underwater blasts. The untreated steel showed a gaping hole; the ERC-treated panel was bent but intact. The ONR scientist could sense a lot of interest, and Cohen later came back to tell Barsoum that his guests had indeed been captivated by the demo. So, apparently, had a few reporters from a defense publication whom Barsoum had spotted. Fearing word might leak out about the technology, he moved to protect the intellectual property. "We filed the patent two days later," he says. The patent, titled "Armor including a strain rate hardening elastomer," was still pending in early 2007.[2]

Additional demos included a handheld explosives detector and technology for coating or "tagging" munitions so that they could be tracked if removed from their depots: many stolen or lost supplies had found their way into improvised explosive devices. Brief descriptions of scores of other technologies from ONR-backed work, the Naval Research Laboratory, and various systems command labs were also compiled in a 254-page catalog. All these innovations were categorized according to when they could be deployed: Available now; 0–3 months; 3–6 months; 6–9 months; 9+ months.

Admiral Cohen and the Office of Naval Research ended the day with an even more heightened sense of urgency to help the war effort. "This meeting at NRL is a watershed," sums up Jim DeCorpo. "I think a bond gets formed between him [Cohen] and the Secretary: this guy is working on my problems." DeCorpo made for an interesting story himself. The former Navy chief technology officer had left the Office of Naval Research less than two years earlier but was returning to become technical director of the newly formed ONR Global in London. From that position he would oversee the organization's international scientific program, which was being greatly expanded as part of Cohen's ongoing management overhaul (see sidebar).

On full exhibit that day was a more overtly military side of ONR far different from its historic thrust of sponsoring longer-term university studies. Despite its relative rarity, though, this aspect of what ONR did seemed to rear its head with astonishing regularity, often bringing with it a newfound appreciation for the research ONR had been supporting and helping the office fend off critics of its programs. As Cohen took to saying: "Every ten years there is a push, we don't need these science projects. Then something comes along called war."

ONR had last been on a war footing in 1991 during the Gulf War, but the build-up had dissipated as quickly as the short-lived fighting. This time, the build-up seemed an almost chronic condition. ONR had gone on high alert after the *Cole* bombing in the fall of 2000. From

ONR Global:
Bridge around the World or a Bridge Too Far?

Since its creation in 1946 ONR has been keenly aware of the need to cultivate ties to scientists around the world. Indeed, its first overseas liaison office was founded in London in 1946, not long after the organization itself was formed. Now ONR's London office is the central hub of a worldwide organization with representatives at major Navy and Marine commands and field offices in Tokyo, Singapore (the new headquarters), Canberra, Australia, and Santiago, Chile. These groups sponsor scientific research, travel programs, and hundreds of conferences and collaborative efforts in scores of countries.

The London office took root as an outgrowth of the close cooperation between U.S. and British scientists during World War II. A Navy captain who reports directly to the Chief of Naval Research has typically headed the office. A technical director oversees the scientific program. This was the job Jim DeCorpo took in 2004, not long after he left Ballston Towers. Staff mix, titles, and areas of responsibility have changed over the years. But working under the technical director in the current era are associate directors, usually a mix of European university professors and scientists dispatched from ONR and other U.S. government agencies. Normally they serve a two- or three-year appointment while on sabbatical from their home institutions, acting as talent scouts who sponsor projects in their fields and keep up with local developments—as well as supporting conferences and providing travel stipends to facilitate exchanges between U.S. scientists and their European counterparts.

Staffing in the London branch peaked around sixty people in the late 1960s. This number was sharply reduced in leaner times and has never recovered. Even in 2006 the office was home to only about fifteen associate directors and eleven additional support or administrative staffers. The entire group operates on a budget of roughly $12 million a year, a little over half of which is overhead. The associate directors dole out the remaining $5 million-plus, always to universities and private industry and not to foreign government organizations. These funds are split almost equally between the 6.1 and 6.2 budget categories, with a small amount of advanced technology development 6.3 monies. To leverage their tiny pot, the associate directors often work in cooperation with the Army and Air Force R&D offices, which are housed in the same building.

The first expansion of ONR's overseas presence took place in 1974, when the organization established an office in Japan, which was fast becoming a technological powerhouse. With the end of the Cold War, the London organization also broadened its horizons and began cultivating ties with Russian, Czech, and Hungarian scientists as well as those in other eastern European countries. To symbolize this wider reach, the office changed its name to Office of Naval Research–Europe. By the early 1990s it further extended its outreach to the Middle East and Africa while the Tokyo office began covering a wider swatch of Asia along with India, Australia, and New Zealand.

All this set the stage for a bigger, more unified organization. In 1997 the London and Tokyo offices, which had essentially existed separately, were merged to form the ONR International Field Office, headquartered in London. A Singapore branch set up shop in 2000. This was followed by ONR Australia in 2001, and ONR Latin America, which opened in the U.S. embassy the following year. Except for Tokyo, which was staffed by three scientific and technical people and an officer in charge, all these branch offices consisted of just one or two representatives.

The most recent expansion of the organization's scope—and apparently its most controversial—came in 2003, when CNR Jay Cohen ordered the International Field Office to merge with two other groups to form ONR Global. The other parties in the merger were the International Liaison Office and the Naval Fleet/Forces Technology Office, both based at Ballston Towers. The former was a small organization actually created to manage and coordinate the branches set up in Chile, Australia, and Singapore. The Naval Fleet/Forces Technology Office included some twenty-five scientific advisors assigned to the major numbered fleets and Marine Corps commands around the world. Their job was to serve as the interface between the commands and the scientific and technical communities but they were usually looking for advances that might be rapidly adopted by the Fleet.

Cohen saw several major benefits to the move. The International Field Office, he explains, consisted of scientists and engineers knowledgeable in their domains and with certain geographic responsibilities. The Fleet/Force science advisors, meanwhile, had only broad scientific knowledge but had great knowledge of what was needed by the military. "So it occurred to me if I combined the science advisors and the ILO, I would get tremendous synergy." A single organization also greatly reduced overhead.

To someone like F. Michael "Mike" Pestorius, who was London technical director at the time, bringing them into the ONR Global fold was not as clear-cut. "A bad, bad idea," he says. His job, Pestorius points out, was to distribute 6.1 and 6.2 dollars, which meant taking a relatively long-term view toward what was funded. The scientific program officers came from "a very short-term, operationally driven viewpoint," he says. "They've got a Mr. Fixit point of view. . . . It just doesn't make for a very good marriage."

In 2006 the headquarters of ONR Global was scheduled to move to Singapore. To Pestorius it was time for a gut check on whether it should be kept open at all. This was partly because of the high cost of overheard relative to ONR Global's budget. But it was also because ONR was finding it increasingly difficult to convince good people to uproot their lives and move abroad for a two- or three-year tour. Overlaid on that was the changing nature of the world.

During the Cold War, says Pestorius, you needed technical scouts to roam around Europe, learn who was doing what, and pay for their travel to the United States to collaborate with American scientists. Today, virtually every university science department has extensive ties with colleagues worldwide, maybe even working on ONR contracts together. It's cheap and easy for U.S. and foreign colleagues to get together, and they can communicate and collaborate readily over the telephone, e-mail, and the Internet.

Cohen understood this argument but felt that the end of the Cold War did not change the essential need for an organization like ONR Global. "The bad guys are looking for asymmetrical threats. They are not going to come where you are strong," he maintains. That means the United States needs to continually examine areas where it is not currently investing. "The way that you get knowledge of that is by having presence. We're not talking spying here. All this is unclassified. You have to be interacting at a personal, I call it get-down-and-drink level. And these need to be sustained relationships."

The story of ONR Global is pieced together from Fargo, "ONRG: A History 1946–2005"; the ONR Global Web site, http://www.onr.navy.mil/Science-Technology/ONR-Global .aspx; and interviews with Cohen, Pestorius, Ramirez, DeCorpo, and Ferreiro.

there, the drive to help the warfighter had only picked up momentum, accelerated by September 11, the U.S. deployment in Afghanistan a month later, and the March 2003 invasion of Iraq.

By the time of the Naval Research Lab demonstrations that December, tens of thousands of U.S. troops were already in harm's way; hundreds were dead or wounded. In addition, some 42,000 Marines were set to be deployed to Iraq the following spring. ONR's scramble to help them was not independent of its push for innovation. Rather, initiatives like SwampWorks and TechSolutions were motivated largely by their potential to deliver quick solutions to the field, and inside these and other programs Cohen switched significant funds from Navy projects to those that more directly benefited Marines—moving money from "blue" to "green," as it was termed.

Well before the county fair, ONR had played an instrumental role in delivering at least one weapon to the theater—the thermobaric bomb. After September 11, it became clear that the United States was going after the al-Qaeda organization in the mountain caves of Afghanistan. Caves present extremely difficult targets. It's hard to get people out of them, and they are exceedingly hazardous for troops to enter. Caves could be bombed, but that risked destroying them and making it impossible to find out who and what had been inside. Even if still intact, they might be structurally weakened, endangering the troops sent inside to mop up.

In October 2001 the Defense Department pushed development of a group of programs that might aid troops in what would be called Operation Enduring Freedom, the campaign in Afghanistan. Projects on this fast track included the thermobaric bomb, which had been under slower-paced development by the Navy for years and even decades, depending on how one looked at it.

Thermobarics are weapons that employ a fuel-rich explosive, often a metal fuel like aluminum. A primary detonation disburses the fuel as a cloud of minute particles that permeate the area in which they are released. A secondary explosion then ignites these particles, creating a super-hot, high-pressure blast. It is particularly devastating in a confined space such as a cave. As retired Air Force major general Don Sheppard described it for CNN, the explosion "sucks air in and out of caves because of the thermobaric pressure that builds up there and the heat." He depicted the weapons as a key to avoiding many hazards of cave-fighting. "It can spread through these tunnel complexes, and, in many cases, without actually destroying them. So it'll kill the people that are in there, but it won't collapse the cave. Then you can go in and find out what's in there."[3]

Russian forces had reportedly used thermobaric weapons in Chechnya. The most promising U.S. work was being done at the Naval Surface Warfare Center's Indian Head division in Maryland. After the call to help Operation Enduring Freedom, the Defense Threat

Reduction Agency put together a response team to fast-forward development of a viable thermobaric weapon. The Air Force took charge of transition planning and requirements. The Indian Head group handled the core technology behind the project, everything from fuze modification to explosives scale-up, loading design, and manufacture. ONR, meanwhile, was responsible for funding development of the weapon's payload system.

The Indian Head weaponization program, which rapidly swelled to include nearly one hundred engineers, scientists, and technicians, was led by Anh Duong. In just sixty-seven days, her team designed, developed, and delivered eleven prototypes of the thermobaric bomb. The first of these laser-guided weapons, known as the BLU-118B, was used in combat on March 3, 2002. An assessment of its effectiveness was apparently classified. Still, the project got right to the heart of what ONR wanted to be about. A working prototype had been developed in barely two months. Yet the bomb drew on years of explosives, materials, and combustion research, much of it funded by the Office of Naval Research. Admiral Cohen constantly used it as an example of the payoffs of long-term scientific research, helping justify ONR's budget and existence. With just a little bit of exaggeration, he termed it the "sixty-day miracle that took thirty years."

The U.S. invasion of Iraq under Operation Iraqi Freedom in the spring of 2003 had raised the stakes for ONR even higher. That fall, just a few months before the NRL exhibition, Navy Secretary England established Operation Respond, which sought to identify critical war-fighting technology gaps and make sure urgent operational needs were heard by the Navy leadership.[4] This was one of the first moves England made upon his return to the Navy Secretary post after an eight-month hiatus. He had resigned the previous January to help stand up the new Department of Homeland Security, where he served as its first deputy secretary. But when his nominated successor, New Mexico oilman and former Marine Colin McMillan, committed suicide after being diagnosed with a recurrence of cancer, the Navy was left with a hole in the job. Facing an impending deadline for filling the position, England was asked back to avoid a crisis.

Operation Respond spurred the creation of a system for rapid procurement and insertion of new technologies to help sailors and Marines in combat. Under its auspices, ONR helped speed a variety of additional innovations to the front lines, many of which were on display at the NRL county fair that December. The exhibit itself had also been inspired by the Navy Secretary. Right after being confirmed for the second time, England informed Cohen that he wanted to ensure that the Marines about to deploy to Iraq had the best weaponry and protection science and technology could make available—be it for counterfire, Humvees, or body armor. He then suggested the admiral hold some sort of event or demonstration day, to which he could invite Navy leadership, DARPA and Homeland Security officials, and representatives from the Army and Air Force.

In the ensuing push to hurry innovations out the door, not everything went as planned, though. Cohen testified to Congress about a USB thumb drive that attached to dog tags, so that medical personnel could quickly access a warfighter's medical records in case of an emergency.

When Rear Adm. Jay Cohen retired in February 2006 after six years at ONR, he was the longest-serving Chief of Naval Research in history. Six months after his retirement, he was confirmed by Congress as undersecretary of science and technology for the U.S. Department of Homeland Security. He retired from that position after the Obama administration took office in early 2009.

John F. Williams/ONR

More than one thousand were issued to the First Marine Expeditionary Force for in-theater evaluation when it was deployed in 2004 as part of Operation Iraqi Freedom. However, the thumb drives were apparently never used. Notes an ONR program officer: "The command surgeon for the Marine Expeditionary Force said there was no problem with patient records and requested that they [the drives] be gathered up and removed from his AOR [area of responsibility], which we did."

A far more successful invention that garnered a lot of press was QuikClot.[5] One of the greatest causes of combat death is blood loss. Both the Army and the Navy had invested in novel types of bandages to staunch bleeding, but nobody had a one-size-fits-all, cost-effective solution, says Hal Guard, head of ONR Code 34, at the time called the Human Systems department. ONR partnered with a private Connecticut firm, Z-Medica, that had come up with a novel solution called QuikClot. Its core ingredient was zeolite, a granular, soil-like mineral that could be carried in a packet tucked inside a pocket. When rubbed into a wound, it acted to remove water from the blood, concentrating the blood's clotting factors. And since the substance contained no biological substances, it also eliminated the risk of transmitting disease.

Preclinical tests, sponsored by ONR at the Uniformed Services University of the Health Sciences, showed QuikClot to be highly effective in curtailing moderate to severe bleeding. It was approved by the Food and Drug Administration for external human use in May 2002 and adopted by the Marine Corps as a first aid treatment a year later, apparently soon after Operation Iraqi Freedom began. The first version left a messy cake over wounds, causing doctors trouble cleaning injuries. That spurred an idea among ONR program officer Michael Given and Hasan Alam, the trauma surgeon-researcher who had conducted the preclinical trials. They suggested placing the grains inside a cloth bag, like a tea bag, to facilitate easy removal from the wound. The company apparently jumped on the concept and produced an improved version called QuikClot ACS (advanced clotting sponge) that would win FDA approval in 2005. ONR also funded further improvements at the University of California, Santa Barbara, which were licensed to Z-Medica the following year.

As the fighting in Iraq dragged on, QuikClot became a standard part of the Marine Corps individual first aid kit. Soon it was in use by all branches of the U.S. military and had been sold to the FBI, CIA, NATO, various U.S. allies, and first-responders such as emergency medical personnel. Cohen couldn't have been more gung-ho about the product. Says he, "It has saved scores, scores, if not hundreds of lives, documented."

When it came to helping the war effort, though, it's likely that no problem received more attention from ONR from late 2003 through the end of Cohen's tour than improvised explosive devices. By the time of the NRL county fair, the United States had been in Iraq nearly nine months and the IED threat was already growing more acute. Only a handful of troops had been killed by the roadside bombs in each of the first few months of the Iraq fighting. But fatalities had jumped that fall, hitting a high for the year of twenty in November, with December on pace to nearly match that figure: IEDs would soon establish themselves as the single greatest cause of Iraq combat deaths.[6]

At least a half-dozen projects geared at countering IEDs were contained in the catalog handed out to guests at the NRL county fair. However, only the system for tagging and tracking explosives often used in IEDs was demonstrated. That was largely because the full extent of the threat had not been realized. It was still widely believed that the Marines going into Iraq would be greeted with flowers and flags, and would spend the bulk of their time helping rebuild schools, sewers, and other infrastructure, says Cohen. Therefore, a lot of what was demonstrated that day related to the broader problems expected in Iraq: ways to detect chemical or biological agents and other weapons of mass destruction, for instance.

In a matter of months, however, the focus changed dramatically. In mid-2004 a gravely concerned Department of Defense elevated a small Army working group to a multiservice task force devoted to countering IEDs. Less than two years later, in January 2006, the task force would become a permanent organization, the Joint Improvised Explosive Device Defeat Organization, with some $3 billion in resources at its disposal.

In the spring of 2004 the Navy and ONR tried to get ahead of the problem. Significantly upping the ante on combating IEDs, Secretary England outlined a challenge to find new ways to predict, detect, defeat, and destroy the devices—all from enough distance to keep troops safe. Short-term countermeasures were well under way. But in a meeting with Cohen, the Navy Secretary said he wanted a more sustained, scientific investigation into the problem, which he felt certain would haunt troops for years. England was thinking of something that marshaled the country's best scientists and engineers, akin to the Manhattan Project that developed the atomic bomb during World War II. According to Cohen, the Navy Secretary asked:

"I wonder how the Manhattan Project was done?"

"You know, Mr. Secretary, we have two scientists at NRL, one is a Nobel Prize winner who participated in it. Would you like to have lunch with them?"

In April of 2004 Cohen and Captain Schubert met again with the Navy Secretary, this time for a small lunch at the Naval Research Laboratory. Joining them were the two lab scientists in question, Nobel laureate Jerome Karle and his wife, Isabella, a National Medal of Science winner. The Karles, both chemists, had worked on the Manhattan Project at the University of Chicago. Out of the hour-and-a-half-long lunch came what was dubbed a "mini-Manhattan project" at ONR to tackle the IED threat. England began a long series of biweekly or monthly meetings with Navy and Marine Corps leadership to keep abreast on developments. That same month Cohen launched a small business innovation research effort to solicit ideas from private industry. ONR received 259 proposals and selected 29 for phase 1 funding.

As the death toll mounted, ONR's work on countering improvised explosive devices continued to expand. That fall Cohen called an all-hands meeting where he laid out the challenges of predicting, detecting, defeating, and destroying IEDs to a packed house. He and Schubert allocated 10 percent of NRL's basic research program—covering physics, chemistry, even psychology—to the mission. Also in 2004 England convened a high-level meeting in his Pentagon office attended by Jack Marburger, director of the White House Office of

Science and Technology Policy, and Arden L. Bement Jr., then director of the National Institute of Standards and Technology and acting director of the National Science Foundation. In 2005 ONR was selected by the Defense Department's Joint Improvised Explosive Device Defeat Organization to lead a multi-million-dollar program of long-term research into the IED problem. This effort, led by ONR chief scientist Starnes Walker, would be canceled the next year as the decision was made to concentrate on shorter-term work. However, the bulk of ONR's longer-term efforts lived on in its own program devoted to countering terrorism (see chapter 8).

The Army and Marines, of course, bore the brunt of the IED-related deaths. As a flag officer in charge of the Navy's long-term science and technology research program, and the son-in-law of a Corps officer, Cohen naturally worried chiefly about the Marines. He was visibly stirred by the numbers of troops injured and killed in combat and considered it his duty to help them.

It was in this period that he began showing the picture of the tired young Marine smoking a cigarette—to remind everyone of ONR's commitment to helping the troops. Just as had happened under his predecessor Paul Gaffney, making the Corps ever more integral to the Office of Naval Research became a centerpiece of his tour.

———————●———————

One object of Cohen's focus on the Marine Corps was George Solhan. A retired Marine colonel, Solhan rode a motorcycle, wore a leather jacket, and swore, well, like a leatherneck. In short, he was an odd duck at ONR. Solhan had come to the organization as part of the union that Gaffney had engineered with Marine Corps Commandant Charles Krulak back in the late 1990s. At the time, Solhan had been running the Marine Corps Amphibious Warfare Technology laboratory in Quantico, Virginia. As part of the deal that brought Brig. Gen. Tim Donovan to Ballston Towers as Vice Chief of Naval Research, ONR had taken over all Marine Corps science and technology programs. That included Solhan's six-person operation, which was split evenly between civilian and military personnel.

Solhan's crew had joined Code 35, becoming the core of division 353, Expeditionary Warfare. Solhan had worked as a program manager for several years before being named division director when his boss retired. Solhan was a believer in the Gaffney–Krulak merger, but it wasn't a marriage exactly built on love. Or, as he put it: "This Navy–Marine Corps thing is a shotgun marriage. It's imperative that this marriage occur, but that doesn't make it easier."[7]

An inherent clash of cultures between the Marines and the Navy lay at the heart of the problem. This rift brought with it a different way of doing business, widely divergent warfighting needs and concerns, and a different outlook toward how science and technology should be used to help the warfighter. Again, in his typical colorful terms, Solhan noted: "We don't push a button to shoot a harpoon, we pretty much shoot the fuckers in the face."

As the sole Marine-trained division head at ONR, Solhan was also keenly aware of the clash of cultures between the vast majority of his colleagues and himself. Solhan had an undergraduate degree. He had fought in Vietnam. Positioned around his office were a few photos of his combat squad. Most of his ONR peer group, by contrast, wielded PhDs, and some had taken student deferments to avoid the draft. Solhan liked getting out in the field. His colleagues preferred a more academic life. They didn't have to publish or perish, like a professor, but they made a good, six-figure income and loved associating with university researchers. Solhan respected the diligence with which most of his counterparts approached their jobs and noted that "many of them do it . . . to very good ends." But as a rule, he felt, they had little concept of real-world warfighting needs and concerns, especially Marine Corps needs.

Solhan felt this disparity keenly throughout 2004, as the death toll mounted in Iraq. Despite a great deal of progress made since Paul Gaffney had taken dramatic steps to better integrate the Marines into ONR, he concluded that in many ways the Corps remained a second-class citizen in Ballston Towers.

In January 2005 Cohen invited Solhan to a strategy meeting. The former Marine had been division director only a few months. Looking around the room, he saw the five veteran ONR department heads and a few other staffers. He was the only division director present. What's more, as Solhan gleaned from glancing at the faces around the room, he wasn't the only one puzzled about his presence.

Then the admiral dropped the bomb. He announced that ONR was going to stand up Solhan's Expeditionary Warfare division as the core of a new department, greatly raising the Marine Corps' representation at the organization. Solhan, the new division director, would overnight become a peer of all the department heads. The Marine checked out his colleagues' reaction. "I look around and they're incredulous," he says.

"What do you think?" Cohen asked one department head.

"Frankly, it does surprise me," came the reply. Solhan guessed he pretty much spoke for everybody.

So here was another punctuated step in ONR's evolution. Gaffney had struck an agreement with General Krulak to install a Marine general as Vice Chief of Naval Research (VCNR) and integrate the Corps better into the organization's structure.[8] Cohen had already taken it a notch further, creating another position, the Assistant Vice Chief of Naval Research, to help the Vice Chief do his job. The position had come about when it became apparent that the Vice Chief could not possibly spend much time at ONR anymore. The Marine Warfighting had grown immensely in the aftermath of September 11, and it was no longer feasible to split time between the two organizations the way Tim Donovan had done. So whoever the Vice Chief was, he needed a representative at the senior level who could speak for him.

Unlike the VCNR, the assistant vice chief worked full time in the Ballston Towers complex. The job was not a military or even technically a government job. It was created under the Intergovernmental Personnel Act, which allowed for a university or other nonprofit to detail an employee to a government position for a set number of years. The first assistant vice chief (and the only one as of this writing) was Paul Gido, a retired Marine colonel who had gone to school with Donovan. He came over on assignment from the Potomac Institute for Policy Studies, a nonpartisan think tank almost around the corner from the Office of Naval Research.

Now, by creating a new department with the Marines at its core, Cohen was upping the ante again on Force involvement at ONR. He had no shortage of reasons for the move. Cohen had been working on a large-scale reorganization for more than a year by that point. He considered it "brilliant" of Gaffney and General Krulak to have established the Vice Chief of Naval Research as a Marine position. But that, he notes, was long before Iraq. Now the improvised explosive devices threat was real and growing. Marines were dying with sickening frequency. It seemed only fitting to increase their standing. "It was time at ONR to solidify the full integration of the Marine Corps with the Navy," he relates. "We did not have a department that had Marine Corps systems command or the Marine Corps as the principal customer, and I felt that had to be corrected."

Cohen reallocated parts of his budget previously aimed primarily at the "blue" Navy to fund the new department. All told, the admiral would devote around 5 percent of ONR's core (not including pass-throughs) budget to Marine Corps issues. This included the Corps' official science and technology budget of roughly $50 million, which represented almost 3.5 percent of ONR's total budget. But this still marked a significant bonus of about $25 million that would be devoted to the Marines.

In addition to giving the Marine Corps better representation, Cohen saw the new department as a way to bring his entire organization front and center in the "GWOT," the global war on terror, as it was known around Washington. It was a shrewd move. Solhan gave the admiral real credit for putting ONR ahead of the curve on this vital issue. And, of course, Cohen was making friends in Quantico and the Pentagon at the same time.

Critically, though, despite having the Marine Corps as its principal customer, the new department was never intended to become a "Marine Department." Cohen had first consulted about this with Gido, who had been at ONR since the fall of 2002. Gido had been serving in the Corps when the VCNR position was created and the Amphibious Warfare Technology unit was transferred to ONR to become division 353. He reminded Cohen there had been talk at the time about creating a Marine Department at ONR, but that General Krulak had vetoed the idea, seeing it as a surefire way for Marines to be shunted off into a separate group and marginalized. Part of the point in creating division 353 had been to integrate the six Amphibious Warfare Technology personnel with the rest of the Office of Naval Research. Most of these staffers had therefore been assigned dual roles in other ONR departments.

As Gido, Solhan, and Cohen talked about this with then Vice Chief of Naval Research, Brig. Gen. Thomas D. Waldhauser, they came to a similar conclusion. The general, who had spent time in Afghanistan and Iraq and strove to wield his operational experience to "influence the way ahead," liked the idea of elevating the Marines at ONR in principle. However, the men decided that while departmental status was good, they still didn't want the new entity to be known as the Marine Department. Says Solhan, "I don't want to be a client state. We need to be totally integrated."

In creating the new department, then, everything augured for a broader mission that went beyond just the Corps. Solhan also lobbied to avoid the term "global war on terror." To him, it was "a term of art used by the White House to obfuscate." He preferred something that spoke more specifically to both defending against terrorist attacks and to going on the offensive against terrorists. Cohen concurred. "He essentially gave me carte blanche," says Solhan.

In this way ONR's sixth science and technology department became Code 30, Expeditionary Warfare and Combating Terrorism. The first part of its title screamed "Marines." But the effort to combat terrorism was much broader and more integral to work going on throughout the organization and the entire Navy.

———————●———————

A few months later, on March 4, 2005, Adm. Jay Cohen and seven former Chiefs of Naval Research gathered at seven o'clock in the morning in a Ballston Towers conference room. Around them were various aides, a documentary TV crew, and a few others. Every chief since 1973 was present except J. R. "Smoke" Wilson Jr. and Marc Pelaez. Cohen called the get-together CNR Day.

After a quick breakfast, they were treated to an overview of what the organization had been up to in their absence. Then, in chronological order of their service, the former CNRs spoke for roughly a half-hour each about their own experiences. Toward the end of the nearly daylong get-together, Cohen presented them with a masterful brief on his "reorg" plans.

The sweeping reorganization was Cohen's grand finale. Designed to make ONR far better aligned with Navy goals and easier for insiders and outsiders to comprehend, it had been in the works for almost two years. As events played out, the plan would take another six months or longer to be finalized, and it wasn't fully approved until early 2006, after Cohen had retired from the Navy.

This overhaul spoke to all the changes of the post–Cold War era and especially those of the last five years, from the terrorist attack on the USS *Cole* to the deadly insurgent fighting in the streets of Baghdad.

At the top of the organization were the Chief of Naval Research and the Vice Chief of Naval Research, as before, a Marine brigadier general. Overseeing the science and technology program sat a technical director/chief scientist whose overall power and responsibility had been significantly reduced from the days of Fred Saalfeld's tenure.

Under them came three senior executives: director of research, director of innovation, and director of transition. These, in essence, represented the three main components of the organization as it had recently evolved—the basic science program (primarily 6.1 research), INPs (primarily 6.2), and FNCs (primarily 6.3).

Below the directors were the now-six science and technology departments, one new and all renamed:

Code 30: Expeditionary Warfare and Combating Terrorism
Code 31: Command, Control, Communications, Computers, Intelligence, Surveillance, and Reconnaissance (C4ISR)
Code 32: Ocean Battlespace Sensing
Code 33: Sea Warfare and Weapons
Code 34: Warfighter Performance
Code 35: Air Warfare and Weapons

The updated department names were visible representations of how ONR had been reconfiguring itself to reflect the modern era. Code 30, with terrorism in its title, was the most vivid example. Code 34, previously Human Systems, had been renamed Warfighter Performance. Previously only one department, Special Warfare, had contained the word "war" or "battle." Now, except for Code 31, they all included a form of those words.

Cohen's intent was to make it much easier for the Navy and Marine Corps (from top officers to enlisted personnel), a university professor, or someone in industry to look at ONR and identify which department likely related to his or her area of interest. Just as important, like both the FNC and INP programs, the new structure was designed to align with the pillars and core components of *Naval Power 21.*[9] For instance, C4ISR (Code 31) lined up with FORCEnet. Ocean Battlespace Sensing (Code 32) supported Sea Shield. Air Warfare and Weapons (Code 35) aligned with Sea Strike.

As Cohen said shortly before his change of command ceremony, "It's all about alignment and relevance. . . . We can now show alignment where any customer knows where to enter, and any sponsor knows where they can find a program officer. If you are a university researcher, you know the relevance to you. If you're a warfighter, you know the relevance."

In fiscal year 2006, the final year of Cohen's tour, the discovery and invention aspect of ONR's program totaled some $713 million. This included roughly $100 million for the Naval Research Lab. The remaining $600-million-plus supported a wide variety of projects, with funding often doled out in relatively small amounts of a few million dollars or less. The FNC program took up the second largest chunk of the budget, called "acquisition enablers." Covering roughly 40 percent of 6.2 monies and two-thirds of 6.3 funds, it represented about $550 million. The smallest core component of the budget was leap-ahead innovations. It included SwampWorks but was dominated by the INPs, which accounted for some $160 million of its $180 million allocation.

This was not the entire ONR budget, however. Another $330 million fell into the directed/pass-through bucket. These were mostly congressional plus-ups and earmarks directed to support specific programs that Congress deemed worthy.

When this was added to the pie, about 40 percent of the organization's total budget was devoted to 6.1 fundamental research, with the rest split almost evenly between 6.2 applied research and 6.3 advanced technology demonstration. But this 40:30:30 ratio was only one way of looking at the budget. Cohen himself thought of it as 40:10:10:40. This represented 40 percent for basic research, 10 percent each for innovative programs and what was mandated by the Office of the Secretary of Defense, with the last roughly 40 percent going to Future Naval Capabilities, what he thought of as customer products. "At the end of the day, I left a barbelled budget that balanced the basic research and the advanced technology," he says.

For those who had feared the 1993 merger and the creation of the FNC program heralded a steady erosion at the gates of fundamental research, this stabilizing of the budget represented good news. Cohen received kudos from senior staff for holding the line against further encroachments into ONR's basic science program.

Despite such moves, though, some insiders felt that a steep price had been paid for starting the FNC program in the first place—a price that went beyond the portion of ONR's budget it took up. Says Tim Coffey, "While all this was happening you could see this change occurring in how the ONR established its value metric for the value of a proposition." What he meant by that, Coffey explains, is that he believes program officers have unconsciously shifted the way they evaluate projects. As he once related, they are "looking for stuff that will pay off in the shorter term, and maybe not looking as much as they should in the longer-term. And that I think is a very distinct difference between the old ONR and the new ONR. In some sense you could say neither of them are necessarily bad or good, but they certainly are different."[10]

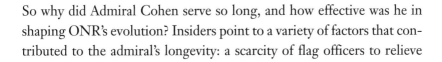

So why did Admiral Cohen serve so long, and how effective was he in shaping ONR's evolution? Insiders point to a variety of factors that contributed to the admiral's longevity: a scarcity of flag officers to relieve him, the shock of September 11 and the enduring war in Iraq that made it less palatable to make leadership changes, his adroitness on Capitol Hill, and his masterful ability to anticipate and deliver what his bosses wanted, resulting in a close relationship with CNO Vern Clark and Secretary of the Navy Gordon England.

Cohen had his enemies, especially at Naval Sea Systems Command after he cut the system command out of X-Craft development. He could live with that. In fact, he was proud that he had taken the time to listen to the dreams of leadership, and felt he was often used by top brass to push things faster, prove new approaches could work, and generally embarrass programs of record (several such programs are profiled in the second half of this book).

"I didn't care who I embarrassed; it was about getting the job done," he proclaimed. "My whole approach to innovation was the Nike motto. 'Just do it.'" Meanwhile, he was a master of visibility and good public relations, unrelenting with his energy, ideas, and catchy turns of phrase. Part of his style was that he unabashedly borrowed ideas from other venues and put his own spin on them. For instance, he adapted the "Intel Inside" motto and insisted on placing a "Powered by Naval Research" sticker on innovations coming out of the office.

Another idea, "Stoogle," was short for "science and technology Google." The plan was to create a system for scouring the Navy's own vast knowledge base for expertise or technology that might be applicable to the war effort. Cohen even tried to get Google founders Larry Page and Sergey Brin to join the effort, but the concept proved too difficult to pull off.

Like the Energizer Bunny, his ideas kept coming, and coming, and coming—and often to good outcome. "There is no question Admiral Cohen has had a major, major impact on this organization," says Bobby Junker, head of Code 31, C4ISR. "I don't think you'll find people in the Navy who haven't heard of ONR anymore."[11]

Fred Saalfeld places Cohen as the latest in an important continuum of CNRs who together made the organization "extremely more valuable" to the Navy. The changes started with Admiral Miller. Marc Peleaz had the job of putting Miller's start into a cohesive whole—

engineering the first big reorganization of the post–Cold War era. Then came Paul Gaffney, who "put spit and polish and focused on delivery to the Fleet and Marine Corps." Finally, he says, Jay Cohen polished up the polish, restructuring to more directly align with Navy goals, thereby taking ONR to another level.

Cohen himself was unsure of his effectiveness. "I don't think I got it right. I don't think anyone can get it right. I don't think anyone knows what right is," he says. All a CNR can do, he adds, is just work his best to make good things happen.

Before he left, though, the admiral went around his organization, which in 2005 moved to relatively swank new offices at One Liberty Place, almost around the corner from Ballston Towers. He asked staffers what they thought his legacy would be. His summary of their responses: "My legacy will be one word: change." Then, Cohen relates, "I asked them was it good change or bad change. Their answer was only time will tell."

No doubt that's true. Still, one central figure in ONR's modern evolution dared to offer a verdict. Jim DeCorpo, at various times in and out of favor with Cohen and a part of the organization for almost all of the post–Cold War period, depicts the admiral as an astute reader of the changes enveloping the world and molding ONR to adapt to them. "There was a time when the Navy had more money and ONR had a lot more flexibility," DeCorpo says. "And now that it is crunch time, you have got to be able to justify and talk the language. And no one does it better than Jay."[12]

Ultimately, adds DeCorpo, echoing Saalfeld, Cohen was a key part of a slow transformation that began when the Cold War ended. "What you see evolve from 1990 to now is certainly a more balanced organization. It has a portfolio—discovery and invention to delivery. Not all people are happy. There are people who miss the old days of, 'Here's the money, go do good things.' Now there's a lot more structure, there's a lot more guidance and churn."

"Which one is better? I don't know. I don't think the old one would have survived."

PART II

DEPARTMENT
AND PROJECT PROFILES

CHAPTER 8

Combating Terrorism

On August 3, 2005, members of Marine Reserve company Lima were on patrol near the western Iraqi town of Haditha, 140 miles northwest of Baghdad.[1] Just a few months earlier, the company had been known as "Lucky Lima." It was no longer so. As their armored vehicles rolled along a desert road approaching the entrance to the city, a brilliant flash erupted in the middle of the convoy. The explosion, from a roadside bomb, blew apart a personnel carrier and ignited its fuel and cargo of explosives. "Huge fire and dust rose from the place of the explosion," according to an Iraqi motorist driving some eighty yards away from the attack. His pickup truck's rear window was shattered by the blast.

When the dust settled, fourteen Marines were dead, along with their Iraqi interpreter, making the attack the deadliest roadside bombing of the war to that point. But that was just a part of the tragic week for the Ohio-based Lima Company and the 3rd Battalion, 25th Marine Regiment, to which it belonged. Two days earlier, the battalion lost six men in a firefight near Haditha and another to a suicide car bombing. As a whole the 25th regiment had suffered twenty fatalities during the previous May and June. The early August assaults more than doubled the number of dead, to forty-one.

The devastating attacks provided a grim reminder for the newly formed ONR Code 30 of the urgency—and the stakes—of the task before it. The department, Expeditionary Maneuver Warfare & Combating Terrorism, had been created earlier that spring after Admiral Cohen's surprise announcement of his intentions to give the Marines Corps higher status at the Office of Naval Research. "We are the primary enter point and belly point for all Marine Corps S&T [science and technology]," says Ashley Johnson, one of the new department's three division heads. "There is stuff done in other parts of ONR, but we're certainly the center of gravity."[2]

At the same time, Corps officials hadn't wanted to become pigeonholed as the "Marine Department." Instead, the decision was to make them the backbone of a broader department that focused on the prime threat the United States currently faced: terrorism and irregular warfare. All you had to do to see the need for such a department was read the headlines from Iraq.

Much of the effort from the beginning had been focused on defeating improvised explosive devices and roadside bombs, building on the momentum started with the "mini-Manhattan" project of the previous year. But the IEDs were just a symptom of the bigger issue of unconventional warfare and terrorism that loomed as the Achilles heel of the U.S. military, according to George Solhan, the former Marine colonel who headed the new department. "We're very good at 'near-peer' competitors. We can kick anybody's ass in the world, at will," says Solhan. However, he adds, "when it digresses into a small war and an insurgent war, we're really not oriented in that direction, and we become reactive."[3]

This point was especially true on land. In the sea and marine environment, while still having to worry about mines and USS *Cole*–like attacks, the United States is for the most part "good to go," in Solhan's words. On land, though, depending on the environment and terrain, things can quickly unravel. The Corps, he says, is unrivaled in the desert. It doesn't perform as well in the mountains and jungles. Fighting in urban settings, however, is even more problematic. A Code 30 PowerPoint slide depicts the desert environment as relatively friendly by shading it in green and a cautious yellow. Mountain and jungle terrain is colored a mix of yellow and red for danger. The urban environment looms as solid red, from city streets to waterfront areas to industrial zones and suburbs.

It was the urban environment, of course, where the war in Iraq was proving excruciatingly difficult. The United States was on the enemy's home court, and Iraqi insurgents were often calling the shots. In truth, the Marines hadn't focused much attention into urban warfare in the past—there had never been a war quite like Iraq. The same Code 30 slide summed up the issue facing Marines and all American forces operating in this landscape: "Most Contested—Least Invested." Therefore, Solhan's overriding goal, and that of ONR Code 30, was to help the United States reorient, invest more, and become proactive when it came to irregular warfare and fighting terrorism, particularly in the urban environment.

———————⬤———————

The military's role in the war on terror closely parallels its efforts to combat irregular warfare. The threats are often the same—including suicide attackers, hidden bombs, sniper fire, and possibly biological agents—as are many tactics for defeating the enemy. This includes a host of S&T initiatives that span surveillance, data mining, psychology and sociology (to understand the terrorist mindset and the social makeup of enemy networks), detecting explosives at a distance, guarding against suicide bombers on land and sea—and much else. The list goes on and on.

Consequently, ONR Code 30 oversees or tries to integrate a hodgepodge of efforts that cut across a far broader swath of S&T areas than those in its fellow departments. Many of these initiatives are not solely, or even chiefly, housed in its confines. This makes getting a handle on its activities or choosing one particular illustrative effort on which to focus extremely difficult. The problem is compounded by the fact that the department is new, therefore many of its efforts are still in the early stages or poorly defined. Finally, because its activities are extremely close to the Here and Now and ongoing conflicts—both the Iraq War and the more general "GWOT," or global war on terror—the most promising projects move quickly into the classified realm. All these factors conspire to make telling the story of Code 30 especially nettlesome.

Even its organization set Code 30 apart. From the start, the new department was arranged battlefield-style, according to nine tactical areas, or thrusts. With certain adjustments made to smooth the way for technology development, these thrusts were conceived to line up with the core principles of the Marine Corps combat development process, which was broken into five essential warfighting functions: command and control, computer; communication and intelligence; fires and maneuver; force protection; and logistics. "That's why we're different, because we're aligned with these warfighter functions," says Solhan.

Virtually all these Code 30 functions reflected the Marine Corps' longstanding interest in what were once called "small wars." In the post–Cold War age, the term of choice was "the long war" or, more typically, irregular or asymmetric warfare. The genesis of the department lay in the urgent need—painfully evident after the Iraq invasion—to better equip the Marines and Navy to fight the long war.

ONR Code 30 Thrusts

Human performance, training, and education: Small unit situational awareness tools; cognitive and physical performance such as fatigue mitigation, nutrition, supplementation, and injury prevention.

Command and control, computer, communication: Mobile networking; tactical situational awareness; small unit location and navigation.

Fires: Enhanced weapons targeting, accuracy, lethality, and mobility in support of distributed operations and urban warfare.

Intelligence, surveillance, and reconnaissance: Sensor nets; data pattern recognition and analysis

Logistics: Better distribution; decreased fuel, water, and energy demands; improved maintenance

Maneuver: Advanced mobility and survivability of vehicles; explosive resistance coatings; unmanned systems

Force protection: Mine countermeasures; body armor; counter IEDs; explosives neutralization

Maritime irregular warfare: Boarding and seizure; riverine warfare; special operations

Operational adaptation: Integrating intelligence gathering, data mining, and understanding of social networks to help military forces adapt to and even shape and disrupt enemy plans on the fly.

Each thrust in Code 30 was typically staffed by just a handful of people: total department personnel numbered about forty-five in early 2007. The program officers in charge of each thrust, contrary to typical ONR practice, managed their work all the way from basic research to transition. That was partly because the department's chief customer, the Marines, were actively engaged in a conflict and needed new technologies as quickly as possible. But it also reflected Solhan's personal management philosophy. Says he, "If you're going to give [a program manager responsibility] for a capacity or warfare area that is also aligned with a lane of technologies, he ought to have the responsibility to integrate the basic research, the applied research, and the technology demonstration stuff within that area."

The rest of the department's structure was also somewhat unique. Program managers in other ONR departments typically reported to division heads, with the divisions responsible for a specific research area. In Code 30, however, because the program managers handled a technology from basic research to technology demonstration, they reported directly to the department head, Solhan. The department's three divisions were left with a more guidance-oriented role according to the stage of development a given project had reached. The Code 30 research division oversaw 6.1 basic research and some 6.2 work. The applications division, overseen by Ashley Johnson, was responsible for 6.2 and 6.3 work—getting it ready for transition to the Fleet or the Marines, usually the latter.

The third division, Combating Terrorism & Naval Enterprise Integration, was even more unique.[4] It oversaw no (or very few) research programs at all. Rather, it had two main jobs. One was to look out across all ONR, and to a lesser extent other Navy labs and establishments, for tools and technologies to support the war on terror. The other was to do the same thing to support the Navy Expeditionary Combat Command, which oversaw some 40,000 sailors and was responsible for riverine and coastal warfare, expeditionary logistics, and more. In short, the division functioned like a business portfolio manager, making recommendations to Solhan, the Chief of Naval Research, and the ONR hierarchy on how to adjust its portfolio in these areas.

The division was led by James McMains, a retired Marine Corps lieutenant colonel and helicopter pilot who had served four years at the Marine Warfighting Lab in Quantico before coming to ONR in 2001 to be the Marine liaison for the Future Naval Capabilities (FNC) program in littoral combat. Later, he was among the core group Brig. Gen. Tim Donovan tapped to help develop the Dragon Eye drone. His long experience with unmanned aerial vehicles (UAVs) was likely to figure in to his new role as a Code 30 division head.

The effort to combat terror was a subset of the broader, much more expensive domain of irregular warfare that occupied the bulk of Code 30 resources. But fighting terrorism spanned many of the same general issues and included taking the point on a significant portion of ONR's counter-IED work, the leading cause of American troop fatalities in Iraq. Its smaller scope and front-and-center place with a major problem confronting the Iraq war effort therefore made combating terrorism a good framework with which to view the new department as it got off the ground and strove to make its mark at ONR.

McMains' division stood front and center in this effort for the entire Office of Naval Research. Every department assigned a representative to the division's combating terrorism executive leadership team, which also included ONR's three high-ranking directors, director of research Patricia Gruber, director of transition Joseph Lawrence, and acting director of innovation Scott Littlefield.

As the new division (and the department that housed it) took shape in late 2005, McMains' team spent nearly nine months—spanning much of the following year—assessing how best to tackle the job of combating terrorism. This included studying national security descriptions of the problem, the Navy's strategic plan, the Marine Corps S&T plan, and a host of terrorism-related documents and treatises. The team also performed an extensive analysis of all ONR programs under way to determine which fell into the combating terrorism bucket.

From this comprehensive assessment, the group identified two overarching functions involved in the fight against terrorism—counterterrorism and antiterrorism. The first comprises direct action against terrorists, the second refers to defensive steps to deter or prevent terrorist attacks. Superimposed on these categorizations were three major capability functions or goals, around which ONR decided to organize its combating terrorism efforts, both antiterrorism or counterterrorism. "When we decomposed this whole GWOT thing into its constituent parts via a pretty rigorous assessment, it appeared to be composed of three major capability areas," says Solhan. These categories were global maritime domain awareness; maritime irregular warfare; and operational adaptation.

Global maritime domain awareness is a broad term that essentially means monitoring and tracking everything in the sea or flying above it, including riverine areas, as well as the land and airspace around ports and urban zones where Marines might operate. From an S&T standpoint, it runs from cell phone and e-mail intercepts to integrated sensor networks like the Persistent Littoral Undersea Surveillance program (see chapter 10) to unmanned reconnaissance drones. Not only does it involve creating better ways to monitor potential enemy activity, it also includes developing complex software algorithms necessary to extract patterns and meaning from the massive amounts of data collected—and doing all this pervasively, persistently, and affordably.

The essential goals and tasks behind global maritime domain awareness are adapted from the CNO's strategic plan, says Solhan. The CNO's vision centered on looking for ships, whether large ocean-going vessels or coastal freighters, typically using aircraft and other overhead resources employing technology in the radio frequency or electro-optic spectrum. "We believe that the naval mission also implies the need to be able to do that in the littoral, down to finding individuals or weapons caches in cluttered environments and urban areas," Solhan notes. The bulk of ONR's work in this area takes place in Code 31 (Command, Control Communications, Computers, Intelligence, Surveillance, and Reconnaissance) or Code 32 (Ocean Battlespace Sensing). Although Code 30 maintains small thrusts devoted to command and control and surveillance issues, the exact role of those efforts in the global maritime domain awareness picture was still being sorted out in early 2007.

Maritime irregular warfare encompasses a similar variety of ambitions, many of which build on the domain awareness outlined above.

"These are the beginnings of the actions, the things you do when you achieve the awareness you need," says Geoff Main, a Code 30 program officer who works under McMains. Say that suspicious cargo or activity was spotted on board a commercial ship, he posits.[5] The vessel might not be obviously hostile, and anything the United States does might have political ramifications. So how do you stop that ship, especially on the open sea, without using lethal force? A lot of the work on this front skirts classified ground. But officials point to things like technologies to take control of the rudder or turn off the ship's engines. "It's a hard problem and thus it's a good S&T problem, because there's no obvious answer for how you do it," says Main. Most of this portion of maritime irregular warfare is handled by Code 33, Sea Warfare and Weapons.

Another aspect of maritime irregular warfare, however, involves boarding a ship and conducting inspection operations efficiently and safely. This might include real-time biometrics—rapidly checking identities through iris scans, for example. Maritime irregular warfare also extends inland where Marines might operate, to investigating or seeking to prevent an IED explosion.

At this stage, things move into the third arena of combating terrorism, operational adaptation. The core idea here is to use the information and abilities gained in the first two stages, especially domain awareness, to adapt to terrorist actions quickly and effectively. "In a nutshell, the premise is that with near-peer competitors who publish doctrine, who have professional military education and we can read and research all that stuff, we can pretty much template what they will do in the friction of combat," says Solhan. But while terrorists might publish ideology, they don't publish doctrine. They change tactics quickly and ingeniously and quickly disappear into the woodwork—so they're hard to predict, track, and counter.

As Solhan's charges completed their assessment and made recommendations to the Chief of Naval Research, they stressed that most of ONR's combating terrorism efforts to date fell into the antiterrorism camp rather than counterterrorism. The group recommended a better balance of projects that included developing more offensive-minded programs.

When it came to the three capability areas outlined here, a solid base already existed in other departments in global maritime domain awareness and maritime irregular warfare. While Code 30 could certainly help with aspects of these efforts, operational adaptation represented more virgin territory. It was this area on which the new department focused its combating terrorism efforts. Pulling it all together became McMains' job.

Observe. Orient. Decide. Act. So goes the "OODA loop," a term coined by an Air Force officer but one heartily embraced by the Navy and Marines in the fight against terrorism. In any combat endeavor, the force or individual warfighter that can cycle rapidly and effectively through these four operations will win the battle. As McMains puts it, the four parts of the OODA loop each represent a battle domain. "To totally dominate an enemy, we need to dominate each domain," he says.[6] Getting inside the OODA loop—disrupting the terrorist's ability to navigate through it while enhancing your own—forms the essence of operational adaptation.

OA, as it is known, comprises some of the most exciting, complex, and interesting ideas floating around ONR. At the same time, it's a concept that requires not only new orientation but also new doctrine and technological tools. Consequently, the entire approach is in such an early stage that the principle itself remains ill-formed, and much of the language used to describe operational adaptation and its relation to the OODA loop is vague. Solhan relates that nonpeer competitors such as terrorists might not even operate in normal OODA loop stages. "They may just orient and act . . . or decide and act. We frankly don't know," he says. "We want to be more adaptable, to get inside of that . . . [have] our OODA work inside their OODA but be able to cycle between their [first] 'o' and their second 'o,' or their second 'o' and their 'd.'" If the United States can do that, he continues, then it would go a long way toward achieving one of its major goals: conducting operations against terrorists in an offensive rather than defensive mode. "Then we can defeat them in an adaptable way, in a proactive way, rather than a reactive way."

If all that sounds confusing, the Code 30 staffers freely admit they are flailing around a bit, unsure of exactly how to achieve their goals. Their first steps seemed to be to create frameworks that helped define and bring order to the problem, forming a core or base around which to craft a long-term plan for achieving their goals.

Part of that framework involves thinking of a terrorist attack, a bomb, or an IED blast as the "event" that lies at the center of everything U.S. forces do. ONR's antiterrorist endeavors and much of its total combating terrorism portfolio are focused on actions to the right of the event—identifying, tracking, and ultimately bringing to justice the perpetrators. However, an increasing amount of activity centers on things to the left of the event, namely collecting intelligence, detecting suspicious patterns of behavior, identifying manufacturing and transportation capabilities, understanding the mindset and social networks of terrorists, and other steps that will either enable U.S. forces to prevent an attack altogether or minimize its effects. This is the counterterrorism side of the ledger. "We are focusing more and more to the left of the boom," Solhan says. The idea is to move as far to the left as possible, hopefully to the point where the enemy can be manipulated into acting in ways that give the United States a decided advantage.

To try to make their still-fuzzy frameworks and concepts more vivid, Code 30 staffers worked up several examples—both left and right of the event—of the way operational adaptation might work in real life. In one scenario, an improvised explosive device is detonated, perhaps killing some Marines and Iraqi civilians and injuring many others. Right now, it takes weeks, if not longer, to sort through the forensics of the site and pick up enough information to go after the terrorist or insurgent network. One goal of operational adaptation is to be able to do this much more rapidly. Suppose surveillance of the area is so good that investigators can rapidly roll back the cameras covering the scene and automatically scan for the likely vehicles or people involved. Says Main, "Now, within minutes or hours, you know whatever sites or facilities were frequented by whom, and what vehicles were involved in this. You could imagine rolling up the network or rolling up a lot more of it really quickly."

The elements involved in such a "right-of-the-event" scenario form a basis for moving to the left of the boom. For instance, if the United States could simply increase its ability to actively monitor the data it was collecting through cell phones and surveillance cameras—before the fact rather than afterward—it would go a long way toward getting ahead of the event and being proactive. Code 30 staffers call this human network mapping. It can encompass watching people transporting materials for bomb-making, say, or delivering IEDs or bombs to the scene of a planned attack, charting phone call pathways to identify ringleaders from minions, and more. "If we can increase our ability to analyze just the data that we're already collecting, that's a big portion of what human network mapping will be," says McMains.

Another concept being employed to this same end is TTL, tagging, tracking, and locating. This spans an entire class of technologies, from sensor networks to geolocation to Internet monitoring, data pattern recognition, and more. Initially, this might involve piecing together terrorist plots and perpetrators after an event, but the more refined the techniques become, the more it enables proactive actions. Says Geoff Main, "These are the hard things that if we can do them it would get you to the left of the event."

Now another scenario comes into play, starting with the first phase of the OODA loop: observe. A Marine patrol is about to enter a village, but pattern recognition software analyzing data from surveillance cameras and sensors placed around the village in real time detects some unusual activity. For instance, audio sensors in the town might be listening to conversations ahead of the patrol's arrival. Speech algorithms sifting through the data might detect a high number of foreign accents in the neighborhood ahead. In Iraq, says Main, there is a strong correlation between insurgency and people native to a different Arab country, so this could indicate an influx of hostile forces. Or video cameras might spot an unusual number of men in the marketplace at a time of day when the area is typically packed with women shopping, again putting the patrol on alert.

All this is treading close to classified ground. "I apologize in advance for us being vague," says Main. But turning something like this into reality points to a class of hardware and software innovations that might be termed situational awareness technologies or, in some cases, cultural sensors. Such an alert might give the patrol a few seconds or minutes of warning, enough to avoid being ambushed, and ideally to enable them to turn the tables on the enemy and gain the upper hand.

If the United States can get far enough to the left of an event, ONR officials note, it might be possible to move into the sphere of battlespace shaping. This refers to the ability to steer and possibly even dictate enemy actions before encountering direct hostility. This is the ultimate goal of operational adaptation because it puts control of the situation almost entirely into American hands.

For instance, Solhan picks up the example of human network mapping from cell phone calls. "The data is huge, and we're not even capable of looking at all of it," he says. But suppose you could refine the analysis to examining all cell phone traffic in the area of an event. By analyzing which are transmitting and which are receiving, you might also be able to identify the ringleaders and begin to predict future behavior—such as where they are moving—and ultimately use that information to tilt the odds in your favor. Or you might be able to somehow stimulate the leaders into making a call and revealing themselves. "If we can energize that network to communicating or activating, we can start to manipulate the outcomes," says Solhan. He calls such a practice information OPS, as opposed to more traditional PSY OPS, or psychological operations, which involves such things as leafleting and propaganda dissemination. "I don't know how we are going to do all that yet, but that's the essence of operational adaptation," he says. And "ONR is the only organization thinking on that."

--------●--------

Code 30 staffers knew from the start that regularly achieving this kind of left-of-the-boom scenario would likely take decades, if it would ever be possible. It would involve fundamental research in psychology and sociology as well as technological advances in fields such as remote sensing and pattern detection, none of them easy. Their approach was not to go for broke but rather to build the foundation for future success by focusing on near-term aspects of the challenge that would be tested and demonstrated. From that, it was hoped, the bigger advances would follow.

Early in 2007 McMains briefed new Chief of Naval Research William Landay III on a far-ranging plan for five demonstrations of the concepts and technologies behind operational adaptation and the wider effort to combat terrorism. After two years of more extensive planning and further development of the technologies involved, these "capability" trials were envisioned to start in 2009 and run through 2013. McMains' colleague Geoff Main described the overall goal: "[It] integrates into a series of demonstrations that range out through the fiscal years as technologies mature, pulling in capabilities that get you ever closer to that mythical point far to the left of the hostility."

Landay agreed to fund at least the first portion of the two-part initial demonstration. The basic idea behind this first demonstration was to kludge together technologies already being funded by ONR and put them into the field with Marines and other warfighters in a quasi-operational environment to see what worked and what might be close to working. It would concentrate especially on global maritime domain awareness–related programs to monitor the seas, skies, riverine, port, and urban areas where Navy and Marine forces would likely operate.

Phase 1, starting in 2009, was to focus on core technologies involved in "ISR," or intelligence, surveillance, and reconnaissance—mainly over water. It would start by using tools very familiar to McMains: unmanned aerial vehicles. The idea was to employ UAVs for monitoring everything inside a two-hundred-mile line in the water, watching both what was on the surface and under it (hunting for mines, for instance) through various sensing technologies. The drones were then to characterize anything they found as friend or foe and relay the information to a command and control center.

The second phase of this first demonstration, which would follow probably in 2010, was to take the same core technologies into urban and riverine environments. McMains posed some questions for this test: Does a drone flying over a city have the smarts without a human operator to pick out someone walking through a crowd carrying a rocket-propelled grenade launcher? Similarly, could it spot a rooftop sniper?

Answers to these questions would depend not just on general UAV technology but on things like automatic target recognition software being funded by ONR.

The second demonstration, designed to move into the area of real-time forensics and human network mapping, would take place in 2010–11. This might involve, for instance, rapidly examining bomb fragments to try and identify the source of the materials used, says McMains. Or, he adds, "It could be fingerprints. It could be blood." On the human network mapping end of things, it might mean tracing cell phone calls and other intercepts after a simulated event took place to try and rapidly identify the participants. But the overarching idea would be to provide tools and technologies for troops to much more immediately identify and go after the terrorists.

The third demonstration would carry human network mapping technologies a step further to try to test the ability to move to the left of the event and provide some forewarning. Here McMains planned to get into the realm of stimulating enemy actions. To give an example from more conventional warfare, he notes that if a Marine platoon were attacking an enemy on a hill, it might fire mortars to force the foe to vacate its positions. The platoon wouldn't know where the enemy would move to, but the main point was to get them off the hill. In an operational adaptation framework, U.S. forces might intercept a phone call that alerted them to an impending terrorist attack. Even though they might not know exactly where the attack would take place or who would perpetrate it, they might be able to add their own call feeding enough bogus information to the network to knock the enemy off his game and disrupt the plan.

With the fourth demonstration, ONR hoped to explore the concept of manipulation. "The key buzz words for the fourth demo are tagging, tracking, and locating," says McMains. There are a variety of ways to do this: fingerprints and other forensics, security monitors, cell phone intercepts, even the idea of an invisible dust that can somehow be used to follow people or equipment remotely. Once the enemy's location is known, and sometimes even if it isn't, the idea is to then manipulate his actions. As opposed to stimulating the enemy into a general action, manipulation seeks to force him into exactly the action you desire, such as funneling him to a battle spot of your choosing. "The stimulation part is easier than the manipulation part," notes McMains.

In early 2007 there was no clear idea of how this fourth demonstration would work. But the fifth demo, set for 2013, was the least defined of all. It gets at the concept of information OPS and digging into the head of the terrorist to understand his or her thinking and behavior. It encompasses more extensive human network mapping, cultural sensors, and more. Historically, the cognitive realm has been the least focused on in the military's counterterror efforts, which tend to specialize in the physical arena. "What we're saying with information OPS is we need to turn that upside down," says McMains.

If the United States can dramatically advance its abilities on this front, he adds, "that is when we can really get in there and manipulate." Then a terrorist network might feel the same vulnerability as a Marine company moving through uncharted territory, not knowing where the next attack might come from.

Despite its focus on a very real threat, the sheer grandness of the operational adaptation vision and the vagueness surrounding exactly how to achieve it stood out as one of the most immense challenges ONR had taken on in the post–Cold War era.

That being said, as Microsoft's former chief technology officer Nathan Myhrvold once observed: "You get more small ideas by thinking big than by thinking small." Operational adaptation seems a prime example of a very big idea likely to yield many valuable smaller ideas before the grand vision is achieved.

CHAPTER 9

New Eye for the New Navy

One hot summer afternoon in 1998 Greg Tavik sauntered across the grounds of the Naval Research Laboratory. Tavik was bound for a special meeting called by his boss, Paul Hughes, head of the Radar division. Walking beside him was another NRL engineer, Steve Lessin. They joined a stream of scores of others: all told, close to one hundred workers crammed into the conference room where Hughes waited.

Tavik was mildly curious about what lay in store. "If I had known, I probably would have turned around and run," he joked years later.[1] Rumors had been swirling of a major new project that was set to be announced. However, as a relatively junior "worker bee," he didn't have the clout to be in on the planning. Neither did Lessin.

That would soon change. The room fell silent as Hughes addressed the gathering. The radar chief acknowledged that the buzz about a big new job was true. He then launched into a description of an endeavor that would almost define Tavik's work life for the next eight years or longer. In fact, in just two years, Tavik would emerge as one of the key players.

As Hughes detailed the plans, Tavik and Lessin shared a glance, an exchange that indicated the two engineers saw things eye to eye: "He has gotta be nuts." A scan of the conference room immediately convinced Tavik that they were hardly alone. Much of the chatter that soon erupted, as Tavik relates it anyway, ran along the general lines of, "This is the dumbest idea we've ever heard."

What Paul Hughes outlined in bold strokes that day would come to be known as AMRF-C, for the Advanced Multi-Function Radio

Frequency Concept. This was a program that might sound mundane to a layperson. But to the engineers and scientists present, as evidenced by their reaction to the news, it was an immense, costly, and hugely controversial undertaking. The idea, in its essence, was to sheer back the "antenna forest" that had sprouted on modern Navy vessels. On a typical 1990s-vintage ship, this had swollen into an array of between 80 and more than 120 electronic systems covering a wide range of functions from different types of radars to communications to GPS and electronic warfare that operated across a host of frequencies or wavelengths. However, rather than consolidating a few with some novel design, the idea behind AMRF-C was to replace them all with two large, multifunctional solid-state apertures, one for transmitting signals and one for receiving them. Each would consist of an array of electronic elements. By activating different groups of these elements, and sometimes repositioning the arrays, it would be possible to perform the functions of all the specialized antennas that currently clogged up a ship—and indeed operate them all simultaneously.

For all its bland engineering-ness, this is the stuff upon which future naval engagements might be decided. The accumulation of antennas on a modern warship acts as a strong reflector of electromagnetic energy. This makes the vessels far more readily observable on enemy radar and therefore more vulnerable to attack. What's more, all these separate antennas, each with its own function, add weight and energy drain to a ship, and require a large contingent of specialized crewmembers to service and maintain. All these factors conspire to slow a ship down, reduce its time at sea, and raise its cost of operation.

Razing the antenna forest down to two apertures would eliminate all of these constraints. A much smaller technical crew would be needed to operate and service the equipment. Add the greatly reduced radar profile and the energy and weight savings, and the cumulative effect would be to make ships quieter, safer, faster, and less costly to operate. It could also make them more deadly. Because moving to a solid-state array makes it easier to fulfill the vision of an all-electric ship, it could eventually help enable new types of weaponry such as the electromagnetic railgun (see chapter 13).

Building such an antenna posed an immense challenge that would require the skills of a host of Navy labs, university experts, and defense electronics firms. The Naval Research Laboratory's job was to act as the systems integrator for this effort. It was primarily because of the program's disruptive potential that so many NRL engineers present for the announcement didn't think AMRF-C stood a chance. Recalls Tavik, "All of us were thinking of all kinds of reasons why this was a bad idea. Not so much that you *couldn't* do it, engineering-wise, but why would you want to? We'd have to first invent such a system, then demonstrate how it could work—how it could be architected, built, and controlled." What's more, he adds, "Politically, it was a huge target. This thing was much different from anything anybody had tried to do in the past."

But somehow the project had been approved. And so began one of the most ambitious endeavors ever spawned by the Office of Naval Research. Typically, ONR projects run on a scale of a few million dollars and occasionally rise into the tens of millions of dollars. By 2007 the price tag for AMRF-C and a major spinoff effort for the Navy's new class of destroyers was closing in on $200 million. The original vision had been changed and aspects of it scaled back as costs rose and practical obstacles reared their heads. However, an enhanced version was poised to take off as a separate, newly funded project beginning in 2008, raising the possibility the approach could transform the way the Navy's ships are designed and built.

"It's not like, 'Build it and they will come.' But it's not far from it, either," says Raytheon's Mike Sarcione, who began work on the effort even before the formal kickoff in 1998 and served as his company's AMRF-C program manager and technical director.[2] "The technology will eventually get to a point where they'll have to adopt it. They'd be crazy not to. We'd be at a significant disadvantage if they don't. And our military will not be caught at a disadvantage."

———————●———————

The roots of "Amerf," as the acronym of the proposed system came to be pronounced, could be traced to the digital computing and semiconductor revolution that stretched back decades before the 1998 meeting at the Naval Research Laboratory. Beginning as far back as the 1960s, the Office of Naval Research initiated a series of basic science and early applied research studies into new semiconductors such as silicon carbide, gallium arsenide, and gallium nitride that formed the foundation for powerful electronic amplifiers and high-speed transistors. One of the hallmarks of these new materials was that they were "tunable," says Max Yoder, who in 1996 became director of ONR's electronics division. That is, when configured in the right way their properties allowed them to handle multiple digital signals simultaneously. This characteristic, says Yoder, was far different from the makeup of the now-familiar silicon chip used in personal computing and other applications. The capabilities and function of silicon semiconductors are determined during fabrication, he says, rendering them not unlike a toy flute that can only emit the specific notes dictated by its preformed holes. The new semiconductor materials, by contrast, enabled chips more like a slide-whistle that could produce a low signal, a high signal, and everything in between. The materials that allowed for this multifunctionality became known as "wide bandgap" semiconductors. Their discovery, says Yoder, "gave us the incentive to look further" and try and learn how to best control their properties.[3]

The hunt to perfect a tunable semiconductor encompassed work at a series of university and industry labs as well as at the Naval Research Laboratory. In 1994 another break occurred. Using indium phosphide, NRL investigators built the first very-high-speed transistor with a clock speed (or switching speed) of one terahertz. This formed the basis for a super-fast logic device that provided the capability to synthesize all of the different signals that a wide bandgap semiconductor produced. Moreover, Yoder says, subsequent studies showed that with the right type of circuitry, not only could the multiple signals enabled by the tunable semiconductor be sent simultaneously through a single antenna aperture, each could be controlled independently in terms of bandwidth, waveform, directionality, and more.

The antenna forest had proliferated in large part because of the single-purpose function of traditional antenna systems. "For years, it was 'Add a function, add an antenna,'" says Raytheon's Sarcione. Given new forms of electronic warfare, satellite communications, radars, and more, the modern ship was awash in antennas of all shapes and sizes—stovepipe, spherical, rotating, fixed—each constructed for one specific application.

To engineers like Yoder and Sarcione, a tunable semiconductor represented a powerful enabling tool. Yoder likens it to a wall socket into which you can plug a computer, toaster, microwave oven, and just about any other appliance. Only this was a military-strength wall socket. "In theory now we could use that aperture for electronic warfare, we could use it for communications purposes . . . or radar surveillance," he says.

It's hard to overstate the potential of such a discovery. In the past, shipboard electronic warfare systems were useless in defending against a wave of sea-skimming missiles that would saturate their systems. Now, with a multifunctional system, says Yoder, "We could cover all those communication signals automatically by computer control to jam or deceive the incoming missiles, giving us operational capabilities that we had never even envisioned before."

Electronic warfare also demanded a lot of power to blanket the airspace around an incoming missile or plane to jam the enemy's systems. With the solid-state aperture and its ability to precisely control pencil-like energy beams, it would be possible to jam exactly on target, greatly reducing energy demands. Indeed, a single gallium nitride chip would draw as little as one-tenth the energy as the eight to ten gallium arsenide counterpart chips needed for the same output.

The somewhat staggering list of benefits didn't stop there. Wide bandgap semiconductors are able to withstand higher voltage loads without sustaining significant damage, enabling higher-power systems. Additionally, a single system dictated just one computer, whereas before engineers had to build separate computers for each function. That saved money and also reduced the likelihood of computer breakdowns and errors. A much smaller crew would be needed, and the repair and maintenance burden would ease greatly. Says Yoder, "Our life-cycle costs are projected to go way down."

The specific idea for Amerf had come from Bobby Junker, head of ONR's Code 31, which was previously called the Information,

Electronics, and Surveillance department and was renamed the C4ISR department (command, control, communications, computers, intelligence, surveillance, and reconnaissance). "I came up with the concept of AMRF-C in 1996 right after the reorganization and I inherited the comms [communications], EW [electronic warfare], and radar programs," Junker relates. "Since all of these were RF waveforms, I asked the question why could we not do multiple functions from the same aperture at the same time."[4] Greatly enthused by the potential now in their hands, ONR investigators had teamed up with Naval Research Lab radar and electronics specialists and other experts and began studying how to best exploit and test these capabilities. By 1997 they had laid out an initial architecture. It wasn't a final design by any means, says Yoder, "but we knew it could be done." Their plan went through a review process and was finally approved in the spring of 1998.

The announcement at NRL that summer marked the real kickoff point for the Amerf project. Greg Tavik still remembers the stunned stillness as Paul Hughes described the idea. Besides the general technical difficulty and disruption the plan entailed, it marked a new type of project for NRL. As Tavik explains, "Typically, NRL gets involved at the beginning of things, trying to come up with some new, maybe crazy, idea." This time, rather than being the inventor, the lab's role was to act as the systems integrator.

An aura of resentment over the project's obviously huge price tag also hovered over the lab. "It's a zero-sum gain," says Tavik. "If ONR decides to spend a lot of money on this one thing, they're not spending it on other things. All the people not working on this job are pissed off because—as they see it—you just took away their money." That resentment lingered well beyond that initial meeting.

The skepticism and somewhat hard feelings surrounding AMRF-C would be with the project a long time. Still, as Tavik and his colleagues dived in, they quickly found a lot to be excited about. The goal of the first phase was simply to devise an architecture or design framework for building the system. The second phase, which would begin in 2000 and run for at least three years, called for the construction of a prototype based on the phase 1 design. The prototype would then be tested under simulated battle conditions at NRL's Chesapeake Bay detachment, a 168-acre site near Chesapeake Beach, Maryland, where the Navy conducted studies in such areas as communications, radar, and electronic warfare.

To save time and money ONR handed the NRL group some predetermined parameters with which to work. These included a mandate to employ active, rather than passive, arrays. Basically, this meant a giant aperture onto which a multitude of electronic elements fitted. By activating different groups of these elements, engineers could in effect form a series of small antennas out of one giant one. Says Tavik, "The thought was that an active array was the most flexible kind of antenna you could get, and flexibility is the name of the game if you want to do a whole bunch of different things."

In addition, as a result of the early studies with NRL radar experts, planners had decided to build separate transmit and receive arrays rather than combine them into a single antenna as most individual radar and communications systems employed. Because you would be transmitting and receiving simultaneously, and because so many of the frequency bands the Navy planned to use overlapped, separating the antennas would dramatically cut down on interference. "Otherwise," notes Tavik, "you'll just jam yourself."

Perhaps the most radical—and ultimately challenging—aspect of the plan was to incorporate elements of related technologies that the Navy was already developing. This was also the brainchild of Bobby Junker. "He didn't want to start from scratch," says Tavik. In particular, the Office of Naval Research and other agencies were already funding advanced solid state technology related to multifunctional active array systems specifically for radar and electronic warfare. The electronic warfare work, overseen by Lockheed Martin, related to the Navy's advanced integrated electronic warfare (AIEWS) program. The fate of this system would have an especially important role to play in the Amerf story.

All of these moves conspired to get things off to a faster-than-might-be-expected start for NRL. Still, the pressure to meet the phase 1 goals kicked off a series of meetings to refine the concept. These were not always pleasant. Relates Tavik,

The thing I remember most was going to these meetings, with EW [electronic warfare], comm. [communications], and radar people there, about fifteen of us in a small room. We would come across some particular topic and somebody just wouldn't want to yield. Either I was yelling, or someone else was yelling, or we were all yelling at each other. We beat the hell out of each other—and at the top of our lungs, "You're an idiot! What are you *talking* about?"

It would go on all morning. Then—and this is the best part—we'd go get coffee together, come back, and do it all over again. There were never any hard feelings; it was all just professional beating-the-pants-off-each-other. Then I'd walk back with Steve Lessin and think, "Why am I working this job? What have I gotten myself into?" It went on like that for over a year.

Tavik believes the naysayers and doubters performed an important function by questioning assumptions and helping to ensure the design stayed on the right track. "They're not all just believers in the idea who are going to go blindly down the path you set them on. They're going to make sure this is going to perform the function you're interested in," he relates. "This [AMRF-C] was designed by committee, which is a miserable exercise. Probably, in the end, it was the best way to do it, but it was a very painful process."

In 2000 Paul Hughes moved up the NRL chain of command and Tavik took the reins as Amerf's technical director. NRL engineers and scientists had long-standing expertise in a wide array of electronics, and work from a few ongoing programs could be tapped to help implement the AMRF-C project. The lab's bigger role, though, was to provide what the new boss refers to as "the glue" needed to bind other existing technologies and components together to create the entire system. In the case of Amerf, this was a software challenge as much as a hardware challenge. That's because the envisioned multifunctional system would have to shift the jobs it was performing from millisecond to millisecond, sometimes handling several tasks simultaneously. Says Tavik, "We had to keep it as generic as possible so at the end of the day we had a system that wasn't a radar system, or a comm system, or an EW system—it was an all-purpose . . . machine."

In that sense, he notes, Amerf was like a personal computer, another all-purpose machine that relies on software for its basic operating system as well as for performing different tasks such as word processing, crunching numbers, surfing the Internet, or playing a game. So for starters, what AMRF-C needed was the equivalent of a personal computer's operating system. "That's what we 'debated' for a year and more," Tavik says. Ultimately, a thirty-person programming team led by NRL's Jim Evins and assisted by Stephen Hagewood at the Naval Surface Warfare Center's Dahlgren division in Virginia, developed just such a system. "You could write a whole book just on the software effort alone," says Tavik. "It was almost like they were running a small software company."

As all this was unfolding, a major hiccup occurred. Initially NRL engineers were mainly investigating low-frequency band systems, concentrating on radar technology with EW and communications further down the priority list. To that end, ONR let several contracts in the low band arena. But in 1999 the Navy deemphasized the radar aspect of the system and decided to concentrate on the high-frequency band, mainly to accommodate more modern communications and EW capabilities. That forced Tavik's crew to change or cancel many of the contracts it had already let.

Still, by early 2002 the Amerf project was in full gear, with more than two hundred people involved in the effort. About half were Navy personnel, divided chiefly between NRL, Dahlgren, and the Naval Sea Systems Command (NavSea) Carderock division, which among other things worked on radar-absorbing coatings for the antennas. The rest belonged to a small army of private contractors led by Raytheon, Lockheed Martin, and Northrop Grumman. All the work was broken into about ten subsystems. Lockheed Martin was responsible for the "front end." This chiefly included the receiving array that would detect and amplify any incoming signals as well as the converter that would transform this analog energy to digital form for signal processing. Raytheon's main role was to build the system to process the signal—

radar, communications, or electronic warfare—and display it for the operators. The Massachusetts-based giant also took charge of the wave-form generator that forms an outgoing signal for transmission. Finally, Northrop Grumman handled the "back end," or transmitting array, including the technology for converting the digitally generated signal back to analog form for transmission. Other groups worked on a variety of components and subsystems.

All the phase 2 designing, programming, and prototype building was nearly complete by the end of 2003. Tavik built a test-bed at the Chesapeake Bay detachment in Maryland, where the various elements of the trial system were installed in the week between Christmas 2003 and New Year's Day 2004. His team then spent almost all of the next year integrating these components and putting the system through its paces, with the first semiofficial trials beginning that May. Testing continued throughout the summer and into the fall as engineers progressively upped the ante on what they asked Amerf to do. At first they tested single functions, then they began layering other tasks on top—radar, electronic warfare, satellite communications, video links. At various points they tested the prototype against simulated missiles. At other times a P-3 Orion early warning radar plane flew against the system.

It all built to a grand finale in concert with Amerf's annual review in early November. The review was usually held at NRL in Washington and typically drew more than one hundred people from the Navy and associated industry players. This time, though, Tavik wanted to hold it at Chesapeake Bay so attendees could see Amerf's first iteration in action. He calls the event "the test-bed's last big bang." As he viewed it, "we've got to have one final one where we tell everybody, 'Here, we've done it, and here's what we've done.'"

Facilities at Chesapeake Beach were much more limited than at NRL, so he spread the event over two days, planning to handle roughly fifty people each day. They started each morning with briefings. A videographer had captured highlights from throughout the year and had woven them into a ten-minute video that was also displayed for the guests. Some real-life demos rounded out the program.

The hub of the live action was nearby Tilghman Island, which served as a base for launching simulated war scenarios and analyzing Amerf's performance. The goal was to demonstrate that Amerf could rapidly shift from one task to another as the situation demanded, and, most importantly, handle several jobs simultaneously. The P-3 was not available that day, but with simulators standing in for enemy aircraft, ground facilities, and ships, the crew methodically demonstrated the system's ability to handle radar detection, satellite communications, line-of-sight communications, radar jamming, and electronic surveillance.

The prototype system was set up atop a cliff overlooking the bay. The simulated attacks came from out over the Atlantic Ocean to the east. Max Yoder was one of those on hand. He had retired from ONR in early 2002 but returned as a consultant for the next five years. Also present were representatives from the major contractors involved: Lockheed, Raytheon, Northrop Grumman, Boeing, ITT, General Dynamics, and others. They were joined by a cadre of admirals from the Pentagon, including the program executive officer (the person handling and overseeing the budget), Rear Adm. Dennis Dwyer.

The trial went fantastically well. Yoder calls it a watershed. Says he, "We demonstrated that we could pull down satellite communications and terrestrial communications, keep track of targets in the area by radar, and jam and deceive other radar and missile threats, all simultaneously."

Not every question had been answered, however. A few months earlier Chief of Naval Research Jay Cohen had decided to call for an independent review of every ongoing FNC program. That included the AMRF-C effort, which still had its fair share of naysayers and doubters.

———————●———————

Enter Betsy DeLong. A civilian engineer, DeLong's involvement with the program had begun the previous June. At the time, she was director of Surftech, an advisory body that represented the surface warfare community in helping the Navy determine its science and technology priorities. It then worked with ONR to pursue those priorities and tried to accelerate their transition to the Fleet.

One day her boss asked her to attend a meeting with Steve Lubard, the new ONR technical director.[5] It proved a fateful request because one of the main items to be discussed that day was Amerf's status. She was completely caught off guard, she says, when Lubard turned to her and asked her to organize an independent review panel of Amerf.

DeLong recalls her shock. "I didn't even work at ONR!" she exclaims.[6] But in fact she was ideal for the job. From her advisory role, DeLong knew what was most important to the surface warfare community, and what needs most desperately needed filling: she had even had some exposure to Amerf, which was just the insight Cohen wanted. His aim was to make sure that resources were poured into the programs that best met and advanced the Navy's vision for the future. In the case of Amerf, perhaps the largest and most costly FNC program, DeLong's job was to serve as an impartial arbiter in that process.

One of the big questions was whether Amerf should continue as a FNC program at all, given its game-changing nature and the still-formidable technical challenges ahead. FNCs, by contrast, were supposed to be mature, low-risk programs that filled an identified capability gap and were on the cusp of moving from the development and demonstration realm into the acquisitions arena as official programs of record. At the same time, the Navy was pushing development of its futuristic, multimission DD(X) destroyer. And many of the Amerf concepts, including solid-state aperture arrays that lowered powered demands and weight, and especially its capabilities in electronic warfare, seemed to fit better into that program.

DeLong held an initial review later that same month, pulling together an expert advisory board consisting of key stakeholders in the issue: acquisitions personnel, representatives from the Pentagon, and various experts in electronic warfare, radar, and other key fields. The panel convened again in early 2005, and things quickly got a little tense. As DeLong puts it, "There was a lot of contention about EW capability, which the DD(X) very much needed." Given the urgency to meet the DD(X) timetable, some of those present pushed hard for AMRF-C to drop the premise of handling multiple electronic functions such as communications and radar and instead focus only on electronic warfare for the DD(X).

Such a notion, of course, struck at the core of the multifunction concept. "They weren't recognizing the benefits," DeLong says of the electronic warfare–only advocates. Still, by airing feelings on the issue, the meeting did break some of the ice between the two camps. It didn't take long for some concrete steps to be taken as a result. The most important was to come to terms with the fact that despite its overall promise and the success of the recent trial, Amerf in its entirety was not yet ready for prime time and did not truly fit the definition of an FNC program. A third very high-level meeting was set for that July to determine its fate.

Chairing this meeting was John Young, Assistant Secretary of the Navy for research, development, and acquisition. Also present were Jay Cohen and Adm. Mark Edwards, director of surface warfare. They were joined by key representatives of all the major players involved in the issue. This session was "much more productive," asserts DeLong. Cohen opened the proceedings by briefing the group on the history of AMRF-C, further helping dispel tensions surrounding the multifunction concept. "There still wasn't what I would call a comfort level with trying to do EW and communications in a common aperture," says DeLong. But, she adds, "there was more of a comfort level with open architecture and multifunctionality."

By the end of the session, Cohen had made some key decisions. First he promised that ONR would make a big commitment to the pressing electronic warfare needs of DD(X) and to its timetable. Because of that, the portion of the Amerf program dealing with electronic warfare would remain as an FNC effort, where it would be poised to transition quickly to DD(X). At the same time, Cohen stressed, the overall concept of AMRF-C should also go forward. Only he proposed that it be moved into the Innovative Naval Prototypes (INP) category because that program was all about pursuing disruptive technologies.

Betsy DeLong was more than eight months pregnant at the time of the meeting, which she describes as "well beyond my pay grade." She would soon go on maternity leave. But in early 2006, not long after her return, DeLong was asked to take charge of a different sort of child than she had imagined. Its name was AMRF-C. Shortly afterward she left Surftech and joined the Office of Naval Research as the newly designated deputy director of the Amerf program.

Admiral Cohen's decision to split the AMRF-C program into two discrete chunks was largely a testament to the bureaucratic and administrative realities of the government–military system. On the one hand, it made a lot of sense. But to Betsy DeLong, Max Yoder, and others who thought the entire program should have been transitioned to the DD(X), the decision still came as a real disappointment. No other Navy had anything like AMRF-C, and its implementation would put the United States far ahead of its rivals, notes Yoder. "As far as I'm concerned, it's definitely the right approach." "But NavSea had never heard of things of this nature before, and getting them educated in time was not possible. They were risk shy."

A big problem, in Yoder's mind, is the way funds are authorized by Congress for specific purposes—radar, electronic warfare, communications, and so on. That works to compartmentalize technologies and predisposes the program officers responsible for each area to fight to protect their own turf. "So," he notes, "the system is not set up that makes it conducive to multifunctional technology. You're fighting bureaucracy from the very beginning, just because of the way funds are administrated."

DeLong echoes this view. She calls it "vision meets PPBE reality." PPBE is the Defense Department acronym for planning, programming, budgeting, and execution, outlining the entire process for prioritizing and funding a given project. Each group responsible for work on its turf is responsible for a very specific set of capabilities—and nothing else. Even if program managers wanted to cooperate, it would be difficult. Says DeLong, "[No] organization has extra dollars lying around to give bonus capability to the other. The difficulty in trying to move something like this forward is 'Who actually does the financial resourcing for it at the Pentagon?'"

Since 1995 ONR had worked with NavSea and other systems commands, as well as those in the Pentagon's program executive office, conducting informational seminars and other efforts to explain the multi-functional antenna concept. But until the test-bed demonstrations in the summer and fall of 2004, many remained highly skeptical of Amerf's potential. As Greg Tavik notes, "To put it bluntly, ONR's looking for a home for all this stuff. They're meeting with some resistance—actually quite a bit of resistance."

The prototype demos went a long way toward dispelling that resistance—but they didn't eliminate the doubters. "It took Chesapeake Bay to convince a few of the admirals," sums up Yoder. However, he notes, "there were still a few who weren't convinced and refused to come out and see the demo." All that skepticism seems to have been reflected in the July 2005 meeting to decide the program's fate.

Even then the decision to retain the EW portion of the program as an FNC effort might not have occurred had the DD(X) had another good choice. Lockheed Martin had been leading development of the next-generation ship's EW system, which was known as AIEWS. ONR had even borrowed or adopted aspects of that effort for the Amerf program. However, in light of mounting costs, the AIEWS project had been killed in 2004, leaving the DD(X) scrambling for EW capability. The new destroyer was being asked to handle so many more tasks than its predecessor ships that there simply wasn't enough room on the deck house for conventional single-function systems. Naturally, program managers turned to AMRF-C to bail them out. "It's the same size equipment, but that size for one function does five functions," says Max Yoder. "Which," he adds, "we'd been telling them about for five years."

It took months of negotiation to work this out. The Amerf backers were unhappy that more of their system was not tapped for the DD(X), which in April 2006 was redesignated the DDG 1000 *Zumwalt*-class destroyer. Worse, even the EW functions were scaled back dramatically. Explains Yoder, "We had hoped to get more of it implemented, but the budgets for the DDG 1000 were too tight to implement the whole works."

The Amerf prototype had demonstrated both sensing and attack forms of electronic warfare. These ranged from passive surveillance to antimissile jamming and other active electronic assaults. However, only its passive electronic surveillance module was initially allocated for the DDG 1000. This system doesn't emit signals of its own. Instead, it waits in listening mode, trying to pick up signals from anything that radiates energy—be it an enemy ship or sub, a missile, plane, drone, or something else. Once something is detected, the system tries to match the object's pulse rate or frequency to signal characteristics stored in its database. If all goes well, it will not only report on the object's direction but will also give controllers an early alert as to what is out there—something along the lines of, "I hear a signal coming from this angle. It appears to be a North Korean cruiser."

While this passive surveillance capability represented only one aspect of what Amerf engineers had been working on in electronic warfare, a great beauty of the AMRF system is that because all its functions are controlled with a single aperture, the capabilities are modular, more dependent on software development than anything else. The hope was to implement more EW function modules over time as budgets allowed. That was the spin, anyway.

For nearly two years following the July 2005 review, panel engineers pressed to refine the surveillance system, which was renamed multifunction electronic warfare, or MFEW. One of the big issues was that the Chesapeake Bay test had used brute force (architecturally speaking) to cobble together mostly commercial off-the-shelf technologies. That made it bulky and ultimately costly. To get it ready for insertion into the DDG 1000, says Yoder, "the push was to integrate a lot of it together so that it could be made smaller, lighter, and more efficient—and better able to serve its ultimate need."

Unlike the test-bed prototype, the idea was to create a far more refined advanced development model. On the test readiness scale used in many government programs, this was to be a 7, in contrast to the test bed's 6. Says Tavik, "Once you're at 7, you're pretty much ready to go into an acquisition program."

As things stood in early 2007, almost all the equipment had been built, with testing and integration under way. The software, too, had been significantly improved. Handoff to the acquisitions community was slated for that fall. "Things are going very well," says Tavik.

———————●———————

As the electronic warfare work for the DDG 1000 progressed, the rest of the AMRF-C program joined the queue for INP funding. DeLong took over from the previous ONR program manager, Keith Craples, who had been asked to take the reins of a different ONR project.

The vision was to expand the main Amerf framework to handle a much wider range of frequencies. Originally, the program had focused on the lower frequency ranges populated mainly by radar systems. The Navy switched gears in 1999, concentrating on higher frequencies for satellite communications and electronic warfare. Now, under the envisioned INP plan, the idea was cover them all.

Officially, the FNC funding for AMRF-C was transferred to MFEW. That left the rest of the program—the part bound for INP status—temporarily without funding of its own. The funding void didn't mean all work ceased. Each FNC program is grouped according to enabling capabilities—separately funded underlying technologies or functions needed to make the FNC successful. In the case of the AMRF-C program, work on enabling capabilities in areas such as electronics technology continued apace. This included size reductions and improvements in efficiency and function of components such as phase shifters, filters, modulators, signal generators, delay lines, and linear amplifiers that formed essential underpinnings of Amerf. Other efforts were ongoing in digital array radar and architecture studies designed to find ways to better integrate systems and bring costs down. A few more basic science and technology programs related to the project also were unaffected.

One of the biggest areas of progress came in amplifiers. An ONR-funded program demonstrated some of the world's first purely digital amplifiers that were able to provide much more signal power output without sacrificing efficiency. This advance was still far too early in its development stage to be used in the DDG 1000. However, the hope was that it would become part of the destroyer's systems down the road—and that it would also be incorporated into the upcoming INP program.

In the meantime, DeLong's job was to flesh out the vision, timeline, and budget for this proposed INP effort. The new proposal would then be taken to the science and technology corporate board, which would make the final decision about whether to officially designate the reborn AMRF-C program an INP. Over the course of the next eighteen months or so, DeLong consulted widely with industry and Navy officials to try and identify the best way to approach the new project. A lot of this work came together in November 2006, when ONR partnered with the National Defense Industrial Association to host an "industry day" workshop that brought together interested Navy and industrial parties to explore the concept.

By early 2007 significant progress could be seen. DeLong's proposal called for the reborn and expanded AMRF-C effort—still without a new name—to move into the INP program from fiscal year 2009 through 2014. Most important, a line item for the program had been incorporated into the rolling five-year budget plan, meaning it had the inside track to become reality. (Author's note: The program received initial funding in 2009 and was officially adopted for the fiscal year 2010. As of mid-2013, the first two prototypes were nearing completion and the program had been renamed InTop, for Integrated Topside.)

One focus of the plan was a companion ship to the DDG 1000, a new class of cruisers designated CG(X). The scope of the revamped Amerf program went well beyond the new cruiser, for which the design would be finalized and construction begun a few years before the INP effort ended. "When we finish in 2014, we will be looking at the thing after the CG(X)," says DeLong. However, a main idea in her proposal was to spiral off some core technologies into the cruiser in much the same way as the EW system spiraled off Amerf for the DD(X)—only with a lot more forethought and planning.

The first technology to be spiraled into the cruiser was a multifunction aperture for satellite communications. A typical modern warship carries twenty or more satellite antennas. Next to radar arrays, these are the largest antennas on a ship. So many are required because a ship needs to link with four or five different satellites—and it needs to ensure 360-degree communication with each of them. This means placing one dish or array for each satellite on each side of the deck house and above it. DeLong didn't yet know exactly what satcom capabilities the CG(X) was being designed to accommodate. However, she notes, "if you could reduce the number of apertures from like twenty-five, twenty-two, down to two, that would be a big savings." Her spiral plan didn't stop with the CG(X), either. The same technology could be used to retrofit satellite communications arrays for existing ships as well.

DeLong called the satellite communications technology "the next spiral out of the Amerf's legacy." She and the ONR hierarchy were ever mindful of the bureaucratic and budgetary issues that could gum up the works. However, in early 2007 they were already exploring the possibility of including the core multifunction aperture technology in the envisioned littoral combat ship, as well as conventional aircraft carriers.[7] "We are spinning on what I could call levels of capability," says Bobby Junker, head of Code 31, which oversaw all the Amerf work.[8]

And even that marked only a beginning. A multifunction array system that integrated electronic warfare, satellite communications, radar, and other capabilities into an energy-efficient, easily managed and maintained architecture fit nicely into the Navy's grand vision of an all-electric ship.[9]

The propulsion systems of current surface warships, submarines, and Marine combat vehicles are powered separately from weapons and auxiliary systems. This leaves the vast amount of power employed for propulsion unavailable for other uses. An all-electric ship would eliminate this inefficiency, freeing energy for sensing and communications and new types of high-energy devices and weapons such as the electromechanical aircraft launch system and the electromagnetic railgun. It would also dramatically improve energy efficiency, enhance the vessel's ability for quiet operations, improve design flexibility, and lower costs.

Junker had already formed a cross-departmental team to explore the best way to pull together AMRF-C and other Office of Naval Research programs to support the all-electric ship concept. Even without this last stage of Amerf's evolution, however, the idea had come a long way from that day in 1998 when Naval Research Lab scientists and engineers convened to hear of the plan. Says DeLong, "The difference . . . is 180 degrees. Folks who were very anti-AMRF-C are now some of its biggest supporters."

Greg Tavik, who was one of those original skeptics but became a leader of the program, put it on a more personal level. "It's hard to know" where it will go, he says. "It's like looking into a crystal ball. I'm pretty confident it has a future. What I hope is that someday someone will look back and say, 'Those guys stirred the pot and generated some new ideas. What they did back there really made an impact.'"

CHAPTER 10

Persistent Littoral Undersea Surveillance

O ff the South Korean coast, a torpedo-shaped craft glides quietly under the ocean. Periodically, it breaks the surface only to dive again. It's been cruising around the sea for months, dutifully accumulating data on currents, water salinity, and temperature at various depths as well taking other oceanographic measurements; this information is regularly transmitted to a shore-based command center when the vessel surfaces. The unmanned vessel also listens to the sounds of the sea. Early each morning, it captures the chug of fishing boats heading out to seek the day's haul. Its recorders also pick up the chirp of dolphins or the high-pitched chatter of whalesong. All the ambient sounds of the ocean continuously permeate its sensors so that they can be filtered and processed by state-of-the-art algorithms programmed into the craft's brain.[1]

One day, though, the routine is broken. An unusual signal is detected, almost lost in the usual whinnies, clanks, and hums. The craft transmits a short message to a fellow glider cruising nearby, one of perhaps another dozen that make up the "school" of undersea vehicles patrolling these waterways. Its mate has also picked up the strange sound, and relays a confirmation that it's on the job. The pair then begin tracking the noise, beaming reports back and forth, seeking to determine its nature. With a shift of a tail fin, they adjust course and glide closer to their quarry; others in the pack do too. As the signal gains strength, there is finally a match with one of the onboard algorithms. One glider blows its ballast and rises swiftly to the surface. Emerging through the waves, its back tips up, so that a tailfin antenna is pointing skyward. It then broadcasts the alert.

An Iridium satellite 485 miles above the Earth's surface picks up the craft's encrypted message. The space platform relays it to a land-based command center. The duty officer, trained in sonar detection, takes one look at the information and is instantly alert: she recognizes the acoustic signature of a diesel-electric submarine, the very kind possessed by the North Koreans. The information is passed up the command chain, and before long a U.S. Navy submarine and a few surface ships in the area are on the way to handle the threat. Whether it's watching North Korea in the Pacific, Iran in the Persian Gulf, or some other potential enemy of the United States in another part of the world, a sensor-rich intelligence system much like this one would give the United States and its allies a formidable edge. Developing such a network is the charge of ONR's Ocean Battlespace Sensing department (Code 32). The system is called PLUSNet, for persistent littoral undersea surveillance network. It was one of the charter INP programs launched in 2005 to bring a powerful new capability to the Navy. The word "littoral" refers to the shallow waters, typically between fifty and five hundred feet deep, within a few hundred miles of a coastline where it is thought most submarine warfare will be conducted now that the days of high seas Russian–American cat-and-mouse games seem over. So in this case, the game-changer is the ability to remotely monitor strategic coastal areas for months on end, without the expense or danger of human deployment, and without the enemy even knowing it is being watched.

The idea behind PLUS, as the project is commonly called, dates back to the early 1990s. At the time, PLUS program manager Thomas B. Curtin was heading ONR's ocean modeling and prediction program. He could see that the work the organization supported was leading to increasingly realistic-looking models of ocean structure. There just wasn't a good way to compare that with real-time observations to see how on target the models were. "The capability to get observations to both initialize these models and also to validate them was not keeping pace at all," Curtin says.[2]

But as Curtin examined the state of the art in computing, it was clear that smaller, more powerful chips, sensors, and other electronic components combined with the latest software might soon make it possible to build mobile sampling systems that would end that disparity. That led ONR to support a variety of projects that advanced the goal of creating real-world monitoring systems to check the accuracy and reliability of computer models. Perhaps the most notable was a late-1990s effort spearheaded by a group at MIT. Jointly backed by the Office of Naval Research and the sea grant program funded by the National Oceanographic and Atmospheric Administration, it was called the Autonomous Ocean Sensing Network. The core concept was very reminiscent of the ideas that would underscore PLUS almost a decade later. Researchers would deploy a series of autonomous mobile sensors to take a variety of ocean readings. The sensors would be ferried around on underwater vehicles called gliders. Several of these had already been developed with support from other agencies, including the National Oceanographic and Atmospheric Administration.

Curtin's twist on this basic approach was to extend the network beyond gathering data on such oceanographic variables as temperature, depth, and salinity to detecting submarines. That would require a different type of sensor—an acoustic sensor or underwater microphone. A variety of other leading-edge sensing, signal processing, computing, and underwater vehicle technologies would also have to be deployed. In essence, what Curtin envisioned was a novel amalgamation of the state of the art, applied to antisubmarine warfare. "A lot of the building block technologies were developed on a lot of these special programs over fifteen years," he says. Sometime in 2004 he took the idea to Frank L. Herr, head of Code 32, (at the time called Ocean, Atmosphere, and Space). Herr enthusiastically supported the idea and was able to cull funds from a variety of programs ONR supported to get it off the ground.[3]

Later that same year ONR issued a broad agency announcement, or BAA, soliciting white papers on how to create the network. Funding priority was given to concepts that could be demonstrated in fiscal year 2006–7. And when the INP program launched in 2005, Curtin's team was able to merge the best approaches into an application for that program. PLUS won approval as an inaugural INP the following year.

Curtin says that pulling all these long-unfolding ideas together into a large program allows the Navy to move more rapidly than it would by continuing to support work more piecemeal-style. It also means a bigger pot of money can be devoted to the problem. First-year funding (for fiscal year 2007) was around $12 million. But much of the $40 million managed by Curtin's group feeds into PLUS in one way or another, he says. So does work from several other ONR departments, although Curtin is quick to add that "more money doesn't always mean faster progress in research and development." PLUS is envisioned to run for six years, with a series of milestones that must be met along the way. Once the first milestone is passed, he says, the Navy can decide whether to fund the next stage.

The driving impetus behind the PLUS concept is the changing nature of warfare since the Cold War. That difference, which involves small regional conflicts and guerilla-type fighting rather than a global battle between superpowers, is easy to see in a place like Iraq. But, at least in the eyes of strategic planners, it will also likely extend under the sea. During the Cold War, the U.S. submarine force largely concerned itself with tracking and neutralizing Soviet nuclear submarines. To help with this job, the country laid a vast array of underwater listening devices, called the sound surveillance system (SOSUS), that was linked via cables to land terminals.[4] The data could in turn be passed on to U.S. submarines, surface vessels, and airplanes that could track and destroy the target if necessary.

Information about SOSUS released after the Cold War ended showed that the United States had been remarkably successful in locating its quarry. But that was largely because the nuclear subs were so noisy that their signals stood out in the ocean from miles away. Now the main threat is from super-quite diesel-electric submarines whose telltale signs are much harder to detect from a network like SOSUS amid the ambient noise from whales, ships, waves, earthquakes, and other sounds of the sea. "Most submarines are quiet enough so that if you're standing in the engine room, you're hard-pressed to hear the engine," says Herr.

Diesel-electric submarines are also far cheaper to construct than their nuclear counterparts, so they have become affordable for a number of nations. Curtin says the Navy anticipates that most of the submarine conflicts in the next twenty-five years or longer will not involve ballistic missiles fired from the high seas. Rather, he says, planners believe submarine warfare will take place in littoral waters, such as in the Persian Gulf or the Taiwan Strait, which were never covered by SOSUS. The SOSUS components still in existence in the twenty-first century are used for academic research.

Since the end of the Cold War, the Navy has made a concerted effort to develop techniques to cope with this perceived new threat. The basic approach is to employ sonar, radar, and other methods for detecting, tracking, and destroying enemy submarines from airplanes, surface ships, or the Navy's own subs. But this costly strategy limits the number of listening posts that can be deployed. Sensor work is also ongoing. However, if the Navy wants to deploy a sensor net in the ocean, it has to drop the sensing devices from a plane into the area of interest. These sonobuoys then drift around gathering data. But the Navy has to keep planes in the air above the target area to receive their communiqués.

Many efforts are under way to improve conventional antisubmarine warfare. For example, engineers are developing sonobuoys that can feed data to a satellite, rather than planes. ONR itself supports an FNC program that also seeks to improve conventional littoral antisubmarine warfare. However, says Herr, the program seeks shorter-term fixes based on what is capable today, not what might be capable tomorrow, as PLUS does. "We have to find ways to multiply our capabilities—what we call a force multiplier—to accommodate this whole issue," Herr says of the INP effort. "And what we're betting on is that we can develop autonomous sensors that move around in the ocean and provide [new] opportunities for sensing."[5]

That vision depends on deploying a fleet of small, relatively cheap underwater craft that act as packhorses for the sensors. These autonomous underwater vehicles (AUV) must be able to stay on the job for months on end, carrying out their tasks with minimal human input. "That's how the Navy works—a carrier task force goes out, stays there for months, comes home," Herr says. ONR is betting that autonomous platforms can work much the same way, but for a fraction of the cost.

Ultimately, Herr and Curtin envision a network big enough to patrol a forty-square-mile area, comparable to what an aircraft carrier covers. If such a system can be perfected, the Navy might then order multiple units so that it could deploy networks anywhere around the globe it saw the need.

Since modern diesel-electric submarines run so quietly, they can't be identified from as far away as old nuclear subs. That's one reason why sensor mobility is so important. The sensors need to get within about three miles of the source of a sound to get a good fix. The PLUS system is being designed to take advantage of the inherent properties of the ocean to improve the chances of detection. For instance, the speed of sound changes depending on water density, which in turn depends on such conditions as salinity and temperature. If the sea is of a uniform density, sound waves typically propagate straight outward from their source, so that it's easy to pinpoint location. But in the ocean, it's not uncommon to find water layers of different densities. When encountering a change in density sound waves often refract, Curtin explains. They can then bounce off the surface or seabed, scattering and losing energy—and making it far more difficult to locate the source of a signal.

One goal of the PLUS program is to use methods of characterizing the ocean environment so that researchers can figure out the best places to deploy the network. "The more you know about the environment, the more you can make intelligent decisions," Curtin says. "The whole question is where to put your assets and where to put them tomorrow, and not just today."

When not tracking targets, Herr envisions that the underwater sentries will pass the bulk of their time gathering data about the ocean around them, surfacing regularly to transmit their information to Iridium satellites. The sky stations will broadcast the raw data to a shore center or surface vessel that will feed the results into dynamic models of the sea. The models will then be crunched to better predict local ocean currents and acoustic properties, using the simulations to redeploy the underwater vehicles to the best spots to gather more data.

All the information accumulated in this way could then be fed back to further improve the models. "If I keep doing that over and over again, then I would have an optimal sampling that would allow the models to be predictive, and the data would help them to be more faithful," Herr says. Oceanographic science should also benefit immensely.

Placement of the sensors is critical. The ocean is too big for dense sampling, says Curtin, so the data must be strategically gathered. He says the problem is not unlike trying to predict weather on the Earth's surface. If you could take just one atmospheric reading for a given area, where would you place a balloon, say, to enable the best forecast? Not only that, but conditions in the ocean are constantly changing. "Where they'll do the most good right now may not be where they'll do the most good four hours from now, or ten hours from now," Herr adds. Here again the feedback loop of the sensors-to-models-to-sensors, and so on, becomes even more important. The idea is for the underwater vehicles to periodically check in at the surface, where they can receive any new instructions about where to position themselves via satellite. "The model is what helps us walk the sensors from one place to the other," says Herr.

The most challenging aspect of PLUS will be developing the signal processing needed to pluck out the signal of a super-quiet diesel submarine from the ambient sounds of the ocean. Both Herr and Curtin call signal processing "the long pole in the tent," meaning it is the critical component that supports the entire concept. Humans constantly perform such signal processing; when people are at a party, with many conversations taking place simultaneously, they're able to easily zone in on the voices of the one or two people in their circle. But perfecting a reliable way for sensors in the ocean to do this autonomously is another matter altogether, especially when the "voice" they're listening for is a barely audible diesel-electric sub.

Leaving the sensors in place for months on end—the "persistence" of the project's title—should help tremendously. When a person enters a forest, Herr relates, at first he or she will only pick out a few sounds. But if they sit still for a few minutes, a variety of new sounds will emerge—birds chirping, a squirrel in the trees, a small animal scurrying through the brush. "When you do that, your mind is doing signal processing to focus the aperture of your ears on a particular kind of signature," he says. "And you recognize it as leaves rustling. It could be a mouse or a rabbit. You didn't see anything, but you heard the effect of it, and you're making a guess on what it might be based on your general, broader knowledge."

So, too, it might be with the PLUS sensors, as they seek to identify the characteristic acoustic signature of an enemy submarine. In signal processing, the key is to construct a library, or database, of specific sound signatures that can be easily searched for a match. Humans accumulate sound libraries throughout their lifetimes, "hearing these signatures, categorizing them, tucking them away, calling them out, realizing that it's something similar we heard before but not exactly," as Herr puts it. The challenge is to automate such filtering and discretionary signal processing and build it into the tiny microprocessor brain of an underwater vehicle. "If you have a sonar operator on a sub, he has 10 to 15 years of experience doing that," says Henrik Schmidt of MIT, one of PLUS's principal investigators. "Here, we have to have a machine doing that."[6]

This ranks as a monumental task. Continuing the forest analogy, it might be equivalent to identifying what caused the rustling of leaves. A gentle, scurrying sound might be caused by a rabbit or chipmunk. A series of loud crunches is probably a person on the move. A stream of slow, steady crunching might mean a hiker, but if the crunches come in rapid succession, the person is likely running. The AUVs have to be programmed to not just track but to classify targets.

If it detects something interesting, especially if the signal is moving, a vessel might determine that it should communicate with other vehicles in its pack to accumulate more information about the sound. The school of AUVs could pinpoint and track the target or even converge on it. The vessels would not carry weapons, but one could be deployed to the surface to feed information on speed and bearing to humans or other automated platforms that do carry weapons.

It's not exactly clear how many AUVs will be required to cover a roughly forty-square-mile area. Herr guesses it will likely take dozens but not as many as a hundred. And researchers must build them so that the hunters do not become targets themselves. "We'd expect these sensors to be quite quiet and near signature-free," Herr relates. They must be small enough, for instance, that an enemy sub would not notice them or figure they were fish. Even if they are identified as sensors, the craft must be numerous enough and cost so little that no enemy could afford to do anything about them. "Our goal is to build sensors that are cheap enough so no target submarine would try to engage them. You don't send a $3 million torpedo against a sensor that may cost a tenth of that," Herr says.

"That's where the real game-changing element is, why this fits the mold of an Innovative Naval Prototype," Herr continues. "This inverts the asymmetry that we find with diesel-electric submarines. They are a very capable but less expensive platform than some of our large surface ships—an aircraft carrier, for example. So for a submarine to shoot a torpedo and sink a big aircraft carrier is a huge victory for a submarine. And all the more reason because the aircraft carrier costs maybe five or ten times the cost of a diesel-electric submarine. But if we can build sensors that cost a tenth or a hundredth or a ten-thousandth the amount of a submarine, then we've inverted this asymmetry."

Another game-changing element lies in the ability to operate clandestinely over long periods of time, in the process adapting to the environment and any targets encountered. That could dramatically alter the psychology behind how the Navy operates, in Herr's view. The ONR department head holds up Operation Desert Storm in the early 1990s as an example. The United States steadily built up some 500,000 troops in Kuwait, spurring much speculation in the press about when a full-out assault would commence. The troops grew anxious; to them, waiting can sometimes be worse than actually going into battle. At some point, it became virtually impossible for there *not* to be a war. This happens in all big systems, Herr says, where decision makers walk up to the edge of an issue and lean over, and then have to determine whether to take the plunge or not.

"It's a big problem, because the decision maker has to realize that it has come to the end of the line," says Herr. In the case of war, he notes, "All of the diplomatic elements have to be wrung out by the time the military forces get to the point where they're leaning over. History shows that militaries that get up to that point, they almost always go because they can't go back. They've already done all this. It takes them so long to get up there that the psychological force is just to go."

A lot of that same psychology applies to antisubmarine warfare, Herr says. Planners will be reluctant to deploy a lot of subhunting hardware into the ocean that's only good for a few weeks unless they are pretty certain they can use it. "All of your psychology is associated with putting them out there quick, getting the information quick, and getting on with whatever you're going to do," Herr says.

With PLUS, however, the system will be out for six months or longer. It doesn't have to be deployed in the conventional sense, so the psychological-strategic issues associated with finely timing the deployment don't exist. If nothing occurs for weeks or months, that's fine. At

PLUS: One of the key pursuits of Code 32, Ocean Battlespace Sensing, is persistent littoral undersea surveillance. Here an autonomous underwater vehicle is lowered off San Clemente Island in the Pacific Ocean.

John F. Williams/ONR

the same time, there's the added advantage that such an autonomous network won't involve the human fatigue that comes with conventional subhunting: fatigue is the biggest problem with having human operators monitoring sonar screens or checking for mines. Finally, having a persistent system in place also makes logistics easier in the event of a military action. "If I can have a persistent sensor that's mobile, that can go out on its own and come back on its own and do all that autonomously," Herr says, "then I don't have to have somebody carry it. And therefore, I don't have to get into the priority line of whether my sensor is more important than your bullets or your food or your water."

All this combines to change not only the psychology of a single military action but also to potentially change the culture of how the Navy approaches its overall job, Herr posits. "The Navy always feels it has too few forces to do the job it needs to do, and in large part that may be true," he says. "All navies feel that way because the ocean is out there and it's very big and everyone is congregated on these few platforms. And that leads to a kind of approach that is different than the approach that air forces typically take or armies take." For example, Herr explains, the Army feels that it can import huge amounts of supplies and weaponry to whatever theater it is operating in, and that it can sustain them for a long time. "But the Navy has always had a philosophy that it sweeps in, does something, sweeps out," he continues. "It sends those planes in to make a strike from the aircraft carrier, does the work, gets back to the aircraft carrier. Goes in again if it wants to, comes back again."

The result is that even though the U.S. Navy has served in various locations around the world for many years, it has rarely built up an infrastructure. "Sometimes, we don't know as much about those areas as we might think we ought to know based on how long we've been there, because the philosophy has been not to pay any attention to the area as a place where we're going to be for a very long time," Herr says. "So what we're suggesting is that we might build kind of an ocean infrastructure that will allow us to understand these things." PLUS would be that infrastructure, or at least the start of it.

Of course, PLUS also holds the potential to alter enemy psychology, which Curtin points out is a key value of unmanned surveillance. Even if the U.S. can only deploy a limited number of sensors, he explains, it can change enemy thinking by creating the appearance of a large network. Says Curtin, "If you can create a perception that there's a barrier here, then you'll probably change the behavior. If you change the behavior, you're already starting to win the game."

A cadre of universities and private labs has been pursuing the research to make PLUS real. Leading the way are two core teams who act as principal investigators. One is headed by William A. Kuperman, an oceanography professor at Scripps Institution of Oceanography in California. The other is directed by MIT's Schmidt, a professor of mechanical and ocean engineering and director of the laboratory for autonomous marine sensing systems. Both these groups conduct their own work, plus subcontract out related work to third parties, including other universities, private labs, and industry. The third leg of the core group is led by Mitch Shipley, a former Navy officer and a research associate at Penn State's Applied Research Laboratory. He acts as the day-to-day program coordinator, handling administration of the various contracts and helping coordinate the research teams. The Penn State group also works on integrating data from the sensor web that will make up PLUS. All these groups report to Curtin.

Kuperman says the Scripps Marine Physical Laboratory, where he works, has a long relationship with the Navy. So do other applied research labs at Penn State, the University of Washington, and the University of Texas. Perhaps a year before ONR issued the PLUSNet broad agency announcement in 2004, the four institutions had decided to form a consortium around the concept of distributed networking in a marine setting. "The four of us got together and proposed the cooperative program among just the four of us, originally," Kuperman says. "I think simultaneously ONR was thinking along the lines of what we proposed and decided to make the program broader. So they put out a BAA on it."[7] As a result, the consortium was one of the first to respond to the ONR call for white papers.

Almost in concert, though, came a proposal from the MIT group. It was collaborating with the Woods Hole Oceanographic Institution on Cape Cod, San Diego-based technical services firm SAIC, and an MIT spinoff, Bluefin Robotics, of Cambridge, Massachusetts. Curtin recognized that the two groups' submissions complemented each other extremely well, so he suggested they work together to put forth a joint proposal. When an ONR program manager makes a suggestion like that, people listen. "So basically Henrik Schmidt at MIT and myself sat down and worked out the details of how we would coordinate these things," Kuperman says.

The pair put the final touches on their joint proposal while cruising in the Mediterranean Sea off the coast of Italy. They were conducting an experiment for an unrelated ONR program, and the deadline was fast approaching, so they seized the opportunity. "We're old friends," Kuperman says. "We wrote a book together, so it wasn't a forced marriage or anything like that."

A contract was awarded in 2005. Kuperman's group at Scripps, now working primarily with Harvard University, is focusing on improved oceanographic modeling. The MIT contingent, meanwhile, is chiefly responsible for the autonomous underwater vehicle side of the project. It is concentrating specifically on developing the cooperative behavior between vehicles, the various sensor technologies, and the onboard processing. Besides its administrative duties, Penn State, teamed mainly with the applied research labs at the universities of Washington and Texas, oversees work on the centralized command and control systems that will integrate the data from all the various inputs. Almost every institution is working on some aspect of signal processing.

In a sense the underwater vehicle work overseen at MIT is the most mature. That's because oceanographic researchers have been using AUVs for decades for a variety of scientific purposes. Several kinds of existing vessels are being adapted and studied for possible use in PLUS, Schmidt says. One type is propeller-driven, so it is able to tow sensing arrays—long strands of wires carrying hydrophones. Submarines also haul such arrays, although because of their much smaller size AUVs pull shorter nets, typically some sixty-five feet in length. The MIT team is working with a group that's developing other types of sensors, called vector sensors, which are specially geared to charting the directionality of sounds. That work, which was field-tested in 2006, is not funded under the PLUS project. However, it is part of related work also being supported by ONR. "One of the things Tom Curtin has done is he's been cherry-picking what he thinks are the emerging technologies that he would like to combine upfront in this moving distributed system concept," Kuperman explains.

One of the most interesting AUV types being studied is hanging above a sofa next to the reception desk in ONR's Ocean Battlespace Sensing department. It's a three-and-a-half-foot-long torpedo-shaped Slocum Glider made by the Webb Research Corporation in Cape Cod, Massachusetts. Painted bright yellow, the glider boasts two narrow wings and a tail fin that houses an antenna. The battery-powered AUV contains no propeller; instead, it moves primarily by adjusting its buoyancy. Hidden in its bowels is a pump that draws in seawater to add weight to the nose, causing the craft to tip forward and dive. Its wings allow the vehicle to "sail" forward as it journeys downward. When the AUV needs to rise again, seawater is pumped out, tipping the nose back up and making the craft more buoyant. The glider travels up and down in a sawtooth or switchback pattern, each turn bringing it closer to its destination. To maximize battery life, it only uses power to operate its pump and to transmit data to a communications satellite. The Slocum Glider excels in shallow water, from about 13 feet to 650 feet in depth.

Researchers at the University of Washington's Applied Physics Laboratory have built another type of glider called the Seaglider, which is designed to trace out a steeper sawtooth pattern that enables the craft to dive far deeper than the Slocum Glider. The Seaglider is a bit bigger than its counterpart, about four-and-half feet in length. It adjusts buoyancy by pumping a light oil back and forth between a pressurized container and a special bladder. To dive, the vehicle moves the oil into the container, rendering the craft denser than water. If the Seaglider is cruising deep under the sea, it pumps the oil into the bladder, which expands and takes up more volume. The AUV then becomes less dense and rises toward the surface. To control pitch and roll, the battery pack inside the craft can shift to alter the vessel's center of gravity. The Slocum Glider used in the PLUS project currently lasts only for about a month. The Seaglider, by contrast, stands as the persistence champion, able to operate in the ocean for up to six months at a time.

When either type of glider breaks the surface, it tips its tail up to point the antenna skyward. The Seaglider's aerial runs three-and-a-half feet, spanning most of the vessel's length. Both craft are outfitted with modems that enable them to transmit and receive data from an Iridium satellite. By using the global positioning system and a computer program, the gliders can orient themselves for their next assignment and determine whether they need to adjust their compass headings. The gliders employ compact flash memory to store computer programs and any data they gather.

Both the Seaglider and the Slocum Glider were originally developed for oceanographic purposes. Indeed, scientific groups around the world routinely use them to accumulate oceanographic data. A sensor pack mounted on the vehicles' exteriors allows them to measure temperature, pressure, and conductivity, although the gliders aren't able to carry as much equipment as a propelled AUV. According to Schmidt, ONR has also funded work with gliders, mainly to map out seabeds in shallow water in order to locate mines. "The work of the last ten years has been completely focused on mine countermeasures," he says. "We're still doing that."

PLUS extends that countermine work to antisubmarine warfare. To locate mines, researchers typically use active acoustics. That is, they send out sound waves and measure what is reflected back—the same as sonar. This basic acoustic technology can also be applied to finding subs, except that the detectors need to operate quietly and remain in listening mode so as not to alert the enemy it is being hunted. In a sense, says Schmidt, PLUS is bringing back antisubmarine warfare, which has been on the wane since the breakup of the Soviet Union. "Since the end of the Cold War, it's basically been forgotten," he says. "It's interesting, because there's a whole generation of antisubmarine warfare people that have been lost in this because they had to go into other areas. There was a lot that was lost in that period."

Between the fall of 2004 and the following spring, investigators at the University of Washington Applied Physics Lab tested a Seaglider in the Labrador Sea. The craft performed a record 663 dives, dutifully taking measurements of salinity and temperature and transmitting its data back to the lab via satellite hookup.

A key goal of the tests was to check how well the vehicles could hold up to persistent use. "The engineering associated with allowing these things to go for a very long time is a real research issue," says ONR's Herr. Battery life is limited. Organisms can attach to the outside of vehicles, disrupting their hydrodynamics. Electrical and mechanical components are vulnerable to failure, even though the craft has few moving parts. All these issues must be resolved if the systems can be expected to spend months at sea.

This is not unlike the challenges faced by space scientists deploying rovers on Mars, Herr notes. Data transmission periods are limited, and controllers have no way to make hands-on repairs. One big difference is that the underwater vehicles are designed to operate autonomously, whereas Mars rovers generally are remote-controlled. But that doesn't make things easier.

Another obstacle not faced by the rovers is weather—in this case ocean currents. The gliders move slowly, going about their paces at a speed of roughly half a knot (half a nautical mile per hour). Tests in the Labrador Sea and elsewhere showed that the craft usually get to where they are directed but that the travel time can be considerable. Not only do the vessels lack a propulsion system, they are so small and weakly powered that they tend to drift with currents. That led ONR to fund development of a new type of beefed-up glider, called the Liberdade XRay. "What we set out to do is to see whether we can build something that's more like a hawk or an eagle than a tiny little sparrow that's all puffed up," says Herr.

The craft is being jointly developed by the Scripps Marine Physical Laboratory and Washington's Applied Physics Lab, with input from various other PLUS partners. The XRay gliders are shaped like huge wings, twenty feet long, that enable them to travel at speeds up to five knots. Their glide slope is 7:1, which means that the craft moves some

twenty-one feet horizontally for every three feet or so it travels vertically, greatly enhancing its ability to cover more sub hunting ground.

All of the flavors of AUVs will likely have their place in a PLUS web,
Curtin says. "They're all good for different things. There's not one that
solves every problem. That's part of the challenge—to get the right mix."

PLUS managers are also banking on advances in the other main
aspect of the project—the oceanographic modeling being pursued
chiefly at Scripps and Harvard University. "Gliders, even though they
are capable of half a knot or five knots, they're not persistent if they're
running around a lot," observes Herr. "That's because there's no real
free lunch here. The amount of energy it takes to move something in
the ocean is based on the drag, the body of this platform. . . . [So] what
we've been dining out on is the possibility of knowing the ocean well
enough so that you can take advantage of the currents in the ocean to
move the systems around appropriately." Better oceanographic models
should help with that a lot, he says. By riding the ocean currents instead
of fighting them or being carried off by them in the wrong direction, the
gliders can increase their speeds significantly without too much penalty
in energy use.

Whether the PLUS researchers can also equip these autonomous
systems with truly adaptive behavior—the ability to track, follow, and
coordinate actions based on what is detected—is another big unknown.
"That's what makes this whole business so risky and so uncertain,"
admits Herr. "Up until this point, the elements of doing this [have been]
from an oceanographic point of view. . . . That's pretty well in hand.
The riskiness is all about being able to translate that into a naval mission
against a non-cooperative target."

As of early 2007 the PLUS program was scheduled to unfold in
three main phases. Phase 1 was ongoing. Its goal: to demonstrate detection of a submarine and develop adaptive feedback mechanisms from
data gathered in the ocean. Another AUV field test had taken place the
previous August in Monterey Bay. Schmidt called it a "plumbing test"
to work out some engineering issues. A land-based control center was
established in Monterey to communicate via a radio link to moorings
set up in the ocean. The moorings, in turn, were outfitted with modems

that communicated acoustically with the underwater vehicles. For the test, the team employed both gliders and propelled vehicles towing sensor arrays, as well as some fixed arrays, although they're not part of the PLUS concept. The goal of the field test was not to simulate each phase of the envisioned network, but to look at overall connectivity. "It's always interesting to get out there, because one of the things that happens when you go to sea with all this new technology, there's always something breaking," Schmidt says. "So there's a lot of on the job training."

A more sophisticated field test was scheduled to take place off the southern California coast in the fall of 2007. This time a surrogate target vehicle would simulate the sounds of a submarine. Planners expected to employ a trio of propeller-powered underwater vehicles towing sensor arrays, as well as a few gliders. The hope was that this network would detect the quarry autonomously—a challenge Scripps' Kuperman calls "picking wiggles out of other wiggles"—and relay the information to a control station. At that point, some two years into the official project, the first phase should be completed. Herr says that the decision to press on to phase 2 will largely depend on how well that test goes. With only a partial success, he notes, it's possible that the Navy will still decide to fund it, but at a reduced level.

Presuming the researchers can show the ability to reliably detect a submarine, the second phase will address how to optimally detect targets. That will entail developing improved sensors that can pick up and amplify extremely quiet sounds. A leading idea is to employ arrays of multiple hydrophones aligned to sense preferentially in one direction over another, filtering out noise from other vectors. This could involve placing the hydrophones on a group of AUVs traveling in formation, not unlike a small school of fish. Already researchers report partial success controlling three gliders in a cluster, ordering them to rotate en masse, or fly closer together or farther apart. "We don't know how to control more than three of these autonomous systems together," relates Herr. "We've deployed more than three together, but the best we've done in a controlling manner is [when] we have three." However, he adds, "We're going to get better at that."

MIT is working to enhance acoustic communications between AUVs. The early data transfer rate between the vehicles was a mere thirty characters per second, barely eclipsing early telephone modems, says Schmidt. That enables the vessels to send out a short message to one or two of their fellows roughly every ten seconds while submerged. "There's absolutely no doubt we'll be able to increase [the data transfer rate] somewhat," Schmidt asserts. "But it's a very different concept of operations because we have to put much more intelligence out there."

A few years further down the road, if things get that far, phase 3 will entail linking multiple vehicle clusters so that they move in coordinated fashion. "It could be that we succeed in all . . . of these phases and get to the last stage and find that we don't know how to control a large number of these systems with the many, many degrees of freedom that they have in order to do the distributed sensing, adaptation, localization search, convergence. I don't know," Herr says. "This is why we've developed this in stages so we can do one step, another step, and another step. And yet it could be that the biggest challenge is this idea of autonomously trying to build the behaviors of the large system."

Another unknown lies in the amount of peoplepower needed to manage these "autonomous" networks. The hope is that it will take just a small team, but that might not be the case. Consider an aircraft carrier. Herr points out it takes a crew of some three hundred to manage such a ship. What does it take to care for a team of fifty autonomous vehicles? Data from multiple AUV clusters will come back every few hours for analysis. It could be that the Navy would need more people than the number of vehicles it deploys to stay up with all that.

An avid cyclist, Herr compares the challenge to the invention of the airplane. "It's not by chance that the Wright brothers were bicyclists," he asserts. One of their rivals, aviation pioneer Samuel Langley, sought to build an inherently stable system that wouldn't roll once aloft. The Wright brothers believed from their cycling experience that an inherently stable system wasn't necessary—that the operator could keep it stable by flying it interactively. Perhaps "flying" the AUV clusters will also require such hands-on control, he notes. Automated software programs could help, but developing these applications would require detailed modeling of the underwater vehicle networks. That research has not been done.

In these times of super-quiet diesel submarines, asymmetric warfare, and suicide attacks, the ability to deploy reliable autonomous sensor networks that could persist in the ocean for months on end could provide the United States with a "mobile infrastructure" in places where none exists today. Ideally such a network would precisely track any enemy submarine or attack vehicle in real time. But even if it falls somewhat short of this goal, the mere existence of a web of AUVs might be enough to alter enemy psychology and deter such an attack because the risks of detection are so great. That, too, could be a game-changing advantage.

CHAPTER 11

T-Craft

A U.S. attack is imminent. Marines will soon be hitting the beaches. From a planning point of view, five words are paramount to a successful mission: close, assemble, deploy, sustain, reconstitute.

These core areas together describe the essential challenges of the principle of sea basing: moving forces and equipment to the right spot at sea; organizing and deploying them ashore; providing ample supplies of food, fuel, and ammunition; and then getting the force back safely. In the future, sea basing will form a critical part of many, if not most, Marine missions. And as with much else in the post–Cold War era of hyperefficiency, one of the leading issues facing the Navy and Marines Corps today is how to do it faster, safer, and more cost effectively. At the Office of Naval Research, raising the bar for sea basing is the prime focus of an INP program run by Code 33, Sea Warfare and Weapons.

At the heart of this effort is a potentially revolutionary transport and landing vehicle called T-Craft, short for the transformable craft. The questions the T-Craft effort addresses push the envelope for a Marine assault. Can a landing craft travel on its own up to 2,500 nautical miles to its destination point without refueling, covering at least 500 of those miles at super-high speeds of forty knots? Can the same vessel maintain its integrity amidst the turbulence of Sea State 4, with its seven-foot waves and winds at twenty knots? Can the craft also take on an unprecedented payload of four M1A1 Abrams tanks and associated personnel—and then once it's loaded be able to traverse everything from sand bars to mud flats and "get boots dry on the beach?"

These are the goals of T-Craft. In short, the idea is to take the best the Navy has to offer in terms of speed, fuel efficiency, seakeeping, and amphibious abilities and combine them into one landing vessel. To pull it off will require pushing the state of the art in areas such as aluminum hulls, composite materials, and propulsion systems. But the payoffs could transform the speed and power of an assault, which is why the effort falls into the INP's game-changing category.

"When we went from sails to steam, that was game-changing," says Kelly Cooper, the ONR program manager leading the T-Craft effort. "And when we were able to launch aircraft from a ship, like the aircraft carriers, that was game-changing. Submerging ships that could surface, that was a game-changer. Screw propulsion." T-Craft falls into this same category, she says, because it represents far more than a landing vehicle. "It's not only a piece of equipment that would allow you to do something in a new way but a concept of operating that would allow you to accomplish something in a new way."[1]

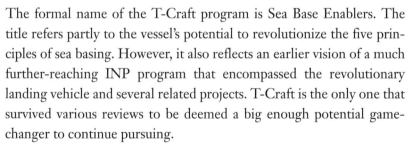

The formal name of the T-Craft program is Sea Base Enablers. The title refers partly to the vessel's potential to revolutionize the five principles of sea basing. However, it also reflects an earlier vision of a much further-reaching INP program that encompassed the revolutionary landing vehicle and several related projects. T-Craft is the only one that survived various reviews to be deemed a big enough potential game-changer to continue pursuing.

The original, broader effort (initially called Sea Basing before its name was changed to the current Sea Base Enablers) was one of four charter INP programs when the initiative began in 2004, along with the EM gun, TacSat (a tactical satellite), and PLUS. (The railgun and PLUS are profiled in this book). Heading the initiative was Navy commander Greg Reed, who at the time served as a deputy division director inside ONR's Code 33. When the INP program got started, a corollary program was ongoing as an FNC effort. Called Expeditionary Logistics, it dealt with some of the same issues in getting forces to the right spot at the right time and with the proper equipment. However, like all FNC programs, it tried to fill identified capability gaps using existing, well-proven technology. As the INP campaign kicked off, Reed's job was to pursue far more radical ideas that really pushed the sea basing envelope.

His first act was to visit Maribel Soto, who had taken over the SwampWorks program and was serving as ONR's acting director of innovation. Reed asked Soto to describe the fledgling INP process. "The answer," he recalls, "was that the process is a work in progress."[2] In other words, wing it.

Reed's approach was to seek out his colleagues working on the FNC effort as well as other key stakeholders in sea basing, including the expeditionary warfare group at the Pentagon later known as N-85 and officials of the Marine Corps Combat Development Command at Quantico.[3] He shared the premise behind the new INP program and its goal of developing a prototype for a leap-ahead concept in four to eight years. Then he asked, essentially, "If you had your choice, what types of concepts would you come up with?"

The question prompted three especially interesting ideas that Reed ended up developing further. One was for a powerful, versatile landing craft that would replace the aging generation of landing craft air-cushion vehicles known as LCACs that the Marines used to ferry tanks and equipment from ship to shore. This became T-Craft. Another idea called for a push-button warehousing system for ships dubbed TransPorts that would enable a pallet-sized load of equipment or supplies, or even something larger, to be rapidly stored or brought to the weather deck for unloading. Much like pushing the controls of a vending machine (A6, for instance), personnel could easily select a specific location in one of a ship's holds, and the pallet would be transported through watertight bulkheads right to where it was needed. Furthermore, items would be moved at game-changing throughput rates of up to 180 pallets per hour.

The third idea involved a "gator" escalator called Personnel Transport that could safely and efficiently carry Marines between transport ships and assault craft in high sea states. The goal was to move up to six hundred troops per hour (or one every six seconds) in Sea State 4, a condition currently deemed unsafe for transfers. "Those were our initial concepts," says Reed. Then, probably in the spring of 2005, a fourth idea surfaced. It came from experts at the Naval Surface Warfare Center's Carderock division in Bethesda, Maryland. Their concept was to create a version of a heavy-lift ship that would act as a way station for staging and loading equipment and personnel onto landing vessels, thereby streamlining the sea basing process in a different way. As with the semisubmersible salvage ship that brought back the USS *Cole* from the Yemini port of Aden, crew members would be able to ballast down this vessel to float things on or off its large flat deck, making it easier to equip and deploy LCAC for the trip to the beach. Currently, LCACs and other landing vessels ready for loading had to be driven into a ship's well deck—an area in the stern that can be opened to the sea. Reed calls using the well deck "very limited." The Carderock idea was called the Intermediate Transfer Station. "It basically gave you some real estate," he notes.

All this came together by mid-2005. Funding for the INP program was due to kick in that October, at the beginning of fiscal year 2006. Nearly $300 million had been budgeted for the Sea Base Enablers program over the next five or six years. But to tap that coffer, there had to be a more concrete plan to fund than just the raw ideas. Notes Reed, "If you don't have a plan for it, a lot of time the money goes away before you get it." Of the four ideas before him, Reed says the greatest doubts surrounded the transportable craft. Its target parameters far exceeded the capabilities of other landing craft in almost every category—from speed to payload to sea state operability. He recalls, "The one big question we had was, 'Is T-Craft even remotely possible.'"

To sort it out, Reed proposed holding an industry workshop to brainstorm with the Navy engineers and commercial ship builders who might produce the craft. He met with some resistance from ONR colleagues who thought it was a waste of time, but Admiral Cohen, the Chief of Naval Research, backed the idea and overrode the doubters. The meeting was held that April at the Naval Surface Warfare Center in Panama City, Florida. Before the get-together, few attendees really thought it could be done. At the meeting, after reviewing the state of technology and sharing ideas on how to best attack the problem, several softened their views a bit. None thought you could completely eliminate the so-called iron triangle of tradeoffs between speed, payload, and range that the T-Craft proposed to overcome. However, most seemed to believe a good start might be possible. Kelly Cooper had not yet joined ONR but attended the meeting representing the Carderock laboratory, where she worked as a naval architect. The new consensus, she remembers: "A craft could do one of these things, but not all."

But even that view soon moderated. Continues Cooper, "Little by little, through the next two or three months, the technology developers, the shipyards, the design agents that had attended that meeting came back and said, 'I'm thinking we could do that.'" Several even volunteered that they might be able to exceed the desired specifications in some areas. By mid-summer, an almost complete reversal had taken place. As Greg Reed sums up, "Almost everyone who attended said, 'You know what? We think we can do something.'"

Buoyed by the increasing optimism, ONR officials decided to go ahead and put out a broad agency announcement (BAA) soliciting design concepts for the envisioned T-Craft. As Reed puts it, "We felt at the time there was enough potential that we could go ahead and put the BAA out on that and see what would happen." The announcement was released in August 2005, along with similar solicitations concerning the other three Sea Base Enablers ideas. Just before the BAAs came out, Reed went on terminal leave, preparing to retire from the Navy. He soon ended his formal ONR posting but would return to work on T-Craft for a private contractor.

As Reed stepped down, Kelly Cooper took over as his replacement. Initially the naval architect had also considered T-Craft a long shot: she had been drawn into the INP effort by helping formulate the Intermediate Transfer Station concept. However, as Cooper grabbed the reins, she found the entire program about to be turned on its head. The other three ideas, once considered better candidates than T-Craft, had begun losing favor. Her own project, the Intermediate Transfer Station, was rendered redundant by a more favored idea called the mobile landing platform (MLP), which was under separate development but served much the same function. The Personnel Transport system for moving troops in high sea states never got off the ground, largely because no good ideas came in from the BAAs. Says Reed, "We just didn't get anything that wowed us enough." Finally, by early 2006, the transports idea for "candy machine" warehousing would be nixed as well by new Chief of Naval Research William Landay III, who found it overlapped other programs trying to automate aspects of warehousing.

In the end, says Reed, "We said the real game-changer here would be T-Craft."

————————●————————

The transformable craft addressed a central element of the Pentagon's vision of the future of warfighting. War planners have moved away from the traditional practice of initiating and supporting ground combat operations from extensive shore bases containing acres of troops and matériel, as was done in preparation for operations such as Desert Storm and Iraqi Freedom.

Instead, the strategy for many forcible entry operations is to move toward sea basing, the idea of creating smaller, more secret staging areas about seventy-five miles offshore where cargo-filled transport vessels would offload troops, weapons, munitions, food, and equipment. This would avoid the long build-up times of establishing shore bases and allow for more rapid strikes that would be supported at sea until heavier joint forces could move in to the airfields and ports secured by the first assaults.

A sea base comprises at least one carrier strike group, at least one expeditionary strike group, various combat logistics vessels, and a squadron of ships known as the Maritime Preposition Force (Future). The exact makeup of the MPF(F) remains unclear. However, it should be capable of supporting and supplying twenty days of stores, including food, fuel, and ammunition for a Marine Expeditionary Brigade and accommodating at least 8,500 troops. There are various scenarios in which a U.S. attack might unfold, including the establishment of an intermediate base (also at sea) as much as two thousand nautical miles from the sea base. But in any scenario, at some point the combat troops, stores, and equipment would have to be transferred from supply and transport ships to sea base strike group ships and the MPF(F) vessels. A final transfer would take place when the assault troops and their equipment move from the MPF(F) ships to landing craft for the push to the beach. One aim of sea basing is to be able to move two battalions, totaling 2,400 Marines and their equipment, to a shore-based objective overnight. To facilitate this, Navy plans call for a novel, still-unbuilt type of ship called the mobile landing platform that would be part of the MPF(F) squadron. It would act as the way station between transport ships and other ships in the sea base, including landing craft like the LCAC. Under the vision, the MLP would sidle up to a "roll-on/roll-off" cargo vessel laden with supplies. The matériel could then be rolled onto this "floating pier." The gigantic platform might well carry landing craft itself. In any case, it would then be able to semisubmerge, like the salvage ship that carried the USS *Cole* (and like the Carderock idea for an Intermediate Transfer Station), allowing for much easier and faster loading and deployment of LCACs and other vessels than possible in the well deck of a supply ship.[4]

While never coupled to the MPF(F), T-Craft nevertheless represented another possible enhancement to the concept, envisioned to overcome some of the major limitations of LCACs and other landing and air vehicles typically used to carry troops and matériel to shore from a sea base. LCACs can operate at high speeds of up to fifty knots. But their range is limited to about fifty nautical miles when fully loaded and traveling at such speeds. This means they cannot get to the sea base on their own: they have to be carried there in the well deck of a mother ship (or, down the road, in an MLP). What's more, when traveling between a sea base and shore, they either have to be supplied with fuel en route or give up cargo space to carry more fuel. Even when not freighting extra fuel, their capacity is limited to one M1A1 tank or twelve to sixteen Humvees—and they can only operate in relatively calm seas. The result is a series of constraints that severely curtail the capacity and flexibility of a landing force. "It seems we could do better," says Cooper.

Doing better—a lot better—is the idea behind T-Craft. First of all, says Cooper, "it would be able to be self-deploying." With a range of up to 2,500 miles at 20 knots and the ability to handle relatively heavy seas, it could travel by itself along with the fleet from an intermediate staging area to the sea base. Once there, it could be loaded at the MLP or in a ship's well deck. However, even when fully laden, it could traverse 250–300 nautical miles to shore and back without the need for refueling. Even better, it could operate in harsher conditions than an LCAC and do all this with a payload of up to 320 long tons, giving it the ability to carry up to four tanks, quadruple the capacity of its sister craft. When the concept was explained to the Marine Combat Development Command, one of the generals, Cooper doesn't remember who, proclaimed: "I'm not a naval architect and don't know the technical feasibility. But if you can do this, this is really what the Marine Corps needs."

Percolating through the T-Craft vision was a series of studies conducted by the Center for Naval Analyses in the late 1990s and early 2000s. Among other things, Cooper says, these evaluations looked at safe standoff distances and sea conditions for sea basing and concluded that these would be severely constrained by LCAC ranges and capabilities. The gist, she says: "We would spend so much operating time refueling that we would lose lift capacity and not be able to meet timelines we had envisioned with safe standoff distances." Even in ideal conditions with a sea state of zero and 100 percent reliability of craft performance, she adds, the LCACs would fall short of the goals of delivering up to 2,400 Marines and the tanks they required under cover of darkness. Says Cooper, "It just seemed more and more like we needed to look at a ship that had a self-deploying capability and had a larger lift capacity."

These assessments made it seem even more imperative to come up with an alternative to the LCAC, serving to bolster Greg Reed's idea of convening industry experts to carefully assess the feasibility of the T-Craft. That idea had led to the April 2005 workshop in Panama City, Florida—and ultimately the BAA that August. Where T-Craft was concerned, the plan with the BAA was to solicit preliminary design ideas. The designs were due October 1, 2005. ONR would then select and fund further development of up to five of the design submissions. Phase 2 called for building small-scale models from those designs and testing them on land and in sea conditions. The third phase involved full-scale technology demonstrations and construction of a prototype craft.

Within a month of sending out the call for proposals, Hurricane Katrina hit the U.S. Gulf Coast, home to several of the ship-building operations expected to submit T-Craft designs. Team members and their families were scattered; the entire region was reeling. A number of companies reported to Cooper that they simply could not meet the October 1 date. ONR delayed the due date a month, but even that proved a hardship. Finally ONR relented, asking only for ten-page outlines of design ideas by November 1, rather than full proposals.

Given that abbreviated format, ten firms made the deadline. Cooper's group quickly turned around evaluations and asked eight companies to go ahead and submit full designs. They extended the due date another two months, until early January 2006. A technical evaluation team, consisting of representatives from ONR, NavSea, the Carderock laboratory, the expeditionary warfare group in the Pentagon, the Marine Corps Combat Development Command, and two Army groups concerned with transportation issues immediately conducted assessments. By that February the evaluation team had recommended several designs for additional funding to the new Chief of Naval Research, Admiral Landay.

Sea Fighter: Test Bed for Innovation

It was a rainy morning at the Port of Everett, north of Seattle and just next door to the Naval Station Everett base. A large gray hull loomed behind a guard shack. Near it was a sign that read: "X-Craft Restricted Area."[1]

The date was May 31, 2005. A ramp was open from the mission bay to the dock, enabling a crowd of people—some twenty-six crewmembers, workmen, and several dozen visitors—to stream onto the spanking new ship. One of those walking up the ramp was former Secretary of the Navy John Lehman. He was joined by Adm. Jay Cohen, the Chief of Naval Research.

This was ONR's latest creation, and one of Cohen's pet projects. Although the sign still read X-Craft, short for "littoral surface craft—experimental," the 262-foot-long vessel had been christened *Sea Fighter* just a few months earlier. Since that time, its crew of twenty-six, including sixteen Navy personnel and ten Coast Guard members, had put the craft through its paces in Puget Sound. Now, with the vessel set to go into operational service, it was time for a more public unveiling. And, oh, how Cohen liked to tell its story.

Sea Fighter was the result of some of the admiral's favorite activities: game-changing and feather-ruffling. Beginning in 2001 he had neatly side-stepped bureaucracy to build the craft, completing it for a bargain-basement figure of roughly $90 million that came out of congressional plus-up funds, not the Navy's R&D budget. The craft had gone on to successfully demonstrate a number of innovative features that held big promise for other ships and programs. To begin with, *Sea Fighter* was the Navy's fastest ship, capable of speeds of greater than fifty knots. Built by Nichols Brothers Boat Builders of Whidbey Island, Washington (a small commercial yard), the aluminum catamaran relied on two gas turbine engines and a pair of propulsion diesels to power the four water jets that moved it effortlessly to top speed. On its test voyage that day, visitors were stunned when the pilot announced the vessel had hit forty-eight knots with barely a vibration felt. "It's the fastest thing on the water, except small speedboats," Cohen says.[2]

The X-Craft, short for "littoral surface craft—experimental," was built for about $90 million as one of Adm. Jay Cohen's experimental, potentially game-changing projects. The 262-foot-long vessel was christened *Sea Fighter* around early 2005. It has a twenty-six-person crew, is capable of speeds up to fifty knots, and has interchangeable mission modules for tasks as diverse as mine countermeasures, amphibious assault support, antisubmarine warfare, and humanitarian assistance. A deployable stern ramp allows it to launch and recover small manned and unmanned vessels, and its flight deck boasts two landing spots that can handle aircraft up to the size of an H-60-type helicopter.

John F. Williams/ONR

The experimental vessel was intended as a floating test bed for other craft designed to operate in shallow coastal waters, most notably the littoral combat ship then in development. In particular, the X-Craft had been built to test futuristic "HME" (hull, maintenance, and electrical) concepts, including evaluating the structural behavior and hydrodynamic performance of high-speed vessels.

It was also breaking ground on a number of other fronts befitting the envisioned future of smaller-scale, asymmetric warfare. The craft was self-deploying, with a large range for a littoral ship of up to four thousand nautical miles without refueling. Its climate-controlled mission bay could hold a dozen twenty-foot "mission modules" that permitted the crew to quickly reconfigure it for different tasks, among them mine countermeasures, amphibious assault support, antisubmarine warfare, and humanitarian assistance. A deployable stern ramp allowed it to launch and recover small manned and unmanned surface and subsurface vessels while its flight deck included a pair of landing spots that could each handle a variety of small aircraft up to the size of an H-60-type helicopter. Supported by an unprecedented level of automation and systems monitoring capabilities, all this could be operated and maintained by an extremely small crew—initially just five officers and twenty-one enlisted personnel.

While such accomplishments might make it sound like the X-Craft should win unanimous praise inside the Navy, such was not the case. The feather-ruffling had come into play because Cohen had launched the project separate from normal Navy R&D processes, and without deeply involving the Naval Sea Systems Command, which had overall responsibility for shipbuilding. According to more than one ONR insider, NavSea officials were upset over another Navy group building ships. Cohen, though, was hell-bent on increasing innovation at ONR and determined to think and act outside the box.

In August 2005 *Sea Fighter* was transferred to San Diego for further testing by the Navy and Coast Guard. While unarmed in its Puget Sound trials, the ship was scheduled to get a fifty-caliber machine gun. Later it was possible to outfit its flight deck with missile systems and other weapons.

Cohen didn't think *Sea Fighter* would be commissioned as an actual operational vessel. Still, he predicted that once transferred to San Diego, the U.S. Coast Guard would be keenly interested in its applicability to intercepting drug trafficking, picking up or rescuing illegal aliens, and conducting anti-terrorism patrols. Moreover, he noted, many of its concepts should prove valuable for use in building the planned littoral combat ship. It proved impossible to verify his predictions: sometime in 2006, the ship and its operations were moved into the classified realm.

The admiral was particularly proud of the X-Craft. In March 2005, the month after the craft was christened, he appeared before the Senate Armed Services Committee's subcommittee on emerging threats and capabilities. During his testimony, Cohen called the ship a "tangible example" of "capabilities that promise to fundamentally change how we prepare for and fight wars."[3]

True, he had ruffled feathers by its creation. But that's often what has to happen for innovation to occur, he says. Those involved in the normal acquisitions process find it extremely hard to take risks because so much rides on success when something becomes a program of record, including individual careers. Taking risks is much easier for a research-oriented organization like ONR because failure is part of many of the early stage efforts it supports. Despite upsetting some brass at NavSea, he figured ONR should take the chance of building X-Craft because otherwise many of the concepts behind it might not be explored, at least not in the immediate future.

"We have embarrassed the status quo, the programs of record," Cohen once acknowledged.[4] He later added, "I didn't care who I embarrassed, it was about getting the job done."[5]

---

1. The author was on board the X-Craft for the test cruise of May 31, 2005. Much of the description is taken from that trip, including the Thomas interview. See also "Navy Takes Possession of Fastest Experimental Ship," *Navy Newsstand*, story number NNS050708–02, July 8, 2005, http://www.navy.mil/submit/display.asp?story_id=19084; "X-Craft . . . in a Class by Itself" (undated ONR document); "X-Craft/Littoral Surface Craft-Experimental (LSC(X)). Fast Sea Frame/Sea Fighter (FSF 1)." *GlobalSecurity.org*, http://www.globalsecurity.org/military/systems/ship/x-craft.htm (page modified August 8, 2005).
2. Cohen interview, May 25, 2005.
3. Cohen, "Statement of Rear Admiral Jay M. Cohen."
4. Cohen interview, December 15, 2005.
5. Cohen interview, December 27, 2006.

With Cooper serving as the ONR program manager, the project itself—meaning all the contractors and subcontractors—was managed by the Naval Surface Warfare Center at Carderock. Ultimately, four T-Craft proposals received phase 1 funding. This primarily covered development of the preliminary design. By August 2007, two years after the BAAs went out, ONR planned to select three to continue into phase 2. This would involve what Cooper terms a "very aggressive" plan to develop and test models on a twenty-four-month timetable. Testing would include computer simulations of various design parameters and land-based tests of such things as the strength and durability of composite materials that might be used in the craft as well as evaluations of small-scale models (perhaps one-quarter scale) in a towing tank at Carderock. Cooper was somewhat vague about what exactly these tests would entail. Because the T-Craft was so revolutionary, Navy engineers still lacked the means to evaluate the models properly. Therefore, concurrent with the model building, ONR was funding development of a suite of tools to help make the necessary analytical and performance assessments. Phase 3, set to begin in 2009 and continue until 2012, was intended to produce at least one full-scale prototype craft.

In early 2007, with phase 2 not yet begun, many question marks surrounded T-Craft, Cooper admitted. "We don't know what's going to work. And each of the proposals proposed a different solution." Indeed, one idea includes a composite hull, another an aluminum hull. And there are wildly different types of craft, including a "wing in ground" design that in effect uses a super-deep keel for stability.

The game-changing goals of the INP program dictated taking some big chances. Still, to mitigate its risks, ONR was investing in a suite of technologies—from the novel propulsion system that would power the craft to super-strong hull materials to a new form of air cushioning to enable it to ride smoother on the waves—that held promise even if the T-Craft failed. The Navy was separately pursuing a more conventional improvement to LCACs under its joint modular air-cushion vehicle effort. Even if the T-Craft didn't pan out, Cooper notes, "some of the things that we're going to be doing in T-Craft could possibly transition to that program."

Cooper was also hedging ONR's bet in a couple of other ways. First, she had assembled a so-called red team to manage the risks of the programs. Rather than acting as an advocate of the program the way the Carderock lab project managers do, the red team acts as an advocate of the government. It independently reviews the claims of performance and examines the various technical components to assess whether what's being attempted is feasible. "We need those independent eyes," says Cooper.

She continues, "The other thing we have thought is that because we have selected such different technology, maybe nobody has the total solution yet. We won't know that until we get through phase 2." Therefore, she notes, planners had structured the program so that ONR could decide to fund further development of specific technologies behind the vessel without going ahead and funding construction of T-Craft itself. "What we have left open is the possibility that we will go forward of full-scale development of technology and not a particular craft." She adds, "I think we have invested in a broad enough range of technology that we might have some ripe fruit."

By mitigating the risks of funding the T-Craft in that way, it made the overall program more palatable to the Naval Sea Systems Command and the rest of the Navy. From the start, ONR has been particularly sensitive to how the program executive office (PEO) for ships will react to the T-Craft. For one thing, the office inherits the maintenance burden for any ship that is built and likes to be closely involved from the start in any plans that might lead to the creation of a new class of ships. In addition, in ONR's view the longtime PEO for ships, Rear Adm. Charles Hamilton, no doubt well remembered the X-Craft, another experimental vessel ONR had built without closely involving NavSea, roiling the leadership there.

When it came to T-Craft, Cooper was determined to have a much better working relationship with Hamilton's office. From the ONR viewpoint, Hamilton had initially taken a stance against T-Craft. That was back when Greg Reed was still program manager, and the X-Craft was under construction. As Reed puts it, "He made it clear that he didn't like ONR building craft of any sort, so this [T-Craft] was by default stupid."

With some hard work and relationship-building, Hamilton's view had changed. Cooper had placed members of the PEO office on the management review group to prevent any surprises and avoid duplication of investment. And ONR would not move into phase 3 without full agreement from the Pentagon. Cooper says, "They will participate in examination and analysis of the technologies and help us avoid risk. In the end, the more they know about the program the more comfortable they will be on the acquisitions side." Transition, she adds, needs to start at the beginning of even a long-range effort like T-Craft. "You have to start back when it is being funded with 6.1 and 6.2 dollars."

Ultimately, she notes, it is better for everyone if the only surprises come when the enemy—and not the Pentagon—experiences the flexibility and capabilities the Navy and Marine Corps can bring to forcible entry operations.

CHAPTER 12

The Virtual Warfighter

I n August 1941, on the eve of America's entry into World War II, the United States expropriated more than three-fourths of the tiny Puerto Rican island of Vieques, some 26,000 acres—encompassing marshes, mangrove areas, and agricultural lands—out of the island's total 33,000 acres. The move was made with the approval of the local San Juan government. But that didn't help the Viequenese, as thousands were forced to vacate their long-held homes and farms. Some congregated in what little room was left inland; others dispersed for the Puerto Rican mainland, Saint Croix, the United States, and elsewhere. Meanwhile, the U.S. Navy quickly established two bases. On the western coast rose a vast ammunition facility. Sprawling in the east, an 11,000-acre weapons training center.[1]

Then the bombing and gunnery practice began.

For nearly the next 60 years the weapons training facility was under fire some 180 days per annum—used by the Marine Corps and Navy for naval gunnery support missions, air-to-ground ordnance exercises, and amphibious maneuvers. Resident resentment swelled with the years. Noise from ship-to-shore gunfire could be numbing, and complaints mounted over the economic hardships endured as a result of the expropriation, including disruption of local fishing, agriculture, and tourism. The environmental cost proved staggering, with extensive damage to the island's natural resources, ecology, and archeological sites. And residents alleged an increased incidence of cancer and other ailments as a result of the chemical pollutants released by the barrage of bombs and artillery shells.

Various lawsuits and other protests forced the U.S. to make some concessions over this time. But in April 1999 a Marine Corps F/A-18 on a training mission mistakenly released two five-hundred-pound bombs on an observation post, killing a civilian Viequenese security guard and injuring four others. The next day Puerto Rican governor Pedro Rossello wrote President Bill Clinton to request the "immediate and permanent cessation of United States and allied activities that entail the use of weaponry anywhere in the vicinity of the Municipality of Vieques, Puerto Rico."[2] That set off a slew of new investigations, legal challenges, claims, and counterclaims. At one point, Marine Corps lieutenant general Peter Pace, commander of the Atlantic Fleet's Marine forces, employed a football analogy to try to explain how badly Vieques was needed. While the Navy maintained other sites to practice blocking and tackling, he said, "the only place where we can scrimmage with the whole team together is Vieques."[3]

But it was fourth down; time to punt. Vieques had become a public relations nightmare. Although the Navy briefly resumed training and war games on the island in 2001, the administration of new president George W. Bush announced that June that it would end military training operations on Vieques by May 2003.[4] (The Navy would actually hold its last island training exercise in January 2003.) In concert with the announcement, Navy Secretary Gordon England stated, "I am directing the creation of a panel of experts to reinvigorate our efforts to find effective alternatives to Vieques for training our forces."[5]

That was a cue for the Office of Naval Research. As the drawn-out battle over Vieques reached a crescendo, England's call galvanized an ONR effort to canvas the state of the art in computer technology to find new ways of simulating gunnery training—post Vieques. The effort was named VAST, for virtual at-sea training. Led by Code 34, the Warfighter Performance Department (at the time it was known as Human Systems), VAST grew over the next few years into a widely deployed training tool that avoids many of the economic, environmental, and public relations costs of traditional weapons training.[6]

By the end of 2006 more than one hundred ship gun crews had been qualified with the system. Even more important, ONR officials pointed to the VAST program as helping pioneer a new business model for how the organization should work with its end "customers" in the Navy to understand real-world needs and conditions and then incorporate that feedback into effective technologies and systems. As 2007 got under way VAST-like training systems were being explored for Marine Corps artillery training, antisubmarine warfare, littoral combat, and—most ambitious—for joint warfare training involving the Navy, Air Force, and Army. Declares Hal Guard, head of Code 34, "This is I think a breakthrough in naval/MILITARY training."[7]

———————●———————

The events that led to this proclamation enveloped ONR in June 2001, even before the public announcement that the Navy was planning to cease training operations on Vieques. Chief of Naval Research Cohen was on a plane trip with Adm. Robert J. Natter, Commander of the U.S. Atlantic Fleet. Somewhere in their conversation, talk turned to Vieques. Natter groused about the impending loss of Vieques and asked Cohen if he had any ideas on how technology might help replace the loss of the range. The ONR head promised to get back to Natter right away.

Task Force VAST, as it quickly came to be called, formed almost as soon as Cohen returned to Ballston Towers. "After the trip, Cohen came back to ONR, organized a group to address the problems posed by a possible withdrawal of the Navy from Vieques," recalls Harold Hawkins, an ONR program officer in Code 34 tapped to participate.[8] The first meeting took place on the top floor of ONR's headquarters in the last week of June. "At the initial meeting, there were thirty-five or forty people," he adds. "The main objective of the initial organizational meeting was to identify what technologies were readily available and which facilities would need to be involved to test a prototype."

Admiral Cohen set an ambitious goal: deliver a working prototype by late July, barely thirty days away. Hawkins was put in charge of the effort, retired Navy captain Michael Dunaway his second in command. Initial funding of $250,000 came from the naval modeling and simulation management office, which routinely provided funds to ONR to sponsor computer simulation and modeling work.

A special sense of urgency underscored this task. Before a ship could deploy, it had to fulfill a series of qualification steps on a training readiness matrix. The Navy had no plans to close its live-fire range in the Channel Islands off the California coast, where Pacific crews trained. On the East Coast, though, Vieques was the only place to qualify. So for the Atlantic Fleet, says Dunaway, "The show-stopper for Navy deployments was the loss of the [Vieques] bombardment range."[9] Speed, he says, was of the essence.

Hawkins' goal from the start was to develop a simulation system that enabled ship gun crews to fire live rounds at sea against virtual targets instead of Vieques. It couldn't be a stand-alone system, either. Because, in real life, naval gun crews would often work in concert with other ships, the Navy needed a system that could simulate a task force or group of ships, all in constant communication with each other.

Rather than bankrolling the invention of new technologies, as was ONR's traditional practice, the idea was to assimilate existing technologies into a vastly improved gunnery training system. In recent years, computer and simulation technology had matured so rapidly that this concept seemed very realistic. Says Hawkins, the technological "pieces were all there, we just had to configure them in the right way."

Hawkins and Dunaway didn't have to look far for the right start. The core technology behind VAST came from the Navy itself. Indeed, the service and simulation technology went back a long way, to around 1931, when the Navy laid out $1,500 to purchase the first fully instrumented flight simulator, the Link Trainer. Since then, it had helped drive the state of the art in training and computer simulation, including ONR's funding of the pioneering Whirlwind digital computer in the early 1950s.[10] In 1953 the Cape Cod System for Air Defense, for which Whirlwind provided the processing power, was able to demonstrate "virtual human-machine distributed interactive simulation" in which radar operators and weapon controllers reacted to simulated targets presented to them as real targets would be in war.[11]

Far more recently, for the past decade or so, the Navy had been using the Battle Force Tactical Trainer (BFTT) system to provide ship-based training in weapons and sensor systems. "Beef-it," as the system was dubbed, was a fairly elaborate system in which the trainee was immersed in a simulated combat environment. Computer-generated scenarios based on video feeds depicted realistic radar displays and geographic imagery. The highly flexible system also allowed for a lot of interactivity so that individuals or units (and sometimes larger groups) could train together. Data was collected in real time, allowing for rapid assessment of performance. As Hawkins describes it, "It generates electronic signals which replicate information the ship receives through sensor systems, such as radar, navigational input, sonar, etc. . . . An example would be a simulation in which the crew sees planes flying towards the ship for a raid. The crew could then activate its weapons systems to engage the targets."

When it came to Vieques-like gunnery training, though, some major problems loomed. First and foremost, the "Beef-it" system was designed to plug into a ship only *after* it had pulled into a pier. That meant it was of no use in supporting live fire, a prerequisite for gun crew qualification: it hadn't even been applied to simulating naval fire support. Another liability, adds Dunaway, "was that it only affected a single ship. There was no way to network."

Although it did not possess the networking and at-sea features the desired gunnery training simulator would need, the BFTT technology did provide the essence of the envisioned system. The Navy and ONR had a long-standing relationship with BMH Associates, a Norfolk-based firm staffed largely by ex-military personnel that had established itself as a leader in interactive simulations for military training. Hawkins chose it as the lead coordinator or systems integrator for VAST; the company would retain this role for the entire lifespan of the program. Ed Harvey, the BMH president, worked closely with ONR on assimilating existing technology for the prototype demonstration. By July 2001 his team had a working system ready for two or three live-fire tests at the Naval Surface Warfare Center in Dahlgren, Virginia, where several five-inch guns pointed out over an open-water test range in the lower Potomac River. The first demonstrations that summer were somewhat down-and-dirty affairs. Admiral Natter did not attend, but representatives of the Atlantic Fleet staff were on hand as well as a few Marine

Corps and Navy officers. Boats were cleared from the firing range area in the Potomac. Hawkins then recalls "a lot of standing around while technicians figured out why the system was not working the way it was supposed to." The bulk of the contingent gathered in a nearby room watching a computer monitor, along with a Marine Corps spotter. The screen displayed a simulated target of a tank traveling across a swath of land. When a shell landed in the Potomac, its location would be geo-translated onto the synthetic environment. The spotter would then call out new coordinates to try and zero in on the enemy vehicle: "500 yards up," or "250 yards left."

The way the Marines worked gunnery fire, the first few shots were spotting shells. Once the spotter had the guns zeroed in, he would "call for fire." The battery would be released, and a fierce salvo would ensue. Hawkins was pleased at how quickly the spotter caught on to the system. "I think a lot of people were quite impressed with the potential," he says.

In the end, although there were several fits and starts, the prototype clearly served its purpose, performing well enough to prove the concept was viable. "Backs were against the wall with Vieques, and [people] saw this captured enough of the training of Vieques," Hawkins says. He and Dunaway were especially happy when they learned one of the Marine Corps lieutenants had reported to his superior at Quantico that he thought it had real training value. Natter's group soon professed its support for the concept, and Cohen quickly provided a capital investment of an additional $1 million to get the project formally off the ground. For the next several years, VAST would be funded at somewhere between $1 million and $1.5 million annually.

Following the initial demonstration, the main challenge was to turn the one-of-a-kind prototype into a more robust and sophisticated software program that could be installed on laptop computers. It needed to be compatible with Navy systems and easy to use by a crew at sea—and it needed to interact seamlessly with special hardware that linked it to the analog world.

The basic idea rested on a ship deploying a network of floating buoys, each outfitted with a hydrophone, GPS receiver, and radio transmitter. The buoys would be positioned at sea, framing the target area.

Meanwhile, on board the ship, as soon as the first shell fell into the sea, the computer would generate a three-dimensional simulated target, projecting its image onto the laptop screen as if it were physically located in the area ringed by the listening buoys. The images seen on the display, which could be based on photographic images of real-life sites, appeared as video feeds. The simulated scene might depict an island such as Vieques or a coastal target such as an enemy gun emplacement, an opposing warship, or an armada. The Navy had plenty of existing models to draw on from other simulation systems such as BFTT. "There is a history of treating visualizations of virtual environments, which goes way back," says Hawkins. "We used that to create the images of battle terrain and targets."

Gun crews would fire at the simulated target depicted on the computer screen. The buoys would listen for the splashes of the incoming fire, transmitting the exact time they detected a projectile's impact and their GPS position at that moment. By correlating the information from the various buoys, the shipboard computer could fix the splash point of the incoming round. Using ballistic flight models, the shell's trajectory could then be calculated, allowing the computer to determine exactly where the projectile would have struck on the computer-generated 3-D battlespace, taking into consideration the target's elevation or height above sea level. It would next conjure up a visual image of the target as it might appear to a spotter on shore or in an aircraft above the target area. Finally, that image would be displayed on a video monitor manned by the forward observer, who would see the shell strike the target, complete with simulated explosion or impact smoke. The observer could then provide feedback to the gunnery crew about how to adjust gun coordinates. In this way an entire team could be qualified in live-fire naval bombardment. This covered the gun crew; the "Glo," or gunnery liaison officer; the shipboard navigation staffers; the Combat Information Center and communications personnel; and the forward observer. (The system would also work in port in a totally simulated environment and without live fire, like "Beef-it".) A forward observer, or spotter, might be on land, in a key vantage point on board ship, or even thousands of miles away watching the action by satellite. He would radio adjustments in fire coordinates to the "Glo," who relayed the instructions to the gunnery crew. True, live-fire rounds fell into the sea. But when compared to striking an inhabited land mass like Vieques, the VAST system allowed for meaningful gunnery training and practice with a minimum of potential human and environmental damage.

The initial prototype demonstration, along with subsequent reviews with Dahlgren and Fleet personnel, identified a series of improvements or enhancements needed by the system. The most pressing need was to raise the graphics and image quality. The BMH team introduced continual improvements in this area over the next several years. Next in line came developing the capacity to use "constructive" or simulated fire with the system in situations where live fire proved impractical.

With these and other improvements being incorporated into the system, several tests were conducted in the Gulf of Mexico in 2002 and early 2003. At one point, Dunaway and Hawkins flew out to the carrier USS *Enterprise* and then hopped a helicopter to the cruiser USS *Gettysburg* to watch it take part in a comprehensive training unit exercise using VAST. By this point VAST was looking increasingly feasible, and not just for East Coast ship crews. It quickly became clear that such a system could also be useful on the West Coast—saving ships based in Guam, for instance, from steaming across the Pacific to the Channel Islands for their certifications. "In many ways, VAST is really an improvement over Vieques," Dunaway told *Popular Science* not long after a Gulf of Mexico trial in late 2002. "Not only are VAST exercises cheaper, we can set them up wherever we want without transporting equipment and personnel long distances." With most naval guns fired at distances of many miles, seeing a real hit wasn't necessary, he added.

Another simulation in 2003 incorporated into the model aerial photography from drone planes flying over a "target" at Fort Benning, Georgia. This urban terrain exercise also involved Air Force and Army units engaged in attacking a small town while being supported by the Navy artillery fire. It revealed formidable obstacles to bringing simulation into such joint exercises. Says Dunaway,

When you start dealing with computer-generated simulations for tactical operations, the systems that you network together may have been systems designed for an open-source environment. As soon as you put them together for military training, [including] how enemies operate, our tactics, individual weapons systems, speeds of flight, you are in the classified realm real fast. One problem is the system design is unclassified, but the purpose is classified. There were a lot of negotiations between the services about what could be done and not done—administrative problems—between the services.

Another key issue was that each service's simulations had their own data base formats, so affordably weaving them together to provide consistent terrain across a wide range of devices proved problematic.

Still, by this point the flexibility, cost savings, and environmental advantages of the system for gunnery training were compelling. By early 2003, when the last exercise took place at Vieques, the Navy had begun qualifying East Coast–based ship crews with VAST. Four years later at least one hundred ships had qualified their gun crews with the system. "Every ship that deploys nowadays qualifies with this VAST system before they go," asserts Dunaway.

Firing shells into the open sea and having a computer figure out how they would have struck a physical target lacks substance and real-world feedback when compared to blowing something up. However, Hawkins estimates that "80 to 85 percent of training requirements can be met in simulated training." It can even prove superior to the real thing in some ways. Gun crews firing for days on end on Vieques, for example, would get used to seeing the same target over and over, limiting the conditions for which they could train. "But by using simulation in which the target can vary and different variables can be added, training can be better than on a live range," Hawkins adds. Plus, he notes, "If you just have to go a few miles offshore, you can get a lot more training done in a short period of time. You don't have to steam 1,200 miles to Vieques, which takes three days, exercise and then steam back. Given that the experience is essentially the same, indirect fire really puts you ahead of the game. It is also far less expensive . . . so you can do the training more often—start and stop scenarios."

Ambitions for VAST kept growing. Even as the Navy increased the number of ship gun crews qualifying with the system, ONR worked to expand the core concept to shipboard damage control training. By 2004 Hawkins' team was also partnering with the Marine Corps to adapt the basic technology for training the crews of the high-mobility artillery rocket system for ground support. "This was the next variant," says Hawkins. It was essentially the same thing except that the weapon that was being fired was a Marine Corps weapon. They called this version VFST, for virtual fire-support trainer. Some $400,000 in funding for the effort came from ONR's TechSolutions program. Within less than a year, VFST was developed and transitioned to Camp Lejeune, North Carolina, where Marine artillery teams train. Guns are positioned along the Atlantic Coast, firing out over a shoreline that includes a nesting ground for turtles and is otherwise rich in marine mammals. The Marines were looking to avoid live fire when possible to save costs and minimize environmental impact, so the VFST system was often used for constructive (virtual) fire.

Heading into 2007 several other major extensions or offshoots of VAST were under way. If successful, they would have an impact far beyond surface ships and even the Navy. One involved an effort to provide integrated antisubmarine warfare training for crew members of SH-60 helicopters. Several of these systems, called the Mission Rehearsal Tactical Team Trainer (MRT3), had been deployed by the end of 2006, including three at Kaneohe Bay Marine Air Base in Hawaii. The idea was to network them together to provide tactical team training.

Another "child of VAST" effort involved working with NavSea, the Naval Sea Systems Command in Washington, to transform the technology for use in a new class of vessel, the littoral combat ship (LCS). These high-speed, multimission ships were being built to operate in shallow littoral waters within a few hundred miles of the coast as a complement to the new generation of destroyers and cruisers, the DD(X) and CG(X), respectively.[12] Their chief jobs envisioned in post–Cold

War scenarios involved mine countermeasures, antisubmarine warfare, and guarding against *Cole*-like terrorist attacks, especially in busy port areas. Crews needed to be trained in these and other core capabilities as well as things like ship maneuvering, maintenance, and damage control. "We are applying what we know to new combat ship classes," says Dunaway. "It shows the acceptance of the technology. It makes our job easier because we don't have to sell every idea." An even more ambitious project centered on creating, in effect, a portable version of the Maritime Synthetic Range (MSR), an instrumented submarine training and test range covering several hundred square miles off the coast of the Hawaiian island of Kauai. The waters there teem with underwater acoustic devices that make it easy to fix the position of a submarine in three dimensions. They track the action as subs practice targeting surface ships or other submarines, making it possible to recreate and evaluate various war games scenarios. Just as with naval fire-support training, however, it often doesn't make sense to steam long distances for such practice: a submarine in Guam, for instance, doesn't want to have to transit to Hawaii just to get basic qualification. "What we are trying to do is replicate that so it can be taken anywhere," says Dunaway.

The U.S. Pacific Fleet, which is headquartered in Hawaii, is driving the initiative, says Hawkins. If Navy training with ships, submarines, and aircraft could be seamlessly woven together, teams in completely different locations could take part in the same exercise. What's more, the training could involve combinations of completely live action, virtual action with live fire, and totally simulated action. "If there's a Holy Grail, that's probably it—at the current stage," says Hawkins, "because it combines the live, virtual, and constructive capability." He adds: "They envision this as revolutionizing Fleet training in the Pacific."

Even this, though, represents merely a step toward the overarching aim of integrating the Navy's virtual training models into an initiative called the Joint National Training Capability. This mega-effort seeks to integrate live and virtual training exercises involving the Navy, Marine Corps, Air Force, and Army. To succeed will entail overcoming some of the same obstacles that surfaced when VAST was part of the much smaller joint exercise at Fort Benning back in 2003. All the services have something to offer. Navy software is great with ships and gun support but not good with aircraft simulations. The Air Force, meanwhile, is really good with models involving things like aerial photography, reconnaissance, flight patterns, and aircraft signatures. "But they don't do ships, of course," notes Dunaway. The Army, on the other hand, employs simulation models that are highly accurate at depicting such things as terrain and foliage, vehicle and armored units, and even infantry deployments.

The obvious goal is to blend the best each has to offer to enable smoother, more realistic joint exercises against a wide array of threats and under a variety of conditions. The problem is that they're built on a host of different systems and architectures that makes such integration a major headache. The ONR team isn't going to solve all this. But as it works on the various Navy technologies, notes Dunaway, the goal is to make sure the Navy and Marine Corps systems are as compatible with the other services as possible. "So what we are trying to do is design the systems so that the engineering actually helps drive that integration."

Despite the growing success of VAST and its progeny, Hawkins and Dunaway seemed at least as proud of the model they had used to develop them as they were of the technologies themselves. "The most important lesson was the business model," says Hawkins. Starting with Admiral Cohen's hastily called brainstorming session about how to help replace Vieques training, VAST represented a marked departure from the way ONR had traditionally gone about its business. "Many people in uniform, if [they] know anything about ONR, it is that developments are ten to twenty years down the line. ONR's current activities cannot do anything for them," he says. "The Vieques issue was the first time ONR really got serious about addressing an immediate problem. There was so obviously a desperate need. It placed a lot of pressure on ONR to develop a better model to meet their needs."

Driven by this imperative, Hawkins and Dunaway worked from the start to partner better with representatives of the Fleet. The goal, says Hawkins, was to "identify very specifically what their requirements are for computer simulations, training, etc." This not only informed the BMH technical team that acted as the project integrator what was needed, it also generated support for the effort inside the Fleet because their people contributed to its design. Continues Hawkins, "You need to be involved with the customer base from the beginning. We develop a first prototype after consultation with the end-user, then provide demonstration to the end-user, and then modify system to address concerns that they have. . . . This continued interaction has been really important. It gets the end-user to feel ownership for the system. We're not knocking on the door and handing them a system because we think they need it."

That sense of ownership and connection definitely eased VAST's path into service, he says. And their success didn't go unnoticed. In June 2003, when Vieques officially closed down, Hawkins and Dunaway were visiting the Naval Undersea Warfare Center in Newport, Rhode Island, to work on developing a VAST-like system for training in shipboard damage control.

As they left the building, Dunaway's cell phone rang. It was the head of their department, Hal Guard, letting them know that Hawkins had won that year's Arthur Bisson Prize for Achievement in Naval Technology. The award, which carries with it a plaque and a $7,500 cash prize, is named after ONR's director of science and technology from 1993 until his death in 1996. It recognizes a current or former Navy scientist, engineer, or science and technology program manager whose achievements best exemplify those of Dr. Bisson—and whose work had a significant and direct impact on the transition of science and technology to Navy operations. Hawkins was the first person from ONR to win the award.

CHAPTER **13**

The Electromagnetic Railgun

wo shots echoed over the test range. In the command room, an operator perched before a control panel had kicked things off with a brief countdown: "Regulating at 8.4 KV. . . . It's armed. Three, two, one—fire." Then the man pushed the fire button, causing the first hollow retort. About six seconds later, the second shot was fired.

An observer standing outside the control room could see two rectangular, concrete-encapsulated chambers about the size of two short covered bridges. They were perched forty or so feet apart against a backdrop of green trees on a clear day, their open ends facing one another. From the right-hand chamber a puff of smoke arose following each shot. Then, almost instantly, a similar puff wafted out of the second confine.[1]

The "bullets" that traveled across the open air between the chambers moved too swiftly for the naked eye to perceive. The retorts from their firing had sounded much like gunshots. But a slow-motion video of the scene showed an odd-looking projectile reminiscent of a Klingon warship streaking across the gap, pursued by some unidentifiable smaller debris. The image then shifted to a head-on view of the second chamber. Inside sat a railcar laden with a long, metal-lined pallet. One hole had already been punched through the metal at the front of the pallet, the result of the first shot. Now came the second projectile, hurtling at supersonic speeds into the same space. A bright flash erupts, and the sand packed inside the railcar goes flying, spewing a small dusty cloud. A few minutes later, a group of nearly two dozen men and women gathers before the camera to celebrate their successful shots.

"Railgun!"

"Hoorah!"

The date was October 2, 2006. The venue was the Electromagnetic Launch Facility at the Naval Surface Warfare Center at Dahlgren. The technology being tested belonged to a novel weapon called the electromagnetic railgun, or EM gun for short. Using powerful electromagnetic forces rather than gunpowder, the railgun fires nonexplosive projectiles at fantastic velocities. Guided by GPS, if successful it will streak to its targets with uncanny precision, relying on the incredible force of impact rather than a warhead to devastate targets as much as 250 nautical miles away, a feat that would extend the current striking reach of naval ships by more than ten times.

The Office of Naval Research has been pursuing aspects of the railgun for a decade or longer. But in 2004 the weapon was named one of the organization's charter INP efforts, the responsibility of Code 35, Naval Air Warfare and Weapons. Since then it has undergone steady improvement and is advancing on a critical milestone test from early 2009.[2] Program manager Elizabeth D'Andrea sees the railgun as one of the most game-changing efforts under way at the organization. "We think it could completely transform the way you do operational support of the ground forces, and for naval forces," she says. "If you think about it you've got essentially a field artillery capability from the sea. So instead of having to deploy people on the ground to get a foothold and establish a beachhead and establish an operational unit to be able to do artillery launches . . . you don't ever have to take land, and you don't ever have to put people at risk on a foreign soil in order to inject firepower on foreign soil."[3]

———————●———————

The railgun gets its name because, in essence, it consists of a bore barrel inside of which run two metal tracks, ultimately twenty feet long, like those on a railroad. A projectile sits on a slide armature positioned between the rails, the way a train car waits on its tracks. The armature itself sits where the explosives powder would reside in a gun, just behind the bullet. An electric current runs along one rail, through the armature and up the other rail, creating an intense electromagnetic field that essentially propels the projectile outward at tremendous speeds. The more energy produced in the barrel, the greater the muzzle velocity and therefore the farther and faster the projectile flies.

At the forces envisioned in a ship-based gun, the projectile would achieve what's called a "hypervelocity electromagnetic launch" of approximately Mach 7.5, sending the newfangled gunnery shell on a ballistic trajectory that would carry it some 500,000 feet above the Earth's surface. It would be able to travel some 250 nautical miles in six minutes and be GPS-guided to its target, allowing extremely precise, relatively low-cost firepower from distances well beyond the reach of most enemies.

The technical director of the railgun project is Roger Ellis, who was detailed to ONR from the Naval Surface Warfare Center at Dahlgren. Ellis had joined Dahlgren's gunnery group after earning his master's degree in mechanical engineering from Virginia Tech. From his point of view, the Navy story surrounding the railgun is one of fits and starts. It goes back at least to the Strategic Defense Initiative days of the Reagan administration during the 1980s.

One popular concept at the time envisioned railguns placed on satellites, able to rain power from above to shoot down enemy ballistic missiles soon after their launch, an idea nicknamed "the Rod from God." Another big effort came from the Army, which in 1985 initiated a program designed to equip tanks with much smaller versions of railguns, mainly for tank-to-tank warfare. Back then the Navy also looked into the possibility of a shipborne railgun. Ships offered more room for the power supply and other associated equipment than tanks. At the same time, a naval gun intended for "indirect fire" at targets well over the horizon required a much more powerful system than a short-range, direct fire tank-to-tank weapon. It just didn't look possible. The Navy put the plan on the back burner, where it was joined by the space-based "Rod from God" idea.

It wasn't until the late 1990s that the picture began to change. The Dahlgren lab where Ellis worked is the historic home of the Navy's guns division. Ellis was doing research into big, sixteen-inch guns in 1997, when the service decided to conduct a feasibility study to take another look at the railgun. The report was hardly encouraging. Relates Ellis, "The answer came back that it takes too much energy: we don't have that much energy on ships we got out there today, and it may not fit."[4] So the service put the technology back on its watch list. As Ellis puts it, "The Navy concluded it wasn't time for the Navy, so we'd just continue to watch the Army."

The railgun had less opportunity to gather dust this time around, as over the next few years conditions changed significantly in a suite of "enabling" areas necessary for the technology to drive forward. First the Navy made a commitment to create all-electric ships. This was originally manifest in the DD-21 destroyer program, later called DD(X) and still later renamed the DDG 1000. Since then the idea has been extended to other ship programs, most notably the new CG(X) cruisers intended to supplant the *Ticonderoga*-class Aegis cruisers. Essential to the electric ship concept, of course, was a powerful source of electric power that was also critical to the railgun. In fact, electric warships are expected to provide eighty megawatts of installed electrical power, more than enough to furnish the fifteen to thirty megawatts necessary to operate railguns. "So for the first time you have a floating power plant," says Ellis. Most of that power would go toward driving the ship, but when the vessel was not steaming from one point to another, he adds, "you've got megawatts of power available for electric weapons. [You can] make not just an electric ship, but an electric warship."

A second enabler came in the form of the advanced projectiles that could constitute the "bullets" of a railgun. These advances were partly the result of a separate ONR program looking into guided munitions for the DD(X), which, like the DDG 1000, will have a 155-millimeter gun system whose shells will be directed by GPS signals. Years of work meant it would finally be possible to fire much more accurate shots from hundreds of miles at sea—just what the railgun doctor ordered.

The third major area of progress, owing mainly to the Army's program, lay in improvements in launcher technology and bore life. Together, these meant it was possible to construct much more stable, long-lasting railgun "barrels" that would withstand repeated use at the tremendous forces needed to fire projectiles. Rounding off the advances in enabling areas were computational improvements that provided algorithms for simulating flight body dynamics and precisely modeling the environment inside the railgun so that designers could maximize its efficiency and design. Says D'Andrea, "We [could] now quickly turn around modeling and analysis."

By 2001 all these advances in the science and technology behind railguns had come together well enough that it now seemed prudent for the Navy to once again revisit the idea of a shipboard system. That November Ellis was asked to help lead the latest reexamination. Joining forces with colleagues at the Naval Sea Systems Command and the Office of Naval Research, the gunnery expert co-organized a railgun workshop at the Institute for Advanced Technology in Austin. The center, part of the University of Texas, served as the Army's center of excellence for railguns. Organizers brought in national and international authorities on everything related to the subject, including experts on launcher systems, projectiles, and pulsed power.

Close to seventy people attended the meeting. Subgroups were formed according to specialty area; Ellis co-chaired the launcher subgroup with the Institute for Advanced Technology's Ian McNabb, one of the world's most eminent figures in railguns. A prime issue the subgroups all considered was whether it was possible to build a large railgun with a muzzle energy of sixty-four megajoules—tank systems, by contrast, were envisioned to operate at about sixteen megajoules— enough power to propel a projectile two-hundred-plus nautical miles. Somewhat to people's surprise, reports Ellis, "The general conclusion was that everybody thought there weren't any insurmountable technology issues."

That conclusion kicked off a new round of studies, several of them prepared for the Center for Naval Analysis, and one published for the Naval Research Advisory Committee in May 2002. These reports essentially confirmed the workshop findings and concluded that it was time for the Navy to take the railgun off the back burner. The enthusiasm caught the attention of Adm. Robert J. Natter, Commander of the U.S. Atlantic Fleet. Natter was on the verge of retirement and wanted to see some progress in railguns before he left the service. He took advantage of a program to help Fleet commanders fund technology trials or demos. The largest railgun facility at the time was at Kirkcudbright (pronounced kir-KOO-bree), Scotland. "How about you go shoot something out there and do it before I retire," is how Ellis sums up the mandate from Natter. "And so that was our charge—go do a demo in less than three months."

Groups at Dahlgren, the Institute for Advanced Technology in Texas, and ONR turned around a preliminary design in one week, then spent another week churning out the final design. "That was exciting," Ellis says dryly of the all-out pace.

By early 2002 the jury-rigged test bed was pronounced ready. Ellis and his colleagues had constructed a launch package that spit out a projectile at 1.3 miles per second, a rate that, if it could be maintained, would traverse 400 miles in about five minutes. A small group of VIPs convened in Kirkcudbright, including Atlantic Fleet Commander Natter and Chief of Naval Research Cohen. It was a fitting place to demonstrate a potentially revolutionary new weapon for the American Navy. John Paul Jones had been born in Arbigland, Scotland, in the stewartry of Kirkcudbright.

For the trial, Natter and Cohen posed for a picture of them loading a projectile into the gun. The picture, later widely distributed, was titled, "How Many Flag Officers Does It Take to Load a Rail Gun?!" Gathering in the control room, the two admirals and a small entourage of others then stood by as the system counted down and a capacitor bank charged up. On the mark, someone pushed a fire button, and a popping noise was heard. "It sounds like a gun, and you see downrange the projectile hitting something and dirt flying, and you say, this is a weapon, this is something real," recounts Ellis.

It had taken the projectile about a second to travel some one thousand meters down range. To the designers' surprise, it had struck with huge force within a couple feet of the target, a feat they replicated during a series of other firing tests. Everyone was enthusiastic, including the brass. Says Ellis, "A lot of people came out of that test series believers."

The successful test indeed spurred interest in the railgun project. Despite the tremendous force of impact, the first trial had showcased a low-powered system, designed to operate at only two megajoules. This was a fraction of the sixty-four megajoules that would be needed in a real shipboard system. ONR followed up by providing additional funding for a new test, raising the bar by requiring planners to show that more power could be trained on a target. For its next test, the railgun was to shoot through three six-inch-thick, reinforced concrete walls that simulated the floors of a building.

In the spring of 2003, roughly a year after the previous trial, the teams again traveled to Kirkcudbright. This time, the system operated at eight megajoules. The upgraded gun worked like a charm. Says Ellis, "The video is pretty impressive because you see the projectile go through one, two, three [walls]. But then it keeps going—and there is all this spaw [dust and debris]. It's pretty dramatic."

A series of issues remained to be addressed before the Navy could think seriously about putting a railgun on a ship. However, based on the successful trials of the past few years, a second Naval Research advisory committee study was soon kicked off. Published in early 2004, it included a basic plan for creating a formal railgun development program. That September Vice Adm. Phillip M. Balisle, head of the Naval Sea Systems Command, was charged by John Young, the Assistant Secretary of the Navy for research, development and acquisition, to establish an executive steering committee to come up with a more detailed structure for such a railgun program. The committee's task included making a specific recommendation about which Navy group should oversee the program as well as diving more deeply into how transition of the weapon system into the Navy should be handled—after all, no ship in existence could accommodate the weapon.

The committee, which included flag officers from NavSea, Chief of Naval Research Cohen, and a couple of others from ONR, met several times over the next year or so. Its final letter of recommendation concluded that because of the high-risk nature, the railgun should be run by ONR in its early stages, not NavSea. Moreover, the group noted that ONR should retain its role as system integrator and coordinator

Thu Jan 31 2008 10:49:53.236 261 S

Employing powerful electromagnetic forces rather than gunpowder, the railgun fires non-explosive projectiles at fantastic velocities. The first photo shows the housing where the projectile is loaded. The second photo shows the projectile in flight during a test shot in January 2008. A shipborne railgun could fire its projectiles at targets far over the horizon. Guided by GPS, they would streak to targets with uncanny precision, relying on the incredible force of impact rather than a warhead to devastate targets as much as 250 nautical miles away, a feat that would extend the current striking reach of naval ships by more than ten times.

John F. Williams/ONR

(not just funder), rather than handing those responsibilities to a commercial contractor, the way it would with a normal program of record. "It really boiled down to the type of money that needed to be spent on it based on the amount of risk," says D'Andrea.

Behind that recommendation, the railgun was selected as a charter INP effort in the fall of 2004. However, funding didn't arrive until the following October, at the start of fiscal year 2006. Some $230 million was allocated for phase 1, which carried the goal of demonstrating by 2011 a thirty-two-megajoule system capable of firing one hundred shots without the launch barrel breaking down.

At ONR the railgun program had existed in a kind of limbo for several years while the executive steering committee was figuring out how to handle it. However, work on the effort had not stopped. As the committee was forming, planners put out BAAs soliciting proposals for building the projectile, launcher, and pulsed power system. With the committee's final recommendation and subsequent formal approval of the program, they used the proposals submitted under the BAAs to quickly get contracts awarded. ONR even held a caucus day to acquaint contracting partners with each other and representatives of NavSea. Admiral Cohen couldn't make it, but he videotaped a message that made it clear how important the effort was to ONR.

The caucus day helped jumpstart the program, according to Ellis and D'Andrea. Boeing and Draper Laboratory took the lead on projectile development. BAE Systems and General Atomics were contracted to oversee development of the launcher and containment systems. These four major contractors in turn teamed up with a variety of other firms as well as with the Naval Research Laboratory.

Code 35's job was to integrate all this work. In September 2005, as the funding started, Roger Ellis was detailed to the organization from Dahlgren to formally assume the technical director role. His first major objective was a new test in Kirkcudbright in which the gun was to fire through a series of six walls. The trial, which took place in February 2006, was specially designed to show the Marine Corps the power of the railgun to provide precision fire support for land-based operations. It wasn't quite as dramatic as the second test because this time the planners had modeled the demo ahead of time and knew what to expect. Still, when the projectile ripped through the barriers, everyone in the control room applauded. "We were all excited," says Ellis.

Shortly after this third test, D'Andrea took over as program manager. The first program head had been Roger McGinnis, a Navy captain. It was not until the spring of 2006, after McGinnis changed roles to become the director of innovation overseeing all the INP efforts, that D'Andrea took the reins. She assumed the lead role from John Kinsler, who had been serving as acting program manager since McGinnis' departure.

The latest test was the last in Kirkcudbright. Ellis and his colleagues began building up a test capability at Dahlgren, closer to home and where the railgun could be better tested for possible Navy applications. D'Andrea was disappointed that she would not get to oversee a trial in Scotland. Jokes she, "I am a golfer, so that was hard for me to do."

One of D'Andrea's first tasks was to meet with new Chief of Naval Research Landay. The ONR leader, an engineer himself, wanted her to lay the groundwork for the smoothest-possible transition of the railgun to the acquisition community—if indeed the weapon ever progressed that far. With a typical basic research program, ONR wouldn't worry much about acquisition matters. But because the INPs were funded with applied research money and targeted at filling specific capability gaps, the goal was to facilitate any future handoff by preparing strategic planning and test documents that spelled out specific project milestones as well as the technologies that needed to be available at each stage.

Normally, the acquisitions community would carry out many of these steps at a later stage of a project's development. But D'Andrea worked with an acquisitions deputy stationed at ONR to create a "lighter" version of a full-on plan. As a result, she notes, the railgun project is more structured than traditional high-risk efforts, planned with transition in mind. "We're trying to eliminate the Valley of Death by putting acquisition-like planning into our basic and advanced research," she asserts. D'Andrea notes that if the effort proved fruitful, the railgun procedure would provide a basis for other INP programs. Says she, "We are setting the template for how INPs will be run."

Over much of the next six months, while D'Andrea worked on transition and acquisition planning, Ellis and a group at Dahlgren performed a series of readiness reviews for the new test bed. The U.S. facility would not be nearly as elaborate as its counterpart in Scotland, and the tests wouldn't be as dramatic. At Kirkcudbright, the railgun had been shot across several hundred yards at targets positioned at the side of a mountain. The "range" at Dahlgren consisted of a railroad car inside a cement and rebar tunnel where the gun sat. The weapon then shot across a short open gap into another railroad car filled with sand. Says D'Andrea, "It's like a catcher's mitt for a baseball game, only it's for a lot of energy."

Finally, on September 30, 2006, the last day of the fiscal year, the facility was approved for testing. Just two days later, the first official trial took place, the one concluding in the "Railgun! Hoorah!" cheers. The initial test shots were fired with a muzzle energy of roughly eight megajoules, the same level of power as at Kirkcudbright. More trials took place throughout the year as the group focused on multishot demos on the same pair of rails.

In January 2007 the facility was formally dedicated at a ribbon-cutting ceremony. By then the railgun had won the praise of many beyond the core group. "It's pretty amazing capability," asserted Capt. Joseph McGettigan, commander of the Dahlgren facility. "The biggest thing," he added, "is it's real, not just something on the drawing board."

Chief of Naval Research William Landay also praised the rapid drive to create a working system: "A year ago, this was [just] a good idea we all wanted to pursue."

———————●———————

With some significant successes to point to, D'Andrea planned to up the ante significantly over the next year, with the goal of testing a twelve-megajoule system in early 2008. That would be about the equivalent to a five-inch gun on a Navy ship and would set a new benchmark for railgun power. She predicted, "We will take the world record in muzzle energy launch in the first quarter of '08."

As D'Andrea and Ellis plowed toward an ever-more-powerful and effective system, however, they identified four core technical challenges to the railgun effort. The first involved the interior of the barrel—extending the launcher life. Next in line were developing the projectile itself and the pulse power supply that would drive the gun. Finally came the daunting challenge of integrating a completely new system onto a Navy ship.

Small groups of experts and stakeholders called interdisciplinary planning teams, or IPTs, were set up to plan how to tackle each of those four areas. However, the primary phase 1 focus was on extending the life of the bore barrel. For one thing, a variety of groups inside the Navy and elsewhere were looking at the other areas. The pulsed power system, for instance, was integral to development of the electric ship and therefore constituted a major area of focus for a number of Navy R&D projects. But no one was focusing on the launcher system needed for Navy railguns.

To pursue this goal, D'Andrea's team used a laser mapper to create an elaborate schematic of the interior bore of the barrel after it has been fired, studying the effects of multiple shots on rails and bores made of different materials. The idea was to get detailed information about what happens in the rails in order to improve the design so that the barrel could handle repeated firings at high energies before needing to be replaced. Extending barrel life was essential before a railgun could be put on a ship, where it must be capable of repeated use over months, if not years, of duty. Employing a favorite catchphrase, D'Andrea said the goal is to "get that risk retired." She added, "We've kind of shown that we can punch through most of the walls."

One of the core issues the group studied was the interaction between the armature and the rail itself. Said D'Andrea, "That is where the challenge is from an interior gun perspective." The Naval Research Laboratory took the lead on post-shot rail analysis, putting together a team that she described as "twenty-one of NRL's best materials and plasma physicists."

Another key area of concern was the containment—the wrapping around the barrel that contains the tremendous repulsive forces generated by firing the gun. Composite materials and fibers have advanced so far in recent years, says D'Andrea, that "we believe we can accomplish that now because of advanced materials."

The launcher barrel initially used at Dahlgren was donated by the Army, a refurbished leftover from the service's 1980s studies. In early 2007 General Atomics and BAE were each developing advanced containment launchers made of lightweight, super-strong composite materials more like those that would be employed on a ship. These two larger launchers, each capable of operating at up to thirty-two megajoules, were scheduled for delivery that summer.

The next major goal, though, was to fire a gun operating at sixteen megajoules in early 2008. Along the way D'Andrea's team would be testing different rail materials and configurations, including lubricant-type materials to help the armature slide along the rail. Based on the outcome of those trials and all the related work, a "go/no-go" decision was set for August 2009, essentially three years into the program.[5]

One issue that needed to be addressed was directing the projectile to a target. When it moves out of the atmosphere, it would basically be unguided. D'Andrea noted that experts estimated the projectiles would reenter the atmosphere about one minute from their targets. "That gives us about fifteen to twenty seconds to do last-minute guidance and navigation updates," she said.

Fred Beach of NavSea, assistant program manager for the project, noted that GPS satellites would issue course-correction information, enabling the projectile to steer itself with movable control flaps or surfaces. "Right now, guns are only as accurate as the targeting of the bore, and now we're talking about two-hundred-plus-mile ranges, so there has to be aerodynamic correction," he said. Both Draper Lab and Boeing were working on that problem. What's more, Beach added, because the high-speed bullet will have to withstand forces of up to 45,000 Gs, all the onboard electronics would have to be super-hardened.

——————●——————

If the railgun development stayed on track, what's called initial operational capability of a sixty-four-megajoule weapon would probably occur between 2020 and 2025, says D'Andrea. That would no doubt be after she and Ellis have retired.

D'Andrea was cautiously optimistic about the chances. The necessary funding has been made available, and a clear path to success has been identified, she said. "We think that we have the right team, and it's the right time to make this game-changer."

As of the spring of 2007 there seemed to be little, if any, disagreement within the Navy or Marine Corps. At one point, Lt. Gen. Edward Hanlon Jr., former commanding general of the Marine Corps Combat Development Command, weighed in with a letter to Navy officials that listed what he would like to see in future science and technology advances: the railgun was prominent on the list.

It's little wonder. The railgun promises a highly effective and inexpensive means of striking distant fixed targets, at least in some cases offering an attractive alternative to sending airplanes to bomb enemy installations and infrastructure—putting pilots at risk and increasing operational costs. Their existence could free planes to strike at moving targets that require a "man in the loop."

The Marines and Navy also love the railgun because it should be able to support multiple operations, spanning everything from conventional warfare to clandestine Special Forces operations to suppressing air defenses and the global war on terror. What's more, it promises to provide "time-critical strike" in any weather, with little propellant, and no unexploded ordnance issues to worry about on board ships.

D'Andrea is unabashed in her enthusiasm: "It completely transforms how we fight."

INTERVIEWS

Vice Adm. Albert J. Baciocco Jr., USN (Ret.)............March 3, 2005
Susan Bales ....February 9, 2005
Roshdy Barsoum.............. February 9, 2006; December 14, 2006
James Blesse ....January 19, 2006
Irv Blickstein......................................January 11, 2007
Will Brown ....January 19, 2006
Gerald Cann................... September 5, 2006; October 6, 2006
Richard T. Carlin ....January 14, 2005
Capt. David H. Cazares ....January 14, 2005
Rear Adm. Jay Cohen, USN (Ret.)..................March 22, 2005;
                        May 25, 26, 2005; December 15, 2005;
                                            December 27, 2006
Timothy Coffey..................January 18, 2006; January 25, 2007
James Colvard.............. September 1, 2006; September 21, 2006
David Comis...July 31, 2006
Kelly Cooper ....December 8, 2006
Thomas Curtin ..... September 18, 2006 at ONR (with Corinna Wu);
                        December 18, 2006 (with Corinna Wu)
Elizabeth D'Andrea ....August 3, 2006; April 9, 2007
James DeCorpo........... November 21, 2005; September 21, 2006
Betsy DeLong............. December 11, 2006 (with Jennifer Boyce);
                        March 6, 2007; March 16, 2007
Michael B. Deitchman............................... May 26, 2005
Maj. Gen. Timothy E. Donovan, USMC (Ret.) ....November 1, 2006
Michael Dunaway..........December 1, 6, 2006 (with Kelly Grieco);
                        January 17, 2007; February 1, 2007
Roger Ellis.............................August 3, 2006; April 9, 2007
Larrie Ferreiro.................................. December 20, 2006
Vice Adm. Paul Gaffney, USN (Ret.) ....July 21, 2005; August 9, 2006
Paul A. Gido...................... January 14, 2005; January 5, 2007
Judas Goldwasser ....May 22, 2006 (with Jessica Karnis)

Patricia Gruber . . . . .September 7, 2006
Harold E. Guard. . . . . January 14, 2005
Georgia Harrigan . . . . December 19, 2006
Harold Hawkins . . . . December 6, 2006 (with Kelly Grieco);
February 1, 2007
Frank L. Herr. . . . . .January 14, 2005; August 3, 2006;
September 15, 2006 at Office of Naval Research
(with Corinna Wu); December 7, 2007
(phone interview with Corinna Wu)
Ashley Johnson . . . . .December 7, 2006
Bobby R. Junker . . . . .January 14, 2005; January 19, 2006
Capt. John Charles Kamp . . . . .February 9, 2005
Robert Kavetsky . . . . September 21, 2006
William Kuperman . . . . November 22, 2006
(phone interview with Corinna Wu)
Vice Adm. William Landay III, USN . . . . .September 7, 2006;
February 1, 2007
Joseph P. Lawrence . . . . February 9, 2005; September 7, 2006
Paul Lowell. . . . . .February 10, 2005
Geoff Main . . . . December 7, 2006; January 29, 2007
Lee Mastrioanni. . . . . .December 7, 2006
James McMains . . . . .February 14, 2007; February 27, 2007
Genie McBurnett . . . . September 12, 2006
Rear Adm. William C. Miller, USN (Ret.) . . . . .May 6, 2005,
September 1, 2006
John Montgomery . . . . April 13, 2005
Charles R. Paoletti. . . . .September 6, 2006
Rear Adm. Marc Pelaez, USN (Ret.). . . . . April 15, 2005;
September 23, 2006
F. Michael Pestorius. . . . . December 14, 2006
Robert Pohanka. . . . . January 14, 2005
Lil Ramirez . . . . .February 10, 2005
Greg Reed. . . . . December 13, 2006; April 9, 2007
Fred Saalfeld. . . . . .April 4, 2005; January 20, 2006; August 30, 2006;
September 21, 2006; October 17, 2006)

Mike Sarcione................undated interview, around March 2007
(conducted by Jennifer Boyce)
Henrik Schmidt...............November 15, 2006 (phone interview
with Corinna Wu)
Capt. Dave Schubert............April 13, 2005; December 22, 2006
Philip Selwyn................................ September 22, 2006
Thomas J. Singleton............................December 7, 2006
George W. Solhan................August 1, 2006; February 2, 2007
Maribel Soto....................... February 10, 2005; May 2, 2005
Capt. Michael Stabile ....January 14, 2005
Gregory Tavik..........March 6, 2007 (conducted by Jennifer Boyce)
Mark Thomas.. May 31, 2005
Lynn M. Torres................................January 14, 2005
Brig. Gen. Thomas D. Waldhauser, USMC.............May 4, 2005
Starnes E. Walker............... February 9, 2005; January 19, 2006
Max Yoder.......................January 25, 2007; March 3, 2007
(conducted by Jennifer Boyce)

NOTES

Chapter 1: The Office of Naval Relevance

1. The account of the attack on the USS *Cole*, Navy designation DDG-67, is compiled chiefly from the *9/11 Commission Report* and the *DoD USS Cole Commission Report: Executive Summary*. Also helpful are Thomas and Squassoni, "Desperate Hours"; Burns, "Navy Chief Backs USS *Cole* Captain"; Gilmore, "Cohen Absolves USS *Cole* Skipper, Crew"; McIntyre, "Sources: Report Finds Cole Commander"; Plante, "Revised Timeline Raises New Questions"; and Radgers and Frieden, "U.S. Official Sees Similarities."

2. Thomas and Squassoni, "Desperate Hours."

3. Ibid.

4. The accounts of Rear Adm. Jay Cohen come from multiple interviews and follow-up correspondence with Cohen.

5. Cohen interview, December 27, 2006.

6. Barsoum's account and all quotes come from Barsoum interviews, February 9, 2006, and December 14, 2006.

7. The account of the exchange between Cohen and Rutan comes from Cohen interview, December 27, 2006.

8. The outcome of Rutan's effort is from Cohen interviews, verified through multiple e-mail correspondences with Rutan and his staff.

9. The Khobar Towers attack is widely documented in news accounts. A good supporting document is the U.S. indictment against thirteen named and one unnamed alleged coconspirators (*United States District Court, Eastern District of Virginia, Alexandria Division, United States of America v. Ahmed Al-Mughassil et al.*, June 2001). It can be found here, among other places: http://www.pbs.org/newshour/updates/june01/khobar.pdf. See also Graham, "Bomb Kills 23."

10. IED statistics from the Iraq Coalition Casualty Count: www.icasualties.org.

11. Prime sources for ONR history are listed in the notes to chapter 2. A good resource for the Bird Dogs and their legacy is Old,

"Evolution of ONR," as well as the classic by Dan Kevles, *The Physicists*.

12. For budget sources, a wide variety of material is available from each organization involved. For a good overview of science and technology expenditures at this time, see National Science Board, *Science and Engineering Indicators*, especially tables 4-11 and 4-12.

13. Tim Coffey views and quotes are from interviews with Coffey, January 18, 2006, and January 25, 2007.

14. For more on the legacy of tension between ONR civilian and military personnel, see Sapolsky, *Science and the Navy*.

Chapter 2: The Bird Dogs and Admiral Bowen

1. Nimitz quotes and the entire account of his view of the future Navy from Nimitz, "The Post-War Navy."

2. Kevles, *The Physicists*, 353.

3. Old, "Evolution of ONR."

4. The account of the Bird Dogs is drawn chiefly from Old, "Evolution of ONR"; Kevles, *The Physicists*, 353–54; and Sapolsky, *Science and the Navy*, 9–20. All remaining quotations are from Old, "Evolution of ONR."

5. In June 1940, before the United States entered the war and a year before the OSRD's creation, Vannevar Bush had convinced President Franklin Roosevelt to form the National Defense Research Committee, which did much of the same job of coordinating civilian research for the war effort. The new OSRD subsumed the NDRC, which continued with its work.

6. Furer background is from Kevles, *The Physicists*, 313; and Sapolsky, *Science and the Navy*, 20.

7. The Navy had been rocked by infringement claims after World War I and was hoping to preempt a repeat. Admiral Bowen had been put in charge of the patent office to give him a foot in the door in planning postwar research: he was primed to take over the newly formed ORI, including the Naval Research Laboratory, which he had directed for much of the war. See Sapolsky, *Science and the Navy*, 23 and following.

8. The account of Harold Bowen is drawn chiefly from Old, "Evolution of ONR"; and Sapolsky, *Science and the Navy*, 21 and following. See also Kevles, *The Physicists*, 354 and following; and Amato, *Pushing the Horizon*, 158–61.

9. Sapolsky, *Science and the Navy*, 25.

10. Ibid., 26.

11. Old, "Evolution of ONR," 35.

12. For details on how the battle to create the NSF played out, see Kevles, *The Physicists*, 356 and following. Also see Sapolsky, *Science and the Navy*, 37 and following, 118–19.

13. Old, "Evolution of ONR."

14. Sapolsky, *Science and the Navy*, 44.

15. Ibid., 45.

16. Most figures from Pfeiffer (1949). See also Kevles, *The Physicists*, 355–64.

17. Sapolsky, *Science and the Navy*, 38.

18. For a good look at ONR and its relations with the newly forming NSF, see ibid., 53 and following. As the new science foundation looked more and more as if it would become reality, some ONR officials, including Waterman, resisted its creation, concerned that the new agency would usurp their own role. However, once NSF was created, ONR officials stated that the new foundation was "almost part of the family" rather than a rival organization. ONR argued that if it did not continue to invest in basic research after NSF's creation, the Navy would be unable to profit from basic research, and the scientific community would no longer consider military needs in their research.

19. Highlights from ONR's various anniversaries from ONR, "50th Anniversary." ONR's sixtieth anniversary was celebrated as this book was being written.

Chapter 3: Urge to Merge

1. The bulk of this chapter, the scenes described, quotes, and emotions, stem from a series of personal interviews with the key figures, often supplemented by follow-up calls and e-mails.

2. Miller interview, May 6, 2005. All other quotes from Miller in this chapter are from this interview and a follow-up on September 1, 2006.

3. At the time, the decision maker in this process was known as O98, a three-star position. Later, the position was changed to O91 and became a two-star position—the Chief of Naval Research. More on this in chapter 5.

4. When NavMat dissolved, another change took place affecting ONR. All the Navy labs as well as the ONT were brought under the ONR umbrella. This arrangement did not last long, however. The huge lab organization threatened to swamp ONR, and it proved too difficult to manage everything under one roof. The central structure was dismantled, and control of the various labs was moved to the systems commands they served.

5. Cann interview, September 5, 2006. All background and quotes about Cann come from this interview, another on October 6, 2006, and follow-up correspondence.

6. About the time Cann took the reins, Navy aviation's worst procurement program debacle in history, involving the next-generation A-12 stealth fighter, took center stage and consumed much of his time. When the procurement problems arose, new defense secretary Dick Cheney abruptly canceled the entire program, leading to lawsuits against the government by the two main contractors, McDonnell Douglas and General Dynamics. "I spent the next ten years involved in the litigation on that," Cann says. Major submarine and shipbuilding headaches surfaced as well. "My whole life was totally consumed by shipbuilding and aircraft," he notes.

7. Navy's lab structure and consolidation, from Cann interviews, McBurnett interview, September 12, 2006. Also see Meyer et al., "Early Evolution"; Space and Naval Warfare Systems Center, "SSC San Diego Command," 11; and SPAWAR website, http://www .spawar.navy.mil/sandiego. The lab closure was itself a convoluted process. McBurnett formed the RDT&E Facilities Consolidation Working Group, a seven-person committee that included several of the major stakeholders involved in this envisioned consolidation.

They included top deputies from the Navy's systems commands, director of Naval Laboratories Jerry Schieffer, a representative from the Chief of Naval Operations' staff, and the new head of the Office of Naval Research, Rear Adm. William Miller, who had only taken the reins that July. The committee's task was about 85 percent done when a monkey wrench appeared in the form of Public Law 101-510, the Base Closure and Realignment Act of 1990, otherwise known as BRAC. Congress had been working on this quarrelsome issue for years. But while one relatively minor round of base consolidations had happened in the late 1980s, procedural requirements had effectively deadlocked the process. The new law set out a much more workable process by which bases could be closed or realigned. However, it also presented a challenge for McBurnett's committee, which was working on many of the same issues, but on a separate track. That forced the committee back to the drawing board to rework its recommendations to make them part of base closure, which they ultimately became.

8. In 1990 there were two categories of 6.3 funding, 6.3a and 6.3b. The former, for advanced technology development funds for such things as proof of concept demonstrations, is now called 6.3. The latter, for far more acquisition-oriented advanced component development and prototyping, became category 6.4.

9. DeCorpo interview, September 21, 2006. All DeCorpo quotes and background in this chapter are from the September 21, 2006, interview, a previous one on November 21, 2005, and follow-up correspondence.

10. In addition to DeCorpo interviews cited previously, the Selwyn interview, September 22, 2006, was also important to putting this picture together.

11. Gaffney interview, July 21, 2005.

12. This and the subsequent quote from the Project Reliance report come from presidential directive paper: "Status of Federal Laboratory Reforms," http://www.fas.org/irp/offdocs/pdd5status .html#V, appendix B; "OSTP Questions and DOD Answers," http://www.fas.org/irp/offdocs/pdd5status-b.html.

13. For Biddle accusations and controversy around the case, Miller interviews; Gross, "Stanford Chief Quits"; Desalma, "In the Center of the Storm"; and Stanford University News Service, "Test of President."

14. Pelaez interview, September 23, 2006. Subsequent quotes are also from this interview and one conducted on April 15, 2005.

15. Selwyn interview, September 22, 2006. Subsequent quotes are also from this interview.

16. Saalfeld interview, January 20, 2006.

17. Ibid., August 30, 2006.

Chapter 4: The New ONR

1. Saalfeld interview, January 20, 2006. Subsequent quotes are also from this interview and one conducted on August 30, 2006.

2. Secretary Garrett had already left office in July 1992 and was replaced that October by Sean O'Keefe, who would serve less than four months. It took until the following fall to find a replacement for Cann as ASN RDA. The choice was Nora Slatkin, reportedly a Diet Coke–swilling workaholic whose all-out style earned her the nickname with some in the Navy of "Tora Tora Nora." She stayed in the office until late 1995, throughout most of Pelaez's tour. She was replaced by John W. Douglass, who served from the fall of 1995 until the fall of 1998.

3. This chapter relies heavily on detailed interviews with Pelaez, Miller, Cann, and Saalfeld as well as some follow-up e-mail correspondence. All quotes and descriptions about the actions of these individuals come from these interviews (see interview list), unless otherwise noted.

4. Coffey interview, January 18, 2006. Additional Coffey quotes and other material in this chapter are from this interview, another one conducted on January 25, 2007, and follow-up correspondence.

5. DeCorpo quotes and background from DeCorpo interviews, November 21, 2005, September 21, 2006, and follow-up correspondence.

6. Selwyn interview, September 22, 2006.

7. Through these meetings it was agreed that the Air Force Office of Scientific Research, which funded basic research for that service, would move in adjacent to ONR. Pelaez considered collocation with this much smaller office one more step to building better interaction between the services and finding new ways to get the most from the Defense Department's science dollars.

8. For one account of Boorda's suicide, see "Navy's Top Officer Dies of Gunshot, Apparently Self-inflicted," *CNN*, May 16, 1996, http://www.cnn.com/US/9605/16/boorda.6p/.

9. Hamilton, "DARPA."

Chapter 5: The Valley of Death

1. Donovan interview, November 1, 2006. All quotes from Donovan, and his general perspective, are taken from this interview.

2. This chapter is written chiefly from extensive interviews with the major players, including Gaffney and Saalfeld, supported by follow-up correspondence. Whenever a quote, impression, or emotion is attributed to them, it is because that is what they represented saying, perceiving, or feeling. Interviews with Gaffney took place on July 21, 2005, and August 9, 2006. Saalfeld was interviewed on April 4, 2005; January 20, 2006; August 30, 2006; September 21, 2006; and October 17, 2006.

3. Singleton interview, December 7, 2006. Other quotes from Singleton are also from this session.

4. This is supported by both the Singleton interview and the Gido interview, January 5, 2007.

5. Account from interviews with Gaffney, Singleton, and Donovan, and from the "Memorandum for the Record: Flag Level Meeting of 24 May 1999 to Discuss Issues Related/Impacting the USMC/ ONR S&T Integration," Document given to the author.

6. For more on WARNET and battlefield data, see Thompson, "'Unplugged' Battlefield"; Gourley, "Expanding the Littoral Battlespace"; Yuhas, "Enabling a Transformation"; and GlobalSecurity .org, "Kernel Blitz," http://www.globalsecurity.org/military/ops/ kernel-blitz.htm.

7. Gates, *Business @ the Speed of Thought*, 380.
8. See notes 5 and 6.
9. Donovan interview; Cohen, "Statement."
10. DeCorpo interview, November 21, 2005.
11. For a look at the balanced portfolio strategy from the horse's mouth, so to speak, see Gaffney, Saalfeld, and Petrik, "Science and Technology." Most of the following discussion, including the description of FNCs, is drawn from this paper, supplemented by comments from Gaffney and Saalfeld. See also ONR paper, "Future Naval Capabilities."
12. This and subsequent quotes from her are from Soto interview, February 10, 2005.
13. This and subsequent quotes from Coffey are taken from my interview with Coffey, January 18, 2006.

Chapter 6: Out of the Box

1. The story of the exchange between England and Cohen comes from Cohen. All Cohen's quotes and actions in this chapter, unless otherwise noted, come from a series of interviews conducted on March 22, 2005; May 25, 26, 2005; December 15, 2005; and December 27, 2006, and follow-up correspondence with him. See also Cohen's U.S. Navy biography: http://www.navy.mil/navydata/bios/navybio.asp?bioID=74.
2. The description of people's perceptions of Cohen are gleaned from numerous interviews with ONR personnel and the admiral himself.
3. Saalfeld interview, date uncertain, possibly September 21, 2006.
4. The description of management changes in the wake of Saalfeld's departure was pieced together from interviews with Cohen, Saalfeld, DeCorpo, Lowell, Soto, and Gido (see interviews list for dates of all these interviews).
5. "Public Law 588: To Establish an Office of Naval Research in the Department of the Navy." *Council on Foreign Relations*, http://www.cfr.org/defensehomeland-security/public-law-588-establish-office-naval-research-department-navy/p20982.

6. Quoted in an Office of Naval Research Science & Technology Overview, PowerPoint presentation prepared by ONR, dated October 2005.

7. Buderi, *Engines of Tomorrow*, 121.

8. Blesse interview, January 19, 2006, with supporting documents from ONR.

9. Much material exists on Innovative Naval Prototypes in the form of various ONR documents. I relied on these but also on widespread interviews with ONR staff (Lawrence, Walker, and Cohen) and a McGinnis PowerPoint overview to the subject, "Innovative Naval Prototypes Overview," dated July 2006.

10. Junker interview, January 19, 2006.

11. The quote is from *Naval Power 21* (http://www.navy.mil/navydata/ people/secnav/england/navpow21.pdf). However, the pillars were actually laid out in a companion initiative called *Sea Power 21* (http:// www.navy.mil/navydata/cno/proceedings.html). The Marines, for their part, issued *Marine Corps Strategy 21* (https://www.mccdc. usmc.mil/futures/Concepts%20Library.htm).

12. Cooper interview, December 8, 2006.

13. Main interview, December 7, 2006

Chapter 7: War Footing

1. Description of the event is taken from interviews with Cohen, Barsoum, Schubert, and Mastrioanni (see interviews list for dates). All quotes are directly from those quoted.

2. The patents were filed under International Application Number: Pct/US2005/01394; and International Publication Number: WO2005103363A2.

3. "Pentagon to Use New Bomb on Afghan Cave," *CNN.com*, December 23, 2001, http://edition.cnn.com/2001/US/12/22/ ret.new.weapon/index.html. Other details on thermobarics come from Duong e-mail; Goldwasser and Cohen interviews; Karnis, "Militarization of Science"; and "Thermobarics—It All Began with Basic Research," *STARLINK*, Autumn 2005. Concerns have been raised that the thermobaric bomb may violate the 1949 Geneva

Convention because the incineration produced could burn individuals to death. The U.S. military has denied that thermobaric weapons violate the convention.

4. Cohen interviews, Cohen, "Statement." See also England, "Remarks by the Honorable Gordon England."

5. Cohen and Guard interviews; Michael Given e-mail correspondence; Z-Medica press kit, http://www.z-medica.com/.

6. IED figures and details are from www.icasualties.org; Miles, "DoD Taps Industry."

7. Solhan interview, August 1, 2006. All other quotes and main details about Solhan and his operation come from this session and an interview of February 2, 2007.

8. Details on the VCNR position and Cohen's creation of the new ONR department around Marine Corps issues come chiefly from Gido and Cohen interviews, supplemented by Solhan and Waldhauser interviews.

9. Also in 2005 Cohen restructured the FNC program to align with *Naval Power 21* pillars.

10. Coffey interview, January 18, 2006.

11. Junker interview, January 14, 2005.

12. This and other DeCorpo quotes from interview of September 21, 2006.

Chapter 8: Combating Terrorism

1. The story of Lima company is from Knickmeyer, "Demise of a Hard-Fighting Squad"; and "14 More Marines from Ohio Unit Die in Iraq," *Associated Press*, August 4, 2005, http://www.nbcnews.com/id/8797271/ns/world_news-mideast_n_africa/t/more-marines-ohio-unit-die-iraq/#.UWhhQcpQbHU.

2. Johnson interview, December 7, 2006.

3. This and all Solhan quotes are from interview of February 2, 2007.

4. The story of the division comes primarily from interviews with McMains, Solhan, and Main (see interviews list for all dates).

5. Main interview, December 7, 2006. All other Main quotes in this chapter are from this interview or a follow-up conducted on January 29, 2007.

6. McMains interview, February 14, 2007. All other quotes from McMains are from this interview or one conducted on February 27, 2007.

Chapter 9: New Eye for the New Navy

1. Tavik interview, March 6, 2007. All other quotes from Tavik are from this interview, conducted by Jennifer Boyce.
2. Sarcione interview, undated. All other quotes from Sarcione are from this interview, conducted by Jennifer Boyce.
3. Yoder interview, January 25, 2007. All other quotes from Yoder in this chapter are from this interview, conducted by the author, or a follow-up conducted on March 3, 2007, by Jennifer Boyce. See also Kemerley, Wallace, and Yoder, "Impact of Wide Bandgap Microwave Devices"; and a PowerPoint presentation by William Gottwald, "An Overview of the Advance Multifunction RF Concept (AMRFC) Test-Bed," April 14, 2004.
4. E-mail from Bobby Junker, May 14, 2013.
5. Lubard was part of a rapid succession of technical directors who replaced Fred Saalfeld when he retired in 2002. He would stay on the job less than a year.
6. DeLong interview, December 11, 2006 (conducted by Jennifer Boyce). All quotes from DeLong are from this interview or follow-up interviews conducted on March 6, 2007, and March 16, 2007, as well as some e-mail correspondence.
7. At the time of this writing, this was another proposed new class of vessel. These super-fast, multimission ships were intended to operate in littoral waters within a few hundred miles of shore as a complement to the DD(X) and CG(X).
8. Junker interview, January 14, 2005. All Junker quotes in this chapter are from this interview.
9. I rely chiefly on "Electric Warships & Combat Vehicles," an undated publication by the Office of Naval Research.

Chapter 10: Persistent Littoral Undersea Surveillance

1. This chapter was reported by Corinna Wu, who wrote the initial chapter draft. Much of the material is taken from interviews with

the key actors. See also Eriksen, et al., "Seaglider"; "$27.7M to Develop PLUSNET Undersea Sensor Network," *Defense Industry Daily*, May 10, 2005, https://www.defenseindustrydaily.com/277m-to-develop-plusnet-undersea-sensor-network-0486/; "Persistent Littoral Undersea Surveillance," *FedBizOpps/Commerce Business Daily*, April 26, 2004; Stewart and Pavlos, "Means to Networked Persistent Undersea Surveillance"; Huergo and Fulton-Bennett, "Schools of Undersea Robots"; Riordan, "Undersea Robots"; and "Underwater Robots Work Together without Human Input," *Science Daily*, August 1, 2006. http://www.sciencedaily.com/releases/2006/08/060801183221.htm.

2. Curtin interview, September 18, 2006 (conducted by Corinna Wu). All quotes and attributions from Curtin are from this interview.

3. Adm. Jay Cohen loves to tell the story of when PLUS was first brought to him. At the time, he says, it was called persistent undersea surveillance. He rejected that name out of hand. "There's no point in me selling a program called PUS," he told the presenters. "But if you'd consider 'littoral' I think you've got a winner."

4. Karnis, "Militarization of Science."

5. Herr interview, undated. Multiple interviews were conducted with Herr, and all quotes and other attributions in this chapter were culled from them. See interviews list for details of interview dates.

6. Schmidt interview, November 15, 2006 (with Corinna Wu). All Schmidt attributions in this chapter are from this interview.

7. Kuperman interview, November 22, 2006 (phone interview with Corinna Wu). All Kuperman material and attributions in this chapter are taken from this interview.

Chapter 11: T-Craft

1. Cooper interview, December 8, 2006. All quotes and other material attributed to Cooper are from this interview unless otherwise noted.

2. At the time described in this writing, the group was called N-75.

3. Reed interview, December 13, 2006. All quotes and other material attributed to Reed are from this interview and a follow-up conducted on April 9, 2007.

4. Background on future sea-basing plans, MLPs and MPF(F), is from Hilburn,"The 'Floating Beach'"; and Boensel and Schrady, "JELO."

Chapter 12: The Virtual Warfighter

1. Many sources have examined Vieques. I cite some specific references later in this chapter, but some general sources that I used include Becker, "Senate Legislation"; Marino, "Death Leads Puerto Rico"; Marino, "Emboldened Protesters"; Marino, "Navy Begins Last Live-Fire"; Navarro, "Uproar against Navy War Games"; O'Rourke, "Vieques, Puerto Rico Naval Training Range"; Miller and Walsh, "Navy Bombing of Vieques"; Rabin, "Vieques"; "History of the Navy in Vieques," http://www.vieques-island.com/navy/; Hernandez, "Both Sides Attack Bush Plan"; and Clark, "Memorandum for Secretary of the Navy."

2. Marino, "Death Leads Puerto Rico."

3. Quoted in Suro, "When Navy Spots Vieques."

4. Allen and Pressley, "Puerto Rico Bombing."

5. England, ""Remarks by the Honorable Gordon England."

6. My description of VAST comes from interviews with the key managers in ONR, including Guard, Cohen, Hawkins, and Dunaway. I rely also on Chisholm, "Vast Improvement"; Atlantic Fleet Public Affairs, "Navy and Air Force Hit Virtual Bull's Eye"; Tiron, "Naval Simulators"; Yardley et al., "Can Under Way Training Be Reduced"; and Zacharias, "VAST Offers Sailors."

7. Guard interview, January 14, 2005. All quotes and material from Guard are from this interview.

8. Hawkins interview, December 6, 2006 (with Kelly Grieco). All quotes and material from Hawkins are from this interview and a follow-up conducted on February 1, 2007.

9. Dunaway interview, January 17, 2007. Multiple interviews were conducted with Dunaway, all contributing to this chapter: December 1 and 6, 2006 (with Kelly Grieco); January 17, 2007; and February 1, 2007.

10. For background on Navy simulation development, see Silberman, "The War Room"; and U.S. Congress, Office of Technology Assessment, *Virtual Reality*.

11. U.S. Congress, Office of Technology Assessment, *Virtual Reality*.

12. As of early 2007 the Navy planned a fleet of 55 LCS ships, with four early versions being built by two teams—one managed by Lockheed Martin and one by General Dynamics. However, that January the Navy ordered a halt to work on the second Lockheed Martin ship because of large cost overruns with its first ship. The status of the ships and program was unclear when this book was written.

Chapter 13: The Electromagnetic Railgun

1. The description of the railgun test is drawn from a video of the test.

2. The story of the railgun development comes largely from interviews with the key participants, D'Andrea and Ellis.

3. D'Andrea interview, April 9, 2007. All attributions to D'Andrea are from this interview and one conducted on August 3, 2006.

4. Ellis interview, April 9, 2007. All attributions to Ellis are from this interview and one conducted on August 3, 2006.

5. Although the milestones described here extended past the period covered in this book, the railgun team had a successful go/no-go in 2009 and achieved a thirty-two megajoule demonstration in 2011. Phase II, from 2012–17, focuses on operation at firing rates of up to ten rounds per minute and involves testing the projectile and barrel and firing at mid-range distances of roughly one hundred nautical miles. These tests would take place at large ranges such as the Yuma Proving Ground in Arizona or the White Sands Missile Range in New Mexico. After that would come full-range tests at sea.

BIBLIOGRAPHY

Allen, Mike, and Sue Anne Pressley. "Puerto Rico Bombing to End in 2003; Navy to Seek New Site for Training Exercises," *Washington Post*, June 14, 2001, A1.

Amato, Ivan. *Pushing the Horizon*. Washington DC: Naval Research Laboratory, 1998.

Atlantic Fleet Public Affairs, "Navy and Air Force Hit Virtual Bull's Eye at Sea," Navy *Newsstand*, November 17, 2002, http://www.globalsecurity.org/military/library/news/2002/11/mil-021117-usn01.htm.

Becker, Elizabeth. "Senate Legislation Proposes to Close Puerto Rico Base," *New York Times*, December 16, 1999, A18.

Boensel, Matthew, and David Schrady. "JELO: A Model of Joint Expeditionary Logistics Operations." Naval Postgraduate School, October 2004, http://oai.dtic.mil/oai/oai?&verb=getRecord&metadataPrefix=html&identifier=ADA428078.

Brooks, Harvey. *The Government of Science*. Cambridge, MA: MIT Press, 1968.

Buderi, Robert. *Engines of Tomorrow*. New York: Simon & Schuster, 2000.

———. *The Invention That Changed the World*. New York: Simon & Schuster, 1996.

Burgess, Richard R. "Enemy of the Status Quo." *Seapower*, May 2005.

Burns, Robert. "Navy Chief Backs USS *Cole* Captain." *Associated Press*, January 8, 2001, http://www.apnewsarchive.com/2001/Navy-Chief-Backs-USS-Cole-Captain/id-122d031a44094b3ce212b4584474c7b3.

Cavas, Christopher P. "Rear Adm. Jay Cohen." *Defense News*, October 10, 2005.

Chisholm, Patrick. "A Vast Improvement in Navy Training at Sea," *Military Training Technology Online Archives* 7, no. 8 (December 1, 2002).

Clark, V. E. "Memorandum for Secretary of the Navy from Chief of Naval Operations on the Cessation of Training at Vieques Naval Training Range," December 10, 2002, http://pr.indymedia .org/news/2003/08/88.php?l=en.

Cohen, Jay. "Innovation & Tech Transition: The View from S&T," PowerPoint presentation dated April 7, 2006.

———. "Statement of Rear Admiral Jay M. Cohen, Chief of Naval Research before the Terrorism, Unconventional Threats and Capabilities Subcommittee of the House Armed Services Committee on Defense Science & Technology in Support of the War on Terrorism, Transformation, and Beyond." March 10, 2005, http://www.navy.mil/navydata/testimony/technology/cohen050310.pdf.

Cohen, William S. "Personal Accountability for Force Protection at Khobar Towers." Washington, DC: Department of Defense, July 31, 1997, https://www.fas.org/irp/threat/khobar_dod/report.html.

Council on Economic Priorities. *Star Wars: The Economic Fallout.* Cambridge, MA: Ballinger Publishing Company, 1988.

Department of Defense. *DoD USS Cole Commission Report: Executive Summary.* Washington, DC: U.S. Department of Defense, January 9, 2001, http://www.dod.mil/pubs/cole20010109.html.

Desalma, Anthony. "In the Center of the Storm at Stanford." *New York Times,* May 10, 1991.

"Despite Protests, Navy Resumes Shelling of Puerto Rican Island," *New York Times,* June 26, 2000, A10.

England, Gordon. "Navy Certification on the Discontinuation of Training at Vieques," Letter to Speaker of the House Dennis J. Hastert, January 10, 2003, available at http://pr.indymedia .org/news/2003/08/88.php?l=en.

———. "Remarks by the Honorable Gordon England Secretary of the Navy Naval Institute Warfighter's Symposium, Virginia Beach, Va., September 29, 2004," http://www.navy.mil/navydata/people/secnav/england/speeches/england040929.txt.

————. "Remarks on Vieques." The Pentagon, Arlington, VA, June 15, 2001, http://www.navy.mil/navydata/people/secnav/england/speeches/eng-vieques.txt.

Eriksen, Charles C., T. James Osse, Russell D. Light, Timothy Wen, Thomas W. Lehman, Peter L. Sabin, John W. Ballard, and Andrew M. Chiodi. "Seaglider: A Long-Range Autonomous Underwater Vehicle for Oceanographic Research." *IEEE Journal of Oceanic Engineering* 26 (2001): 424–36.

Eriksen, Charlie, and Peter Rhines. "SG014: Subpolar Atlantic Surveys Davis Strait/Labrador Sea (14) 24 Sep 04." *Glider Information and Navigation Assistant-University of Washington School of Oceanography.* 2005. https://seaglider.ocean.washington.edu/cgi-bin/deployment_summary.cgi?mission_id=5&deployment_id=3&AT=1&starting_dive=1&ending_dive=663&compute=Recompute.

Fargo, Elizabeth A. "ONRG: A History 1946–2005." Manuscript prepared for ONR Global. May 2005.

"14 More Marines from Ohio Unit Die in Iraq," *Associated Press*, August 4, 2005, http://www.nbcnews.com/id/8797271/ns/world_news-mideast_n_africa/t/more-marines-ohio-unit-die-iraq/#.UWhhQcpQbHU.

Gaffney II, Paul G., Fred E. Saalfeld, and John F. Petrik. "Research in a Mission Agency." *Program Manager*, November/December 2000.

————. "Science and Technology from an Investment Point of View." *Program Manager*, September–October 1999.

Gates, Bill, with Collins Hemingway. *Business @ the Speed of Thought.* New York: Warner Books, 1999.

Gilmore, Gerry J. "Cohen Absolves USS *Cole* Skipper, Crew." *American Forces Press Service*, January 22, 2001, http://www.au.af.mil/au/awc/awcgate/dod/n01222001_200101222.html.

Gourley, Scott R. "Expanding the Littoral Battlespace," *Sea Power*, June 1990.

Graham, Bradley. "Bomb Kills 23 Americans at Saudi Base," *Washington Post*, June 26, 1996, A01.

Green, Constance McLaughlin, and Milton Lomask. *Vanguard: A History*. Washington, DC: National Aeronautics and Space Administration, 1970.

Gross, Jane. "Stanford Chief Quits Amid Furor on Use of Federal Money." *New York Times*, July 30, 1991.

Gruber, William H. *Factors in the Transfer of Technology*. Cambridge, MA: MIT Press, 1969.

Hamilton, Charles S. "DARPA—Arsenal Ship Lessons Learned." Distribution statement, December 31, 1997. Available from Defense Acquisition University at https://dap.dau.mil/policy/Documents/Policy/001EB001DOC.doc.

Handler, Philip. "Introduction to the Symposium." In *Science and the Future Navy: A Symposium*, ed. U.S. ONR, 1–2. Washington, DC: National Academy of Sciences, 1977.

Hernandez, Raymond. "Both Sides Attack Bush Plan to Halt Bombing on Vieques," *New York Times*, June 15, 2001, A1.

Hilburn, Matt. "The 'Floating Beach.'" *Navy League of the United States*, June 2006. http://www.navyleague.org/sea_power/jun06-20.php.

Huergo, Jennifer. "Media Advisory: Michael Tinkham Awarded the Fred E. Saalfeld Award for Outstanding Lifetime Achievement in Science." *Office of Naval Research*, April 15, 2005, http://www.onr.navy.mil/en/Media-Center/Press-Releases/2005/Tinkham-Awarded-Fred-Saalfeld-Award.aspx.

Huergo, Jennifer, and Kim Fulton-Bennett. "Schools of Undersea Robots Give Oceanographers New Eyes and Ears in the Sea." *MBARI Press Room*, August 23, 2006, http://www.mbari.org/news/news_releases/2006/mb06.html.

Karnis, Jessica Eve. "Militarization of Science and Mirror Imaging: The Innovation of SOSUS." Cambridge, MA: MIT, 2005.

Kemerley, Robert Tim, H. Bruce Wallace, and Max Yoder, "Impact of Wide Bandgap Microwave Devices on DoD Systems." *Proceedings of the IEEE* 90, no. 6 (June 2002): 1059–64.

Kevles, Daniel J. *The Physicists: the History of a Scientific Community in Modern America*. Cambridge, MA: Harvard University Press, 1987.

Knickmeyer, Ellen. "Demise of a Hard-Fighting Squad." *Washington Post*, May 12, 2005.

Lederman, Gordon Nathaniel. *Reorganizing the Joint Chiefs of Staff: The Goldwater-Nichols Act of 1986*. Westport, CT: Greenwood Press, 1999.

Leslie, Stuart W. *Cold War and American Science*. New York: Columbia University Press, 1993.

Little, Robert. "A Race to Get New Bomb for Cave War." *Baltimore Sun*, August 4, 2002.

Locher, James R. *Victory on the Potomac: The Goldwater-Nichols Act Unifies the Pentagon*. College Station: Texas A&M University Press, 2002.

Marino, John. "Death Leads Puerto Rico to Seek End of War Games," *Reuters*, April 20, 1999.

———. "Emboldened Protesters Digging in on Vieques; Civilians Control Gate, Decry Clinton Decision," *Washington Post*, December 9, 1999, A3.

———. "Navy Begins Last Live-Fire Exercise on Vieques Island; Protests, Hard Feelings Continue; Cleanup an Issue," *Washington Post*, January 14, 2003, A2.

Matthews, William. Polymer Protection Spray-on Armor: Lighter, Cheaper, Even Stronger Than Steel? *Defense News*, April 26, 2004.

McGaughey, Sean. "Battle Force Tactical Training after Action Report," 2001 Interservice/Industry Training Simulation and Education Conference. Abstract and link to full article at http://www .simsysinc.com/TS_Abstracts1.htm#_Toc529446875.

McIntyre, Jamie. "Sources: Report Finds Cole Commander Didn't Take Basic Steps to Protect Ship." *CNN*, January 3, 2001, http://archives.cnn.com/2001/US/01/03/cole.security.failures/ index.html.

Meyer, Robert L., Stephen G. De Sart, Mary K. Quinlan, and Kevin B. Perkins. "Early Evolution of the Naval Undersea Warfare Center/Norfolk Detachment." Appendix I in "Navy Laboratories: Concerns Regarding the Naval Undersea

Warfare Center's Suffolk Facility." Washington, DC: Government Accounting Office, June 1994, http://archive .gao.gov/t2pbat3/151959.pdf.

Miles, Donna. "DoD Taps Industry Know-How in Ongoing Counter-IED Efforts." *American Forces Press Service*, January 24, 2006.

Miller, Bill, and Edward Walsh. "Navy Bombing of Vieques to Resume; Federal Judge Rejects Puerto Rico Bid to Keep Military Exercises off Island," *Washington Post*, April 27, 2001, A6.

Morison, Elting. "The Navy and the Scientific Endeavor." In *Science and the Future Navy: A Symposium*, ed. U.S. ONR, 12–17. Washington, DC: National Academy of Sciences, 1977.

National Commission on Terrorist Attacks upon the United States. *9/11 Commission Report: Final Report of the National Commission on Terrorist Attacks upon the United States*. Washington, DC: GAO, 2004. http://www.9-11commission.gov/report/911Report.pdf

National Research Council of the National Academies. *Identification of Promising Naval Aviation Science and Technology Opportunities*. Washington, DC: National Academies Press.

National Science Board. *Science and Engineering Indicators*. Arlington, VA: National Science Foundation, 2004.

Naval Surface Forces Public Affairs and 3rd Fleet Public Affairs, "FOCUS: Sailing the Simulated Seas," *Surface Warfare*, Spring 2003, http://permanent.access.gpo.gov/lps15447/www .navsea.navy.mil/swmagazine/summarytmp.aspx-iDataPrime ID=853&showmore=true.htm.

Navarro, Mireya. "Uproar against Navy War Games Unites Puerto Ricans," *New York Times*, July 10, 1999, A8.

"Navy Attributes Fatal Bombing to Mistakes," *New York Times*, August 3, 1999, A12, http://www.nytimes.com/1999/08/03/us/navy-attributes-fatal-bombing-to-mistakes.html.

"Navy Suspends Use of Vieques," *Pittsburgh Post-Gazette*, March 2, 2001, A7.

"Navy Takes Possession of Fastest Experimental Ship." *Navy News-stand*, story number NNS050708-02, July 8, 2005, http://www

.globalsecurity.org/military/library/news/2005/07/mil-
050708-nns01.htm.

Nimitz, Chester W. "The Post-War Navy." *The Naval Review* (U.K.) 30,
no. 1 (February 1942): 31–39, http://www.naval-review.co.uk/
issues/1942-1.pdf.

Old, Bruce S., "The Evolution of the Office of Naval Research." *Physics
Today*, August 1, 1961. doi: 10.1063/1.3057690.

Office of Naval Research. "Electric Warships & Combat Vehicles."
Arlington, VA, n.d.

———. "50th Anniversary: ONR, Investing in the Future." 43-page
PDF supplied by ONR. 1996.

———. "Future Naval Capabilities—Sustaining Technologies for the
Next Navy and Marine Corps." Arlington, VA, August 3, 2001.

———. "Science and Technology from an Investment Point of View."
Arlington, VA, n.d.

———. "X-Craft . . . in a Class by Itself." Arlington, VA. N.d.

O'Rourke, Ronald. "Vieques, Puerto Rico Naval Training Range:
Background and Issues for Congress" *Congressional Research
Service Report for Congress*, December 17, 2001, http://www
.history.navy.mil/library/online/vieques.htm.

"Pentagon to Use New Bomb on Afghan Cave." *CNN*, December 23, 2001,
http://edition.cnn.com/2001/US/12/22/ret.new.weapon/
index.html.

Pfeiffer, John E. "The Office of Naval Research." *Scientific American*
180, no. 2 (February 1949).

Pickering, W. H. "Technological Opportunities and the Next Generation
Navy." In *Science and the Future Navy: A Symposium*, ed. U.S.
ONR, 37–41. Washington, DC: National Academy of Sciences,
1977.

Piore, Emaanuel R. "ONR Research Policy." *Research Review*, April
1954.

Plante, Chris. "Revised Timeline Raises New Questions about USS
Cole Security." *CNN*, October 20, 2000, http://archives.cnn
.com/2000/US/10/20/cole.report/.

"Puerto Ricans Protest Fatal Bomb Accident," *New York Times*, May 9, 1999, A16.

Rabin, Robert. "Vieques: Five Centuries of Struggle and Resistance," Vieques Historical Archives (n.d.), http://www.vieques-island .com/navy/rabin.html#ENGLISH.

Radgers, Walter, and Terry Frieden. "U.S. Official Sees Similarities between USS *Cole* Blast and Embassy Attacks." *CNN*, October 23, 2000, http://archives.cnn.com/2000/US/10/23/ uss.cole.01/.

Riordan, Teresa. "Undersea Robots Glide Into New Realm of Marine Research." News@Princeton, August 24, 2006, http://www .princeton.edu/main/news/archive/S15/63/64G05/index .xml?section=featured.

Salkovitz, Edward I., ed. *Science, Technology, and the Modern Navy: Thirtieth Anniversary 1946–1976*. Arlington, VA: Department of the Navy, Office of Naval Research, 1976.

Sapolsky, Harvey M. *Science and the Navy: The History of the Office of Naval Research*. Princeton, NJ: Princeton University Press, 1990.

Schank, John F., Harry J. Thie, Clifford M. Graf II, Joseph Beel, and Jerry M. Sollinger. *Finding the Right Balance: Simulator and Live Training for Navy Units*. Santa Monica, CA: RAND, 2002. http://www.rand.org/pubs/monograph_reports/MR1441/.

Sherwin, C. W., and R. S. Isenson. *First Interim Report on Project HIND-SIGHT (summary)*. Washington, DC: Office of the Director of Defense Research and Engineering, 1966.

Silberman, Steve. "The War Room," NPS News Archive, September 2004, http://www.wired.com/wired/archive/12.09/warroom .html.

Smith, Leighton, Charles Wilhelm, Philip Coyle, Richard Hawley, Richard Heamey, Sherri Goodman, James Perkins, and John Tilelli. *Future Naval Training Environments*, CNR D0006280. A4/2REV. Alexandria, VA: CNA, November 1, 2002. http:// www.cna.org/sites/default/files/research/D0006280.A4.pdf.

Space and Naval Warfare Systems Center. "SSC San Diego Command History Calendar Year 1997." Technical Document 2895, January 1998.

Stanford University News Service. "Justice Department Decides Not to Join Paul Biddle's *qui tam* Suit." News release, January 4, 1994.

———. "Stanford, Government Agree to Settle Dispute over Research Costs." News release, October 18, 1994.

———. "Test of President Donald Kennedy's Resignation Letter to the Board of Trustees." News release, July 29, 1991.

Stein, Harold. *American Civil-Military Decisions: A Book of Case Studies.* Tuscaloosa: University of Alabama Press, 1963.

Stewart, Marc S., and John Pavlos. "A Means to Networked Persistent Undersea Surveillance." Paper presented at the Submarine Technology Symposium, Johns Hopkins University Applied Physics Laboratory, May 2006.

Suro, Roberto. "Navy Bombing Range Deal Reached; Puerto Rico Negotiates Aid and a Vote on Vieques's Future," *Washington Post*, February 1, 2000, A7.

———. "When Navy Spots Vieques, It Sees a Bull's-Eye; Puerto Rico Resisting Renewed Bombing; Hill Threatens to Close Base," *Washington Post*, October 2, 1999, A3.

Sweeney, Annie, and Lynn Sweet. "'They Tried to Break out Spirit'; Gutierrez Back in Chicago for Rally after Three-Day Ordeal in Puerto Rico," *Chicago Sun-Times*, May 2, 2001, 1.

"Thermobarics—It All Began with Basic Research." *STARLINK,* Autumn 2005.

Thomas, Evan, and Sharon Squassoni. "Desperate Hours." *Newsweek*, March 26, 2001, 36.

Thompson, Phillip. "The 'Unplugged' Battlefield." *Sea Power*, March 2000.

Tiron, Roxana. "Naval Simulators Designed for Training While at Sea," *National Defense Magazine*, November 2003, http://www.nationaldefensemagazine.org/ARCHIVE/2003/NOVEMBER/Pages/Naval_Simulators3724.aspx.

"$27.7M to Develop PLUSNET Undersea Sensor Network." *Defense Industry Daily*, 10 May 2005, http://www.defenseindustrydaily .com/277m-to-develop-plusnet-undersea-sensor-network-0486/.

"Underwater Robots Work Together without Human Input." *Science Daily*, August 1, 2006, http://www.sciencedaily.com/releases/ 2006/08/060801183221.htm.

Union for Concerned Scientists. *Empty Promise*. Boston: Beacon Press, 1986.

U.S. Congress, Office of Technology Assessment, *Virtual Reality and Technologies for Combat Simulation—Background Paper*, OTA-). BP-ISS-136 (Washington, DC: U.S. Government Printing Office, September 1994, http://govinfo.library.unt.edu/ota/ Ota_1/DATA/1994/9444.PDF.

"Vieques Protest Continues with More Arrests," *Washington Post*, July 3, 2005, A5.

Willard, Robert F., W. L. Nyland, and John J. Young Jr. "Memorandum for the Chief of Naval Research. Subject: Department of the Navy Science and Technology (S&T) Guidance." May 3, 2005.

"X-craft/Littoral Surface Craft-Experimental (LSC(X)). Fast Sea Frame/Sea Fighter (FSF 1)." *Global Security*, http://www .globalsecurity.org/military/systems/ship/x-craft.htm.

Yardley, Roland J. Harry Thie, John F. Schank, Jolene Galegher, and Jessie L. Riposo, "Can Under Way Training Be Reduced? The Use of Simulation for Training in the U.S. Navy Surface Force," *Research Brief*. Santa Monica, CA: Rand, 2005. http://www.rand .org/pubs/research_briefs/2005/RAND_RB7567.pdf.

———. *Use of Simulation for Training in the US Navy Surface Force*. Santa Monica, CA: RAND, 2003. http://www.rand.org/pubs/ monograph_reports/2005/MR1770.pdf.

Yuhas, John S. "Enabling a Transformation in Joint Operations." *Military Information Technology* 7, no. 1 (January 17, 2003).

Zacharias, Maria. "VAST Offers Sailors Surface Fire Support Training Virtually Anywhere," NAVSEA News, March 7, 2003, http:// www.globalsecurity.org/military/library/news/2003/03/ mil-030307-navsea02.htm.

Web Pages

AN/USQ-T46(V) Battle Force Tactical Training System, http://www.globalsecurity.org/military/systems/ship/systems/an-usq-t46.htm.

"Attack on the USS Cole." *Yemen Gateway*, http://www.al-bab.com/yemen/cole1.htm.

"AUV Lab History." *AUV Laboratory at MIT Sea Grant*, http://auvlab.mit.edu/history.html.

"DDG 67 Cole: Determined Warrior." *Global Security*, http://www.globalsecurity.org/military/agency/navy/ddg-67.htm.

"DDG-1000 Zumwalt/DD(X) Multi-Mission Surface Combatant Future Surface Combatant," *Global Security*, http://www.globalsecurity.org/military/systems/ship/dd-x.htm.

Department of the Navy. "1997 Posture Statement," http://www.navy.mil/navydata/policy/fromsea/pos97/pos-pg06.html.

"Formal Surrender of Japan, 2 September 1945," Department of the Navy, Naval Historical Center, http://www.history.navy.mil/photos/events/wwii-pac/japansur/js-8e.htm.

"History of the Navy in Vieques," http://www.vieques-island.com/navy/.

"IED Fatalities by Month," Iraq Coalition Casualty Count, http://icasualties.org/Iraq/ByMonth.aspx.

"Kernel Blitz." *Global Security*, http://www.globalsecurity.org/military/ops/kernel-blitz.htm.

"Liberdade Xray Advanced Underwater Glider." ONR Media Fact Sheets. http://www.onr.navy.mil/en/Media-Center/Fact-Sheets/Liberdade-XRAY-Advanced-Underwater-Glider.aspx.

"Monterey Bay 2006 Field Experiments." *Monterey Bay Aquarium Research Institute*, August 10, 2006, http://www.mbari.org/MB2006/UPS/mb2006-ups-links.htm.

"Naval Technology Achievement Award," Public Affairs Office of the Office of Naval Research, June 24, 2004, http://www.onr.navy.mil/Media-Center/Press-Releases/2004/Naval-Technology-Achievement-Award.aspx.

"Persistent Littoral Undersea Surveillance." *FedBizOpps/Commerce Business Daily*, April 26, 2004.

"Report to the Secretary of Defense of the Special Panel on Military Operations on Vieques," October 1999, http://www.defense .gov/news/oct1999/viq_101899.html.

"Seaglider." Applied Physics Laboratory, University of Washington, http://www.apl.washington.edu/projects/seaglider/summary .html.

"Slocum Glider." Webb Research Corporation, October 26, 2005, http://www.webbresearch.com/slocum.htm.

"Vieques, PR," http://www.globalsecurity.org/military/facility/vieques .htm.

Other Sources

Gottwald, William. "An Overview of the Advance Multifunction RF Concept (AMRFC) Test-Bed." PowerPoint presentation, April 14, 2004.

McGinnis, Roger. "Innovative Naval Prototypes Overview." PowerPoint presentation, July 2006.

"Memorandum for the Record: Flag Level Meeting of 24 May 1999 to Discuss Issues Related/Impacting the USMC/ONR S&T Integration." N.d.

ABOUT THE AUTHOR

ROBERT BUDERI is founder and editor in chief of Xconomy, an online business news company. He previously served as editor in chief of *Technology Review* magazine and as *BusinessWeek*'s technology editor and was a Fellow in MIT's Security Studies Program. Bob also served on the National Innovation Initiative and as an advisor to the Draper Prize Nominating Committee, and is the author of three previous books about technology and innovation.

The **Naval Institute Press** is the book-publishing arm of the U.S. Naval Institute, a private, nonprofit, membership society for sea service professionals and others who share an interest in naval and maritime affairs. Established in 1873 at the U.S. Naval Academy in Annapolis, Maryland, where its offices remain today, the Naval Institute has members worldwide.

Members of the Naval Institute support the education programs of the society and receive the influential monthly magazine *Proceedings* or the colorful bimonthly magazine *Naval History* and discounts on fine nautical prints and on ship and aircraft photos. They also have access to the transcripts of the Institute's Oral History Program and get discounted admission to any of the Institute-sponsored seminars offered around the country.

The Naval Institute's book-publishing program, begun in 1898 with basic guides to naval practices, has broadened its scope to include books of more general interest. Now the Naval Institute Press publishes about seventy titles each year, ranging from how-to books on boating and navigation to battle histories, biographies, ship and aircraft guides, and novels. Institute members receive significant discounts on the Press's more than eight hundred books in print.

Full-time students are eligible for special half-price membership rates. Life memberships are also available.

For a free catalog describing Naval Institute Press books currently available, and for further information about joining the U.S. Naval Institute, please write to:

Member Services
U.S. Naval Institute
291 Wood Road
Annapolis, MD 21402-5034
Telephone: (800) 233-8764
Fax: (410) 571-1703
Web address: www.usni.org